GRAIL
ALCHEMY

"I am very impressed by Mara's combination of scholarly research, easy style, and practical esoteric insights and instruction. She provides a very comprehensive coverage of the legends of the Holy Grail from ancient Celtic mythology, through medieval Arthurian literature, to 20th-century involvement of occultists such as Dion Fortune and Wellesley Tudor Pole at Glastonbury."

GARETH KNIGHT, AUTHOR OF *THE SECRET TRADITION IN
ARTHURIAN LEGEND* AND *MAGIC AND THE POWER OF THE GODDESS*

"A fascinating wellspring of lore, stories, and legends of the Celtic mystery tradition with wonderfully inspiring Vision Journey meditations following each chapter. From cauldrons, cups, swords, and gods/goddesses to Glastonbury and its legacy of Dion Fortune, and more, *Grail Alchemy* is a Celtic literary *temenos* of our time, a sacred space to further explore one's own inner journey and transformation. Highly recommended."

KAREN RALLS, PH.D., MEDIEVAL HISTORIAN, OXFORD UNIVERSITY, AUTHOR
OF *THE TEMPLARS AND THE GRAIL* AND *MEDIEVAL MYSTERIES*

"*Grail Alchemy* encourages the reader to take up the quest in search of this most enigmatic symbol of spiritual healing and integration. Mara's richly detailed text documenting the Grail's mythic and cultural history is harmoniously balanced with a series of beautiful and powerful meditations and rituals that enable the seeker to open to the Grail's deeper Mysteries. Mara marries these elements with depth and wisdom, offering an experience of the Grail as a living, transformative presence at the heart of Self and Creation. A wonderfully inspiring book."

PHILIP CARR-GOMM, CHIEF OF THE ORDER OF BARDS, OVATES,
AND DRUIDS AND AUTHOR OF *DRUIDCRAFT, DRUID MYSTERIES*

"Mara Freeman has written a beautiful and comprehensive book, drawing on many years of study, reflection, and spiritual practice. She turns this jewel, examining its many facets, from ancient origins to Christianized myth to 20th century. Carefully constructed meditations and rituals provide the reader an opportunity to contact and be nourished by the inner reality of the Grail and, in turn, to share that grace with others. All who seek the Grail will find herein helpful direction for the quest."

JOHN PLUMMER, PH.D., AUTHOR OF *LIVING MYSTERIES* AND
THE MANY PATHS OF THE INDEPENDENT SACRAMENTAL MOVEMENT

"Wisewoman and scholar Mara Freeman is a most skilled and intuitive guide to the Celtic Grail mysteries. Her comprehensive course of study offers the reader a valuable overview of the tradition's folklore and literature. More importantly, though, Freeman opens experiential portals to the deep and often veiled teachings embedded in the millennia-old bardic tales."

SIOBHÁN HOUSTON, ED.D., AUTHOR OF
INVOKING MARY MAGDALENE AND COAUTHOR OF *GNOSTIC HEALING*

"Mara Freeman's *Grail Alchemy* is a fascinating and well-researched book that weaves the many threads of both the historical and spiritual aspects of the Grail legends into a harmonious whole. It's a "must have" for anyone interested in the history, lore, and spirituality of the Holy Grail."

MARGIE MCARTHUR, AUTHOR OF
WISDOM OF THE ELEMENTS AND *FAERY HEALING*

"In *Grail Alchemy,* Mara Freeman brilliantly weaves together a wealth of accessible scholarship, thoughtful commentary, and great stories and includes meditations and exercises to give the reader a personal experience of the Great Mystery of the Sacred Feminine. This is a remarkable book, beautifully and elegantly conceived and written."

LARA OWEN, AUTHOR OF *HER BLOOD IS GOLD*
AND *GROWING YOUR INNER LIGHT*

"Mara Freeman's sure and steady hand will guide the reader through the mysteries of the Grail to the understanding that the Grail is the soul itself—held open to receive the purified, inspired, and golden state of Divine consciousness."

NICHOLAS R. MANN, AUTHOR OF *THE ISLE*

"In this remarkable book, Mara Freeman leaves no stone unturned in her thorough and readable investigation of the often veiled historic Grail lore of the West, disclosing its perennial yearning for the restoration of the Divine Feminine. There is a timely call too, to embrace the Grail as a corrective to our current aggressive attitudes and plundering of the planet's natural resources."

PATRICK BENHAM, AUTHOR OF *THE AVALONIANS*

GRAIL ALCHEMY

INITIATION IN THE CELTIC MYSTERY TRADITION

MARA FREEMAN

DESTINY
BOOKS

Destiny Books
Rochester, Vermont • Toronto, Canada

Destiny Books
One Park Street
Rochester, Vermont 05767
www.DestinyBooks.com

Text stock is SFI certified

Destiny Books is a division of Inner Traditions International

Library of Congress Cataloging-in-Publication Data
Freeman, Mara.
  Grail alchemy : initiation in the Celtic mystery tradition / Mara Freeman.
    pages cm
  Includes bibliographical references and index.
  Summary: "An experiential guide to the spiritual path of the Holy Grail" —
Provided by publisher.
  ISBN 978-1-62055-191-2 (pbk.) — ISBN 978-1-62055-192-9 (e-book)
  1. Grail. 2. Spiritual life. I. Title.
  BF1442.G73F74 2014
  299'.16—dc23

                                                          2013022168

Printed and bound in the United States by Lake Book Manufacturing, Inc.
The text stock is SFI certified. The Sustainable Forestry Initiative® program
promotes sustainable forest management.

10 9 8 7 6 5 4 3 2 1

Text design and layout by Virginia Scott Bowman
This book was typeset in Garamond Premier Pro and Gill Sans with Gills Sans
and Benguiat used as display typefaces

To send correspondence to the author of this book, mail a first-class letter to the
author c/o Inner Traditions • Bear & Company, One Park Street, Rochester, VT
05767, and we will forward the communication, or contact the author directly at
www.avalonmysteryschool.net.

Do not let it be forgotten that there is a native Mystery Tradition of our race which has its mature aspect in the sun-worship of the Druids and the beautiful fairy-lore of the Celts, its philosophical aspect in the traditions of alchemy and its spiritual aspect in the Hidden Church of the Holy Grail, the Church behind the Church, not made with hands, eternal in the heavens.

DION FORTUNE

Contents

Acknowledgments

Honor and heartfelt thanks are due to all those intrepid pioneers in Spirit who rekindled the lamp of the British Mystery Tradition for the modern era, especially Dion Fortune, Wellesley Tudor Pole, Christine Hartley, W. G. Gray, and the Avalonians . . . and also to Gareth Knight and John Matthews, who carried it forward to light the way to the Grail Castle.

The Perennial Grail

The Holy Grail won't go away. This mysterious prize is as fascinating today as it was in the Middle Ages, when tales of King Arthur and his knights were all the rage. For in the words of mythologist Joseph Campbell, the quest for the Holy Grail is "the founding myth of Western civilization." The Grail myth persists throughout the centuries like a recurring dream that must be brought fully to consciousness where it can be understood and resolved.

Where did the Grail spring from? From what depth in the ocean of the collective unconscious did it arise, and when? The etymology of the word "Grail" may provide a clue: in the first Grail literature from twelfth-century France, the word appears as *gral* or *graal*. The origin of this word is not known for sure, but many scholars believe it may come from the medieval Latin *gradale,* meaning "in stages"—a name given to a serving dish or deep platter used to bring courses serially throughout a meal. Others believe it derives from a Greek word, *krater,* a shallow cup with two handles. Yet whatever its origins in the mundane world, the Grail is clearly no ordinary container but rather a numinous vessel with miraculous properties. According to different versions of the legend, the Grail is described as a cornucopia that can provide unlimited amounts of whatever food and drink is desired, it can heal wounds, and even confer immortality.

Because of its wonder-working nature, the Grail has been plausibly traced to the magical vessels of Celtic myth and legend.[1] As we will see in the following chapters, we can trace the origins of the Grail to the Cauldron of Plenty that never runs dry and the Cauldron of Rebirth that can bring the dead to life. The Grail's beginnings can also be discovered in tales of Otherworld cups that hold water from the Well of Wisdom, falling apart when a lie is told and magically reassembling when truth is spoken. The Grail can be glimpsed in the myth of a faery woman who bears an "emerald cup of virtues" with life-giving and protective properties. It is there in stories of the goddess who personifies the land itself and chooses the next king by offering him a cup of red ale. The Grail is, in essence, a radiant Mystery, which flows from the wellsprings of Celtic magical tradition into every corner of the Western world.

Wandering minstrels from Brittany first brought these tales to continental Europe. They were descendants of British and Welsh refugees who had fled across the English Channel to escape the invading Saxons in the fifth and sixth centuries. These *conteurs* earned their living by entertaining people with their music, poetry, and stories at castles, markets, and seasonal fairs. The best of them ended up in the courts of France where they enjoyed the patronage of the wealthiest nobles in the land. By the twelfth century they were delighting the royal households of Champagne, Anjou, and Aquitaine with their rich heritage of Celtic and Arthurian adventure and romance. Ancient stories were translated and modernized in order to appeal to a refined and sophisticated audience who extolled the noble ideals of chivalry. Fortunately for us, these ancient voices were preserved for all time through the skills of French and German poets who wrote down these episodic adventures in a corpus of literature that became known as "the Matter of Britain."

In this milieu, the Grail underwent many transformations. Under the pen of the twelfth-century French poet Chrétien de Troyes, author of the earliest written Grail romance, *Perceval* or *Le Conte du Graal,* the Grail became a golden serving bowl studded with jewels. In the imagination of the thirteenth-century German poet Wolfram von Eschenbach, author of the romance *Parzival,* it became a precious stone sent from heaven. Within the scriptoria of medieval monks, the magic

Celtic vessel took on new symbolic life: it was reinvented as a *ciborium* (a container for the communion wafer); the cup from which Christ drank at the Last Supper; the dish upon which the Paschal lamb was served; and the vessels which caught the blood of the crucified Christ. A popular and enduring medieval legend tells of Joseph of Arimathea bringing Christ's cup to "the Vale of Avalon," as if, in the end, the numinous vessel had to be returned to its mythic roots in the Celtic Otherworld.

THE RETURN OF THE FEMININE

Looking beyond the last two thousand years, it is clear that the ideals inherent to the Grail are as old as creation. A rounded, womblike or breastlike container, it belongs to the family of symbols—bowl, cauldron, vat, well, cup, or crucible—that are all images of the divine feminine, the Mother Goddess whose womb holds the waters of life, found as far back as the Neolithic era and in cultures from ancient India to classical Greece.[2] The Grail is also a symbol of the soul, which is a feminine noun in many languages, for instance: the Latin *anima,* which gives the Gaelic, *anam;* the Greek *psyche;* and German *Seele.* The Grail invites us to gaze into the hidden depths of our own soul and drink deep of the waters of wisdom therein.

The Grail stories arose when Western religion had been dominated by male god-forms for over a thousand years. The natural longing of the Western mind for a connection with the divine feminine could not be assuaged by the prevailing worldview that separated masculine and feminine, spirit and matter, heaven and earth. The wisdom of the feminine teaches us the unity of all life, including the sacredness of the body and the Earth. It embraces the interconnectedness of all living beings and honors the natural cycles of life and death. Inclusive, intuitive, and receptive, it is the antithesis of the drive to conquer and control, preferring rather to dance to the flowing music of the Great Mystery.

By way of compensation, the culture of *fin'amors,* or "courtly love," emerged in twelfth-century France, which honored and elevated the feminine ideal through art, music, and poetry. The Church followed suit by sanctioning the burgeoning cult of the Virgin Mary, which led to the magnificent cathedrals in Europe dedicated to the Mother of God. The most famous of these, Chartres Cathedral, is a treasure-house of glorious icons to Marian devotion, with relics and shrines, luminous rose windows, and Black Madonnas. It became known as the "Seat of the Virgin Mary on Earth."

This was a fertile climate in which the story of the Grail could take root. A mysterious life-giving vessel lay hidden in the hinterland of collective consciousness that, when found, promised to redeem the barren, waiting soil of the European soul. New stories, enshrining the secret wisdom of the ages, sprang up and gave voice to this shared longing. The quintessential symbol of the feminine emerged as the Holy Grail, an icon that, while able to assume many shapes, has always been most popularly conceived as a vessel filled with an unearthly radiance of divine origin. Containing life-giving forces, it could heal wounds and bestow immortality upon those worthy to gaze into it. Tales of the Grail flourished among both the high- and low-born of medieval Europe, for the human thirst for the divine feminine was something that could not be assuaged by the Church with its one-sided masculine authority.

THE RAPE OF THE WELL MAIDENS

A basic theme in the majority of the medieval Grail romances is that the Grail lies hidden in a castle surrounded by a barren and blighted country. It can only be restored to life when the Grail is found by a worthy knight. Among the narratives that attempt to explain how this sorry state of affairs came about is a little-known thirteenth-century text called *The Elucidation*. An anonymous author tacked this manuscript onto Chrétien de Troyes' romance *Perceval*, which he left unfinished, probably due to his death. Despite its humble position in Grail literature, it goes to the heart of the significance of the myth for the Western world, both in the past and for today.

The story tells how long ago in the forests of the rich country of Logres (from *Lloegr,* the Welsh word for "England") travelers could find refreshment at sacred springs. The guardians of these holy springs were known as the well maidens, who served the weary wanderers abundantly from golden goblets and dishes. But one day, the evil King Amangons raped one of the maidens and stole her golden cup, and his men followed suit. After this the forest sanctuaries lay abandoned and empty; the wells dried up, and the countryside was stricken with drought: "The kingdom turned to loss, the land was dead and desert in suchwise as that it was scarce worth a couple of hazelnuts. For they lost the voices of the wells and the damsels that were therein."[3]

Another effect of this desecration was that the court of a mysterious personage called the "Rich Fisherman" was withdrawn from the world:

> In such sort was the kingdom laid waste that thereforth was no tree leafy. The meadows and the flowers were dried up and the waters were shrunken, nor as their might no man find the Court of the Rich Fisherman that wont to make in the land a glittering glory of gold and silver, of ermines and minever, of rich palls of sendal, of meats and of stuffs, of falcons gentle and merlins and tercels and sparrow-hawks and falcon peregrine.[4]

The reference to "voices of the wells" suggests that the maidens were dispensers of oracles. Sacred springs throughout the world, from India to Greece, have attracted pilgrims seeking guidance and healing from their indwelling spirits, hence the common notion of the "wishing well." As late as the seventeenth century, it was not unusual to find a holy well in England under the charge of a "priestess"—usually a highly respected old woman who looked after the place and gave oracles in return for crossing her palm with silver.

Yet the poem also says that the maidens "issued forth" from the wells, which suggests they themselves were the spirits dwelling within its waters. Sacred springs and holy wells have always been considered entrances to the Otherworld, and sacred vessels were frequently found in the care of one or more supernatural women who lived beneath or beyond water, as we shall see later.[5] The violation of the well maidens severed the channels to the Otherworld, leaving the Earth cut off from immense reserves of numinous power. Both material and spiritual riches, once so freely given to humankind, were withdrawn, and the terrible loss soon became apparent as the land became blighted and barren. And we have inherited this sad legacy today: because we no longer hear the voice of the feminine, we experience the state of spiritual impoverishment that is now endemic in Western civilization.

Centuries later, King Arthur's knights came to this region, hoping to avenge the maidens. In the forest they came upon a number of young women, each with an attendant knight who protected her by attacking any approaching armed stranger. One of these knights, defeated by Sir Gawain in a jousting combat, was taken prisoner and sent to Arthur's court. He turned out to be a master storyteller called Blihos Bleheris, who described how he and the other knights and maidens were descendants of the raped well maidens. They had been forced to wander through the forest forever, awaiting the coming of those who could find "the Court from whence shall come the joy whereby the land shall again be made bright."[6]

So begins the quest for the hidden court of the Rich Fisher, or Fisher King, as he is known in some romances, by whose redemption the Wasteland will be made fruitful again. It is within his domain that the Holy Grail, the primary archetype behind the well maidens' cup, lies hidden.

NO SOUND OF WATER

The profundity of this sad story is made clear when examined in the light of Celtic beliefs about right relationship with the land. In Celtic society, a prospective Celtic chieftain or king had to be accepted as the consort of the goddess of the region. It is easy to see how the rape of the well maidens turns this ancient wisdom tradition on its head. The balance between the human world and the world of nature is overthrown, as the king and his men violate the maidens and seize their freely given cups for their own gratification. Because the maidens personify the fruitful earth, this brutal act has the inevitable result of rendering the land infertile.

This extraordinary little tale could not make its point more clearly: violence done to the feminine reverberates on all levels of human experience. This fatal imbalance has been the tragic theme sounding throughout the history of Western civilization, and continues unabated today in our war-torn, ravaged, and polluted world. The rape of the well maidens and the theft of their life-giving vessels is an apt metaphor for a culture in which individuals and nations, perceiving themselves as separate from each other and all forms of life, wage continual war on Nature, destroying and consuming all her treasures. The health of the Earth has already been drastically compromised by the continual plunder and pollution of her vital systems: water, air, forests, and seas. The importance of using Earth's resources wisely and giving back in return is something we have forgotten—with disastrous results: turning away from what our ancestors knew to be a vital interdependence has set us on a catastrophic course likely to end in irreversible damage to the only home we have.

It is no wonder that the image of the wasteland is as relevant today as it was seven hundred years ago. T. S. Eliot used this theme when he sounded the anguished note of the modern era with his great poem of the same name. Although written in the context of the aftermath of World War I, the image has lost none of its clarity and relevance for us today.

> *What are the roots that clutch, what branches grow*
> *Out of this stony rubbish? Son of man,*
> *You cannot say or guess, for you know only*
> *A heap of broken images, where the sun beats,*
> *And the dead tree gives no shelter, the cricket no relief,*
> *And the dry stone no sound of water.*[7]

Later on in the poem there is a reference to the violated well maidens, whom Eliot conceives of as:

> *. . . voices singing out of empty cisterns and exhausted*
> *wells.*[8]

These dry and depleted vessels are not images from a distant mythology. The well maidens are aspects of the *Anima Mundi,* "the Soul of the World," who has always been perceived as feminine. Throughout the world she is called Pachamama (Mother of the Universe), Nokomis (Grandmother), Magna Mater (Great Mother), or simply Mother Earth. Esotericists have referred to her as the Planetary Spirit or the Planetary Being, while more recently, in a scientific context, she has been given the name of the Greek goddess, Gaia. Stolen cups and dry wells are also descriptions of the inner emptiness of the modern soul. Disconnected from our spiritual source, we thirst for life-giving waters in the desert of modern life. As the Soul of the World is feminine, so is the individual soul within each of us. To seek the Grail is to go in quest of the essential Self that has been devalued and disregarded in a world that values material possessions over psychological and spiritual health.

Because things are out of balance, there is discord at every level of human existence. This state of affairs is brilliantly articulated by Jungian author, Anne Baring:

Where there is no relationship and balance between the masculine and feminine principles, the masculine principle becomes pathologically exaggerated, inflated; the feminine pathologically diminished, inarticulate, ineffective. The symptoms of a pathological masculine are rigidity, dogmatic inflexibility, omnipotence, and an obsession with or addiction to power and control. There will be a clear definition of goals but no receptivity to ideas and values which conflict with these goals. . . . We can see this pathology reflected today in the ruthless values which govern the media, politics, and the technological drive of the modern world. We can see the predatory impulse to acquire or to conquer new territory in the drive for global control of world markets, in the ideology of perpetual growth, in new technologies such as the genetic modification of food. We see exaggerated competitiveness—the drive to go further, grow faster, achieve more, acquire more, elevated to the status of a cult. There is contempt for the feeling values grounded in the experience of relationship with others, with other species, and with the environment. There is a predatory and compulsive sexuality in both men and women who increasingly lose the capacity for relationship. There is continuous expansion in a linear sense but no expansion in depth, in insight. The pressure of things to do constantly accelerates. The result? Exhaustion, anxiety, depression, illness which afflict more and more people. There is no time or place for human relationships. Above all, there is no time for relationship with the dimension of spirit. The water of life no longer flows . . .[9]

This deadly imbalance is the impulse behind the quest for the Grail. It is the primary myth that gives voice to the collective unconscious of the Western psyche, which recognizes the loss of a priceless spiritual treasure. That this story never dies and is still as alive today, continuing to provide fresh material for authors, poets, playwrights, and film producers, is testimony that the Grail has never really been found. More than ever, we are beginning to realize we have no choice but to heal the split between masculine and feminine, heaven and earth, ego and spirit that has plagued Western civilization for so long. We must continue to seek the Grail in order to reclaim the Western soul, heal the Wasteland we have made of modern life, and restore the Courts of Joy.

A TWENTY-FIRST CENTURY GRAIL QUEST

The influential twentieth century magician W. G. Gray wrote, "the story of the Grail is the story of the Western Inner Tradition." For the legends of the Holy Grail open up paths to the spiritual dimensions like no other body of lore has ever done before or since. They reveal an initiatory path leading to the highest realms of consciousness. With this in mind, this book is designed to do two things:

- To take you on a journey through story, legend, and lore into the landscape of the Grail, so that you can understand the profound significance behind the primary myth of Western culture.

- To enable you to set forth on your own Grail Quest through simple, yet powerful practices, meditations, and ritual forms rooted in Western Esoteric Tradition.

This time-tested path of initiation will reveal a long-hidden inner landscape of beauty and wisdom that will lead you to become aware of your true identity as a soul, teach you magical knowledge, and lead you to higher consciousness.

Many of the exercises consist of meditations called VisionJourneys, which are designed to help you learn about the esoteric meaning of the Grail and contact the inner powers associated with its various aspects. These can be found at the end of each chapter. There are many deep layers of meaning encoded in the symbols and images of the VisionJourneys in this book. It is recommended that you do each one a number of times to get its full benefit.

Further practices can be found in the final chapter. These are focused on what is referred to in medieval texts as "attaining" the Grail. This is nothing less than achieving full consciousness of the soul—the essential Self beyond time. In sacred alchemy this is known as the "Lesser Work." When we are aligned and identified with this, our true nature, we can open to receive the in-pouring influence of the divine. Then with steady practice and a strong commitment, you may choose to become a Grail Bearer, one who is capable of bringing the Light of the Grail into the world for healing of self, others and our Earth. In alchemical terms, this is the "Greater Work."

BEFORE YOU BEGIN:
A NOTE ON THE VISIONJOURNEYS

A VisionJourney is a form of meditation in which you use imagery to take you into the inner worlds that lie beyond the realm of the five senses. The VisionJourney is a traditional tool of Western esoteric practice originally associated with the Qabalah and known as "pathworking." It is similar to guided meditation, but much deeper: the guided meditation usually takes you only into the personal subconscious to explore your own psychology, whereas the VisionJourney takes you deeper into inner levels beyond the individual psyche. Doing a guided meditation might be compared to looking at a movie on your inner screen that gives you information about your personal life. The VisionJourney is like entering a movie that is clearly about a different dimension of reality and fully participating in it. Here you will come across landscapes and places that you can explore and beings with whom you can interact.

Focus and Imagination

Two skills are required to take a VisionJourney. These include first of all the ability to focus and concentrate and, secondly, the use of the imagination. A word needs to be said about the latter: our precious and remarkable imaginations have been devalued and maligned in modern society. From an early age we are told that the "imaginary" is inferior to the "real." If something is "all in your imagination" it means you have made it up, or you are simply being deluded. But in fact, the imagination is the *language of the soul*. It is the equivalent of our most important sensory organ—sight—only turned inward rather than outward. Every nonphysical thing that exists expresses itself as energy, or Force. The imagination is a creative mechanism that enables us to give Form to the Forces of the nonphysical planes.

In the guided VisionJourney, the images are supplied for you in the narrative. As in a novel, the powers and places of the inner dimensions are drawn so that you can see them in your imagination. As you learn to build them into reality on the imaginal plane (also called the astral plane), they will be "inhabited" or "ensouled" by the Forces they encode. (If you build it, they will come!)

Another thing to note is that "visualizing" here means much more than using the "mind's eye," or visual imagination. We have more inner senses than inner sight: inner hearing, inner touching, inner tasting, and inner feeling (sensing); and you can draw upon these to make the journeying real. For the heart of your experience with the VisionJourneys lies not in watching them play out on the screen of your mind, but in your active participation with whatever you encounter. Each one is designed to provide opportunities for you to have your own experience, which will probably include elements not found in the narrative, as each person's response to the journey will be quite unique. The insights and understandings arising from each meditation will be completely your own.

Taking the VisionJourney

There are several ways to approach the VisionJourney. If you're alone and reading the journey, you can read it a number of times, jot down the order of events and then begin, perhaps opening your eyes and looking at your notes once in a while. If you prefer to relax and be led through the exercise, you can access recordings of each VisionJourney, read by Mara Freeman, as MP3 files from www.chalicecentre.net/recordings. html. Alternatively, you can record them yourself or have someone read the script aloud to you, which is quite effective if you are doing this in a group. Whichever method you use, you will need to allow pauses in the narrative in order to allow your own inner experiences to emerge.

Make sure you are sitting in a quiet and comfortable place where you will not be disturbed by people, ringing phones, or other distractions. Take some deep breaths, relax, and gently withdraw your attention from your body, your feelings, and your thoughts. Let yourself drop into the peaceful place of stillness that underlies the constantly changing movie screen of everyday consciousness. This process, known as "Entering the Silence," will enable you to access the inner world called *Annwn (anoon)* from Welsh tradition that translates as "the deeps," "the in-world," or "the not-world," which is the Void that lies before and beyond time, space, and all of creation.

Be sure to write your experiences down afterward as VisionJourneys take place on the astral plane, which is where we go in our dreams each night, and like dreams, they can sometimes vanish with the light of day unless they are anchored by pen and paper. You may want to dedicate a journal solely to your spiritual journey into the wisdom of the Holy Grail so that you can consciously learn and grow from these inner experiences.

1

Seeking the Cauldron

One of the earliest versions of the Grail quest is found in a Welsh poem in which King Arthur and his warriors seek a wonder-working cauldron from the Otherworld. This first story of an Arthurian quest for a precious vessel is called *The Plunder of Annwn* (*Preiddeu Annwn*) from the fourteenth century *Book of Taliesin*. Its language, however, is much older, possibly dating it as somewhere between the eighth and eleventh centuries. Haunting and evocative, yet incomprehensible in parts, it has been called "a mosaic of Welsh bardic lore about the Other World."[1] The narrator of this tale is the Welsh bard, Taliesin, who tells how Arthur sets sail with a band of warriors in his ship, *Prydwen,* hoping to seize the cauldron of the Chief of Annwn.

The epic adventure is fraught with supernatural perils as the company arrives in a strange landscape in which they encounter what appears to be eight *caers,* meaning "castles" or "citadels," although this could also be interpreted as one castle with eight names that describe its different qualities. The cauldron is dark blue and rimmed with pearls, and "kindled by the breath of nine maidens." It will only cook food for the brave. The poem seems to suggest that Arthur and his warriors are unsuccessful in their attempt to seize the cauldron, and only seven of their band return from this ill-fated expedition. Let's take a closer look at this strange tale, which may be the prototype of the later medieval Grail romances.

THE TOPOGRAPHY OF ANNWN

The poem is set in the Welsh Otherworld called Annwn (a-noon) sometimes found in its older form, Annwfyn (anoo-vin). It translates as "the deep," for it is often located below the earth or beneath the sea. The caers of Annwn are named below in Welsh and English, but their meanings are a subject of scholarly dispute:[2]

Caer Sidi	The Faery Castle
Caer Pedryvan	The Four-cornered Castle
Caer Vedwit	The Castle of the Mead-Feast
Caer Rigor	The Castle of Hardness? Frigidity?
Caer Wydyr	The Castle of Glass
Caer Golud	The Castle of Concealment? Impediment?
Caer Vandwy	The Castle of Manawydan? The Divine Place?
Caer Ochren	The Enclosed Castle?

We will take a look at the caers on this list whose meanings most scholars agree on, since together they form a clear picture of what will later become the landscape of the Grail Quest:

Caer Sidi

Caer Sidi means "the faery citadel" or "castle of the faery mound." The Welsh "sidi" is the equivalent of the Irish "sídhe," pronounced *shee* and Scottish "sithean" (pronounced *shee-an*). This word originally referred to the dwelling place of the indigenous pre-Celtic Irish spirits called the *aes sídhe,* the "people who live in a mound," referring to the prehistoric burial mounds scattered about the landscape of Ireland and Britain. The mysterious and beautiful faery race that lived within them came to be called simply the Sídhe. Within these "hollow hills," as they have been poetically called, the Sídhe lived in a realm of splendor that was illumined by a radiant, unearthly light. It was a timeless dimension where no one grew old, an earthly paradise where joy and peace reigned in an eternal summer. In an Irish tale, *The Adventures of Connla,* a faery woman tells of her home. She says, "I come from the lands of the living, where there is no death nor sin nor transgression. We eat everlasting feasts without toil, and have peace without strife. We are in a great sídhe, and are therefore called 'people of the sídhe' . . ."[3]

In Irish folklore there are strong warnings against entering sídhe mounds, for although they were portals to a world of alluring beauty, only those skilled in *druideacht,* or "Druid magic," could find their way out again.

Caer Pedryvan

Caer Pedryvan describes a castle with four corners, peaks, or towers. We can learn more about the significance of fourfold castles or islands by looking at stories from early Ireland. Within the repertoire of the Irish bards is a class of narratives called *immrama,* literally meaning "rowings-about," which tell of voyages to enchanted islands across the sea. The four-cornered design of Caer Pedryvan is found in a number of these. In the *Voyage of Bran,* the island of Emain Ablach stands on "four pillars." In *The Voyage of Teigue mac Cian,* the goddess takes the travelers to a palace in whose center is a courtyard with four doors, and in the *Voyage of Maelduin* is an island with four fences made of precious materials: gold, silver, brass, and crystal. This creates four divisions: one containing kings, another containing queens, a third containing warriors, and the final part containing maidens.

The fourfold pattern arises out of the One, the undifferentiated whole, the eternal matrix of Being that exists beyond time and space. This unity divides itself into the two primal opposites, which divide again to create a fourfold design—a template of the perfect world. A place built according to this design becomes a *temenos,* "a sacred enclosure." The fourfold Irish Otherworld Island and the Welsh realm of Annwn later became the blueprint for the castle of the Grail as we shall see.

Caer Vedwit

Caer Vedwit is the "caer of the honey-mead" or "mead-feast." This sweet, heady wine made from honey was a favorite drink for the Celts in their feasting halls, and they believed there was an endless supply of delicious food and intoxicating drink in Otherworld castles. Mead was more than a hedonist pleasure, however. Norse bards drank the "Mead of Poetry" to get divinely intoxicated and inspired, and it was also the drink offered by the "Lady with the Mead Cup," a figure associated with the sacred marriage between the king and the land, which she represented—a theme explored in the next chapter.

Caer Wydyr

Caer Wydyr translates as the Fortress of Glass or Crystal Castle, a typical feature of the Celtic Otherworld. In Irish stories about magical journeys, the traveler may sail in a crystal coracle to an island where palaces shine with crystals and gemstones. In a folk-tale from Brittany, *The Crystal Palace,* the hero comes to a hall entirely made of crystal so bright, he is dazzled by its light. Glastonbury, the physical location most popularly associated with the Grail, was once known as *Ynys-witrin,* "the Glass Island." This association of crystals with the spirit world is common among primal traditions throughout the world. Australian medicine men believed that crystals were "solidified light," thrown down to Earth from a celestial city so they could be used to take the initiate on a spirit journey to the sky-realm. In Siberia, shamans placed crystals within their bodies for the soul-flight over "a celestial landscape, bathed in light."[4] Archaeological evidence suggests that many of the sídhe mounds were covered with white quartz, the most famous of these being the Brú na Bóinne, or Newgrange, in Ireland, the largest chambered mound in Europe, considered to be more than five thousand years old. Archaeologists now consider the idea that it was not only a burial mound, but also a place of religious ceremony for the Neolithic, Bronze Age, and Celtic peoples. It is believed to have been covered originally with chunks of white quartz crystal, which have been partially restored today. Visitors can still gaze in wonder at the gleaming mound ringed by standing stones, its mysterious dark entranceway guarded by a horizontal stone slab carved with spiral designs. Such a place may be what the author of *The Plunder of Annwn* had in mind when he wrote about the caers of the underworld.

CAULDRONS OF CHANGES

Turning now to the coveted cauldron, we first have to ask: What was so special about a cooking-pot that Arthur and his men risked life and limb in its pursuit? Cauldrons played a central role in ceremonial feasting and rituals from the late Bronze Age to medieval times.[5] Symbols of plenty and power, cauldrons were cooking-pots that were given an honored place in the palaces of Irish chieftains. The success of a chieftain's reign depended on forging a sacred contract with the goddess of the region, so a full cauldron meant he was an able ruler whom she had accepted as a worthy consort.

Magical cauldrons abound in Celtic mythology, as shown by the following examples:

The Cauldron of Plenty
This famous cauldron was brought to Ireland by the Tuatha Dé Danann, one of the early semi-mythical races of the country. It belonged to their chief god, the Dagda, and contained an inexhaustible supply of food, so that "no company ever went from it unthankful."

The Cauldron of Discernment
This cauldron only served brave warriors, like the cauldron of Annwn that "would not boil the food of a coward." A similar cauldron from Wales belonged to Dyrnwch the Giant: "If meat for a brave man were put in it to boil, it would boil quickly, and if it was put in for a coward, it would never boil."[6] To the Celts, who upheld the virtues of the heroic warrior society, the feminine, nurturing function, represented by the cauldron, would only nourish the brave of heart.

The Cauldron of Rebirth

Another wonder-working Celtic cauldron is found in the story of *Brânwen, Daughter of Llyr,* found in the collection of Welsh medieval tales known as the *Mabinogi,* in which the god-hero, Brân, owned a cauldron that originally came from the bottom of a lake. Warriors who were slain in battle were thrown into it. The next day they climbed out alive and well, although without the power of speech: for only the initiated may tell what they have seen in the Land of the Dead.

Images of deities, animals, and ritual scenes are depicted on the silver cauldron, dating from the second century BCE, found preserved in a peat-bog in Gundestrup, Denmark. Photo by David J. Watkins.

The Cauldron of Inspiration

One of the most revealing cauldron stories from Wales concerns the cauldron of Ceridwen, a woman of supernatural power who lived at the bottom of Llyn Tegid, known today as Bala Lake, in North Wales. We shall take a closer look at this story as it seems her cauldron was none other than the cauldron sought by King Arthur in Annwn.

There are a number of versions of this tale; the oldest comes from the thirteenth-century *Book of Taliesin*. Although differing in detail, the stories tell how Ceridwen had two children: a beautiful daughter called Creirwy ("Beloved") and a son called Morfran ("Sea Crow") who was so ugly he was nicknamed Afagddu ("Utter Gloom"). Out of pity for her son, Ceridwen consulted her magic books and concocted for him a special brew in her cauldron that would yield three drops of Awen. The usual translation of Awen as "poetic inspiration" fails to convey its meaning to the modern mind: in the Celtic world, the poet was trained to enter into ecstatic states of consciousness in which he could communicate with the spirit world and acquire magical powers, such as shape-shifting, seership, and prophecy. In Ireland, this was an important stage in the training of a Druid, and successful graduates were known as *filidh*, "poet-seers."

The elixir in the cauldron had to brew for a year and a day, so Ceridwen hired a local peasant lad, Gwion Bach (Little Gwion), to stir the cauldron. When the potion was almost ready, Ceridwen stationed Morfran beside the cauldron to receive the drops that would spring out of the cauldron, but Gwion shoved the boy out of the way so that they landed on him instead. In a flash he was filled with Awen and could see all things past, present, and future.

The cauldron uttered a cry and burst into two. A black liquid oozed out, dowsing the fire, and trickled away in a black stream, which poisoned all the land and the horses that grazed there. Ceridwen, who had been asleep, sprang to her feet in a fury and pursued the thief, who by this time had raced out of the door. She ran like the wind, but with his newfound magic powers, Little Gwion turned himself into a bounding hare and sped away. Ceridwen changed herself into a greyhound, whereupon Gwion leapt into a river and became a fish. Ceridwen turned into an otter and dove in after him. He flew into the sky as a crow, but she became a falcon and swooped down on him from above. At the last moment, fearing death, Gwion spied a heap of winnowed wheat on the floor of a barn. He dropped down into it and turned himself into one of the grains. But Ceridwen turned into a hen, and scratched her way through the heap until she found him and swallowed him up. But that was not the end of Little Gwion. In her own shape again, Ceridwen became pregnant with him, and nine months later, gave birth to a baby boy. Not having the heart to kill him outright, she bundled him into a basket of hide and flung him out to sea.

The basket eventually floated to an estuary where it got tangled up in a fishing net belonging to one Elffin, the son of a local chieftain. Elffin was hoping to catch a salmon, and was surprised to find a strange bundle in his nets instead. He slit the hide wrappings and was astonished to see inside a baby boy with a radiant light about his brow. He cried, *"Tal-iesin!"*—"Look at that shining forehead!" The baby replied, "Taliesin it is!" and opened his eyes on a new life in which he grew up to become the chief bard of Britain.*

A TALE OF INITIATION

The story of Taliesin's birth begins to look suspiciously like a thinly disguised account of druidic initiation from an earlier period in Wales, veiled in poetic allegory. Ceridwen may have originally been one of those magically empowered women in Celtic myth who serve as initiators to great heroes. In Ireland, Cúchulainn of Ulster was trained by Scathach of Skye while Fionn mac Cumhaill (popularly known as Finn McCool) was raised and educated by two druidesses in the forest. Perhaps there was once a ritual in which a neophyte bard such as Little Gwion invoked Ceridwen, the Muse of the Welsh poets, by drinking a consciousness-altering brew from an actual physical cauldron.

Ceridwen takes away Gwion's life then gives it back by transforming him into a more glorious state of being as a prophet and bard of the highest degree. His radiant brow marks him as a "Shining One," for in Celtic tradition, light around the head was a sign of one filled with the inspiration of the Otherworld. His initiation begins when he undergoes the shape-shifting battle with Ceridwen. The sequence of events

---

*There was also an historical sixth-century Welsh bard called Taliesin, some of whose poems have survived to this day.

describes a process of "uncreation" or reverse evolution. In Western esoteric teachings, the act of creation is seen as a descent through the four
elements, beginning with fire, primal energy; through air, the mental
plane; water, the imaginal plane; and finally earth, the physical plane.
Gwion first becomes a creature of the earth as the hare, then of water
as the fish, of air as the bird, and lastly as a fiery spark of potential life,
symbolized by the grain of wheat. He is literally devoured by the goddess and reborn again as her child, which initiated him into the mysteries of death and rebirth. Yet his initiation is not at an end: her final act
is to cast him out to sea, another feminine symbol of primordial Being.
This last transformation also carries echoes of the myths of early agrar-
ian cults, like those of Attis and Osiris. The primary theme is that a
young god, consort of the Earth Goddess, appears to die like the seed
buried in the earth, but rises again as the new grain in the springtime.

This sequence may also hold the memory of the initiation rites of
the Near Eastern mystery schools of late antiquity. In Egypt, for example, initiates had to pass through the twelve hours of the night, corresponding to the sun's sea-journey below the horizon. Their emergence
was like the dawn's rebirth each morning. This underworld journey
took the candidate into the realm of the Great Goddess as receiver of
the souls of the dead and giver of new life. Gwion's transformation into
Taliesin is prefigured in his first name, Gwion, which derives from a
root word meaning "white" or "shining," like the name of Fionn mac
Cumhaill, his Irish counterpart. It refers to the soul that is often portrayed as a shining light. Gwion's initiation through the cauldron of
Ceridwen can be viewed as an allegory of the death of the egoic self
and the awakening to consciousness of the immortal soul, which tran-
scends time and space. On his return, he was said to be "twice-born,"
that is, first born of a human mother, then reborn of the goddess. But
in the Welsh story, Gwion is actually "thrice-born"—first from his
earthly mother, then from Ceridwen, and finally from the ocean. There
is something peculiarly Celtic about this; the number three is the most
sacred number, just as the power of the brew was contained in three
drops.

In another section of *The Book of Taliesin*, he describes the transformational states of consciousness that he experienced during his initiation:

> *I was in many shapes before I was released:*
> *I was a slender, enchanted sword . . .*
> *I was rain-drops in the air, I was star's beam;*
> *I was a word in letters, I was a book in origin;*
> *I was lanterns of light for a year and a half;*
> *I was a bridge that stretched over sixty estuaries;*
> *I was a path, I was an eagle, I was a coracle in seas; . . .*[7]

Gwion washes up at an estuary, a liminal place where land and water meet—a suitable place to re-enter the physical world. The fisherman who rescues him does indeed land a fish: Little Gwion has been reborn as the all-knowing Salmon of Wisdom! His transformation via Ceridwen's cauldron from ignorant neophyte to the archetypal Celtic poet, druid and seer is complete. What is more, it is clear that Ceridwen's cauldron is one and the same as the cauldron of Annwn sought by King Arthur in *The Plunder of Annwn*, for, in that poem, Taliesin declares how his Awen came from that very vessel:

> *. . . my poetry was uttered from the cauldron.*
> *By the breath of nine maidens it was kindled.*[8]

In the words of Celtic scholar, Patrick Ford:

He has been all things, knows what is, what has been, and what will be; he will endure till doomsday. He is, therefore, the repository of supernatural and otherworldly knowledge, the ultimate divine projection of the Celtic poet whose intensive wisdom (the literal meaning of . . . derwydd, "druid" . . . and other words associated with the scope of poetic activities among the Celts) was his hallmark.[9]

ROBBING THE GODDESS

The Birth of Taliesin points to Ceridwen's original identity as a Great Mother, coeval with primordial goddesses of the ancient world from neolithic Europe through Sumeria, Babylon, Egypt, and India, where she is still worshipped today as Kali. Ceridwen's children, in their polarized qualities of darkness and light, personify the opposites: the Two that emerge from the One to form the world of creation as we experience it. Celtic goddesses had two faces: the dark and the light—life-giving and death-dealing, womb and tomb. They were the midwives of the continual birthing and dying of the phenomenal world, forever spinning time's spiraling web of life-death-rebirth. Ceridwen's cauldron is a symbol of these opposites, being both the womb that gives birth to Taliesin, and also an instrument of destruction whose spilled contents poisoned the streams and the animals that drink from them. Vessels of all kinds are world-wide icons of the goddess, and in early British paganism they often take the form of a large kettle or cauldron. Where Celtic goddesses depicted in iconography on the European continent tend to bear cornucopias, their British counterparts are more likely to carry a large vat. Celtic scholar Miranda Green writes of such vessels: "It may be that the symbolism of the vat on the Celtic goddess images represents not only the presence of wine but specifically of red wine and therefore blood, death and resurrection."[10]

Arthur's assault on the Cauldron of Annwn is but one of many Celtic stories about a male warrior seizing a precious vessel belonging to women of the Otherworld. In another medieval Welsh tale, Arthur sails to Ireland and captures the cauldron of a giant called Diurnach, which subsequently becomes one of the Thirteen Treasures of Britain. Celtic scholar John Carey, in his book, *Ireland and the Grail,* shows Diurnach was originally a woman named Dorn whose gender was switched in successive retellings of the tale.[11]

A story about the Irish warrior, Fionn mac Cumaill, describes how he and two companions force their way into a sídhe mound where they encounter the daughters of Bec mac Buain, owner of an Otherworld

well whose waters bestow wisdom. One of them is carrying a vessel containing these waters, and as the daughters struggle to keep the
intruders out, water spills into the mouths of the three men. They are
immediately filled with *imbas forosna,* "the wisdom that illuminates,"
or visionary knowledge of the spirit world.[12] In another version, each of
the three daughters bears a cup filled with the "liquor of inspiration."
This is clearly the same fluid as the Awen imbibed by Gwion Bach from
Ceridwen's cauldron in the Welsh tale, which is another example of this
theme since Ceridwen intended the contents of her cauldron for her son,
not the hireling. Fionn is in fact the Irish counterpart of Gwion—both
names mean "white, bright, shining." It is clear that these Otherworld
women with their sacred cups or cauldrons were the prototypes of the
raped well maidens in the Grail story.

The repetition of this theme suggests memories of a matrifocal era,
perhaps in the Neolithic Age when tribes lived in Northern Europe by
growing crops and domesticating animals. These people came from the
Mediterranean and Eastern Europe where there is evidence they worshipped a Great Goddess of life, death, and rebirth.[13] Around 700 BCE,
the continental Celts began to move into the British Isles, bringing with
them a warrior-based culture that valued kingship and heroic exploits.
They still had goddesses, but these were now subordinate to male gods.
Stories about stealing the sacred vessel or its contents may be shorthand
for the appropriation of the indigenous cultural and religious symbols
by the Celtic invaders. Like the well maidens, these great goddesses, no
longer invoked or worshipped, withdrew into hidden Otherworld loca-
tions on far-off islands and deep within the Earth.

THE NINE MAIDENS

We can gain a further understanding of the goddess and her sacred vessel
by turning to the Nine Maidens, whose breath kindles the fire beneath
the cauldron of Annwn. First, let's look at the significance of the number nine which figures in practically every aspect of Celtic sacred traditions. The early Celtic cosmos was made up of nine elements; nine hazel

trees border the Well of Wisdom, the sacred source at the heart of the Otherworld; nine angels are frequently invoked in healing incantations; nine herbs were plucked to make healing charms potent; nine sacred woods cut for the kindling of the sacred fire in Scotland at Beltuinn, the festival on the first of May, and a bannock divided into nine sections baked for the feast; nine flowers are thrown into the midsummer fires in Cornwall—the list is endless. As to why this number is associated with magic, a number of theories have been put forward, the two most popular being:

Nine is the sacred number three multiplied with itself to amplify its power.

A child is nine months within the mother's womb, completing the cycle of human birth.

Author Stuart McHardy researched this subject exhaustively for his book *The Quest of the Nine Maidens* and found that companies of nine women abound in Northern mythology and cosmology. There are nine Valkyrie in Norse myth; while in Greek mythology there are nine Amazon warrior women, and nine muses of the arts. In Greenland, there is evidence that the seers known as the Völvas traveled around the country in companies of nine. In Siberian shamanism, the shaman takes a female partner from the spirit world who assists him in his magical work. She becomes his "celestial wife," while nine other feminine spirits called "the nine daughters of Ülgän" confer magical powers upon him. When a human being dies, these nine spirits "come down to earth, take his soul, and carry it to the heavens."[14]

Groups of nine women abound in a number of traditional tales of the Celtic Otherworld. In the *Voyage of Brân mac Febal,* an Irish chieftain sets sail for a paradise island inhabited by three times nine supernatural women. A tale from the book of place-name origins, *The Metrical Dindshenchas,* describes how Ruadh mac Righdonn sets sail in three boats for the land of Lochlann (the name given to Norway, but which can also refer to the Otherworld). Halfway across the sea, the ships are magically becalmed. Ruadh dives into the sea where he finds nine beautiful women: three under each boat, keeping them from moving. They carry him off and he lies with each of them for nine nights.

> *Nine women of them excellent and strong*
> *Hard it was to approach them;*
> *He slept nine nights with the women*
> *Without gloom, without fearful lament*
> *Under the sea free from waves*
> *On nine beds of bronze.*[15]

Another British tradition of nine sisters can be found in the legend of Peredur, a Welsh Grail romance dating from the fourteenth century, yet containing much older elements. The young hero, Peredur, is trained in the arts of warfare by the wild and fearsome Nine Witches of Caer Loyw (the modern city of Gloucester), yet another example of heroes and warriors receiving their initiation from women of magical power.

THE SISTERS OF AVALON

One of the most well-known companies of nine women appears in the *Life of Merlin* by the twelfth-century cleric, Geoffrey of Monmouth. Taliesin once again is a central figure in this story, and in one section he tells Merlin about a country called *Insula Pomorum*, the Island of Apples, also known as "The Fortunate Isle." It is a typical Celtic Otherworld: a timeless realm of abundance and beauty, covered with apple orchards and flowering plants, where no one grows old and all live in harmony and joy.

Taliesin goes on to recount how Arthur was taken to this isle to be healed of his battle wounds by a group of nine women skilled in magic:

> That is the place where nine sisters exercise a kindly rule over those
> who come to them from our land. The one who is first among them
> has greater skill in healing, as her beauty surpasses that of her sisters.

Her name is Morgen, and she has learned the uses of all plants in curing the ills of the body. She knows, too, the art of changing her shape, of flying through the air, like Daedalus, on strange wings. At will, she is now at Brest, now at Chartres, now at Pavia; and at will she glides down from the sky on to your shores. . . . They say she had taught astrology to her sisters—Moronoe, Mazoe, Gliten, Gliton, Glitonea, Tyronoe, Thiton and Thiten, famous for her lyre.[16]

The Queen of the Apple Island eventually becomes Morgan le Fay (Morgan the Faery) in the later Arthurian romances. In these she is often portrayed as scheming and malicious, yet the original Morgen is described as a wise woman and healer. And what of her sisters? With Morgen as the ninth, it is clear that all their names begin with the same initial, sorting them into three groups of three. Moronoe's name begins with the first three letters of Morgen's, "mor" deriving from the root word for either "great" or "sea." The three sisters whose names begins with the letter "g" may be related to an Irish Otherworld island queen, Clíodhna Fair-hair. Tyronoe may also have links with the sea, given the similarity of her name to Tyro, daughter of the ocean, whom Ulysses meets in Hades in Homer's Odyssey. Thiten with her lyre is reminiscent of Terpsichore, one of the nine Greek muses who played a stringed instrument called the cithara.[17]

The Isle of Apples, which elsewhere Geoffrey calls Avalon (from the Welsh *aval,* meaning "apple"), is another aspect of Annwn. In Welsh tales it is also described as being a paradise island across the sea. In fact, an early manuscript from Wales calls Morgen "goddess of Annwn."[18] Annwn and Avalon, like all Celtic Otherworld islands, is also a Land of the Dead where the souls of the departed take their rest after their sojourn on Earth. When Arthur is fatally wounded in his last battle on Camlann field, he is borne across the water to Avalon to be healed by Morgen and her sisters. In this respect, they play the same role as the nine Valkyrie who bring the souls of dead warriors to Valhalla in Norse tradition. Unlike his first voyage to Annwn—another version of Avalon—Arthur is doomed never to return to our world until the end of time, when, it is said, he will sail back to save his old kingdom in its hour of greatest need and usher in a new Golden Age.

PRIESTESSES OF THE ISLES

The ninefold sisterhood was not only a group of divine beings—there is also evidence that groups of nine flesh-and-blood women formed companies of priestesses in the ancient world, not only in the British Isles and Ireland, but in many parts of the world, including Greece, Scandinavia, Russia, and Romania.[19] The nine sisters, in fact, hold the key to the most ancient mysteries of the divine feminine as Mother of Creation, and afford us a clue as to how she was once worshipped. A description of nine priestesses dwelling apart on an island near Brittany can be found in the writings of Pomponius Mela from the first century CE:

> The island of Sein, facing the coast of Osimi, (Finisterre) was renowned for its Gallic oracle, whose priestesses, living in the holiness of perpetual virginity, are said to be nine in number. They were called Gallicenae, and were reputed to have extraordinary powers to rouse the wind and sea with their incantations, to turn themselves into whatever animal form they choose, to cure diseases which among others are incurable, and to know and predict the future. But they rendered their services only to those who traveled over the sea expressly to consult them.[20]

At the time Pomponius was writing, this account was a local legend, so there is no hard evidence of the existence of a priestess cult of shape-shifters, weather-workers, healers, and seers. Early Christian texts suggest that nine was a standard number for groups of holy women in the Celtic church, a custom that might have continued on from pagan religious practices.

A Scottish tale describes nine maidens who accompanied Saint Brighid from Ireland when she was invited over to Scotland by the King of the Picts. In one version they are called the nine virgin daughters of Saint Donald, who were all holy women. One of the daughters is called

Mazota, recalling Mazoe, one of Morgen's companions on Avalon. On their deaths, they were all buried beneath an oak-tree. Saint Brighid is closely associated with the oak, since her abbey was built at Kildare, which means the "church of the oak-tree." The oak was widely associated with pagan religious practices throughout the Celtic countries. Brighid presided over a fire sanctuary at Kildare, which was kept exclusively by her nuns, recalling the pagan tradition of the vestal virgins more than any Christian custom. These nuns were nineteen in number, although some commentators have suggested they may have originally been nine, or possibly there is significance in that $19 = (2 \times 9) + 1$, the last being Brighid herself.

The Ninefold Sisterhood has also given its name to sacred places in the landscape of Britain. In many parts of Britain are stone circles and even a stone row called the Nine Maidens; both the circles and the stone row date from the Neolithic age, over 4,000 years ago. Some of these, like the Nine Ladies stone circle in Derbyshire, are said to be dancers who were turned to stone for dancing on a Sunday.

The Nine Maidens Stone Circle, Cornwall. From Illustrations of Stone Circles and Chromlechs, etc. *by William Cotton, London, 1826.*

A number of Nine Maidens wells can be found in Scotland. A holy well at Sanquhar in southwest Scotland, dedicated to Saint Bride (Brighid), was visited each *Beltuinn* (the first of May) by girls who placed nine white stones within its waters.[21] (Since this festival is associated with love and fertility, they were most likely hoping that Bride would bless them with a husband and family.) Were these mysterious sites once the meeting-places of nine women who, down the ages, gathered to worship the ancient creator goddess in her ninefold aspect?

THE COSMIC MILL

In order to fully understand the significance of the Nine Maidens and the cauldron of the deeps, we must turn to Scandinavian mythology. In Norse tradition, the *axis mundi* was sometimes pictured as the "World-Mill," whose handle extends from the Pole Star in the heavens all the way to the bottom of the ocean. This kind of mill is called a "rotary-quern," which was invented in late prehistoric times. It has a flat, non-moving, lower millstone and an upper stone that is rotated by turning a handle at the center. In early Northern cosmology, the lower stone was seen as the Earth, a stationary disc, while the upper stone was seen as the sky, revolving around the celestial axis, marked by the Pole Star. The World-Mill is rotated by nine maidens at the bottom of the sea, who create the material universe by grinding out the blood and bones of Ymir, a dead giant who was made of clay. This image most likely entered Celtic mythology as the revolving castle of the Irish king CuRoí, a king of Munster; the castle rotated in accordance with the turning of days and nights: "In what airt* soever of the globe CuRoí should happen to be, every night o'er the fort he chaunted a spell, till the fort revolved as swiftly as a mill-stone. The entrance was never to be found after sunset."[22]

The revolving castle entered Welsh mythology as Caer Pedryvan, the fourfold island-castle which Taliesin describes in *The Plunder of Annwn*:

Airt means "direction" or "point of the compass."

I am one who is splendid in (making) fame: the song was
  heard
In the four-turreted fort, fully-revolving.[23]

It seems that the original Nine Maidens who kindled the Cauldron
of Annwn belonged to a long-extinct cosmology of the Northern world,
where they were seen as creative forces of the physical universe.

THE CAILLEACH

These nine creator goddesses were remembered in Scotland as the
Cailleach (pronounced "kal-yach") and her eight servants. *Cailleach*
originally meant "veiled one," a name often given to those who belong to
hidden worlds, although the name has come to mean "old woman," "hag,"
or else refers to a veiled nun. Celtic legends suggest the Cailleach was
once a creator goddess who gave birth to the mountains of Scotland and
Ireland. On the *Sliabh na Caillighe* (pronounced "shlee-uv nuh kal-ee"),
or "Hill of the Hag," in County Meath, Ireland, stands a cluster of *cairns,*
or "earth-chambers," dedicated to her. They are ornamented with carvings
of mysterious spirals, chevrons, and other Neolithic designs and appear
to have been both burial places and centers of ritual worship. On the side
of the largest cairn is a great stone slab known as the Hag's Chair where
people sit in order to make a wish. Stone "seats" such as this are also found
in Scotland, and were originally visited by women wishing to conceive a
child, for they represented the life-giving, fertile aspect of the Cailleach.

The Cailleach also embodies the forces of destruction as well as the
forces of creation, not unlike the Hindu goddess, Kali, with whom she is
often compared. In Scotland she was said to have had eight "hag-servants,"
thus forming another magical company of nine women. Together they
flew about the mountains on black goats calling up storms in the winter months. Like Kali, too, she is described as dark-blue in color:

There were two slender spears of battle
upon the other side of the carlin

her face was blue-black, of the lustre of coal,
And her tufted tooth was like rusted bone.

In her head was one deep pool-like eye
Swifter than a star in winter
Upon her head gnarled brushwood
like the clawed old wood of the aspen root.[24]

Her one eye identifies her as a primal being, who, like Ceridwen, has her origin in the unified dimension that exists beyond the world of opposites. Her name suggests she had her origins in a proto-Indo-European death goddess, Kolyo, "The Coverer," who was beautiful and hideous at the same time.[25] Also like Ceridwen, the Cailleach has two aspects: giver and taker of life. She is both womb and tomb, the dolmen gate through which the ancestral dead make their last journey and from which new souls are called forth into the world. The destructive aspect tends to be ignored or played down in modern times, yet in Celtic tradition it was considered the first dynamic in the cycle of life, for in order to create anew, the old must be destroyed. Thus the Cailleach presided over the dark half of the early Celtic year, which began in Scotland at Samhuinn, "Summer's End," on November 1, and continued until Bealtuinn, the start of summer on May 1. The fierce destructive rains and gales of winter were seen as a necessary cleansing and emptying out of all the energies of the old year, to make way for a new cycle of growth.

The Cailleach also has a cauldron, which in this case is a whirlpool close to the southwestern coast of Scotland. The whirlpool is known as Corryvreckan, the cauldron of Bhreacan, for it appears to be ceaselessly churning a vast vat of boiling water. Local legend describes the whirlpool as being the breath of the Cailleach beneath the waves. When winter gales make the waters even more turbulent, the Cailleach is said to be washing her white plaid in the whirlpool. The first winter snow on the mountains is said to be the plaid laid out to dry. Corryvreckan does look like an actual cauldron at certain times of the year, and the whirlpool creates a spiral effect on the surface of the sea whenever the tide runs. The spiral, of course, is a primal symbol found in Neolithic art, especially in the great earth chambers of Brú na Bóinne and Sliabh na Caillighe—and also on the Scottish mainland quite near to Corryvreckan itself.

From this we can see that the Nine Maidens who guarded the Cauldron of Annwn have their origins in the tremendous forces of pre-creation which are continually engaged in the cycles of destruction, transformation, and recreation of the universe. They are primal creator goddesses, continually giving birth to the world of Form out of Chaos. With their breath, a metaphor for the cosmic life force, they kindle the cauldron of creation and bring our world into being. *Awen* also derives from the word for "breath," just as *inspiration* literally means to "breathe in," or "in-spire." This means that we as human beings, like Taliesin, can also imbibe the generative power of the divine feminine to ignite our own inspiration and bring other creations into manifest form.

Arthur's quest for the Cauldron of Annwn is revealed as a search for the cosmic power which underlies all manifest life and is embodied by the divine feminine and her sacred vessel. It is this that lies at the heart of all later stories of the Holy Grail.

VisionJourney I
The Cauldron of Creation

Journeys to the Celtic Otherworld usually involve a crossing by water. This invisible country lies beneath a spring, at the bottom of a lake, or below the waves of the sea. Arthur and Taliesin sail to Annwn, while Arthur is taken to Avalon in a barge. In similar tales, the inner-world voyager may have to find a way through a magical mist or dive into the depths of a well. In many cases, the Hidden Country is found through entering a hill or burial mound, in which there may be an underground river that has to be crossed.

The crossing by water is an esoteric reference to the change of consciousness from the sensory world to the astral plane in which only the inner senses can be our guide. This first VisionJourney takes you over the inner seas to Caer Sidi, the faery island of Annwn.

Sit in a comfortable position, relax and quiet your mind. . . . Take some deep breaths and imagine you are breathing in a beautiful, silvery violet light. The light fills your body and swirls around you like a mist. . . .

The mist lifts and you see you are standing on a beach at midnight, looking out to sea. The waters stretch away toward the horizon, and there is a gentle swell that gives little hint of the sea's restrained power and mysterious depths. A full moon like a gleaming pearl sheds its light over the vast expanse of the sea, creating a path of dancing silver lights on the water that leads right up to where you are standing. Your feet are bare and you are aware of the cold sharp stones beneath them. You listen to the waves sucking at the pebbles as they draw back from the shore, and then crash as they break once again a few feet from where you stand, spraying you with foam. Taste the tang of salt water on your face, and inhale deep draughts of the sea air.

You start to count the wavelets as they break on the beach: one . . . two . . . three . . .

When nine waves have passed, you find yourself floating effortlessly across the waves. Out of the corners of your eyes, you are aware of shimmering shapes, as if the People of the Waves are making themselves visible to you . . . and you may even hear the sibilant whispers and laughter of the Mermen and Merwomen—the Merrows—and the Selkie folk.

Before too long, you arrive at the shore of an island, and you know that it is Caer Sidi, the Faery Island of Annwn. You appear to be all alone, but there are voices on this isle—soft voices that accompany you with low chanting as you walk, as if in a dream, through an orchard of apple trees glowing silver in the moonlight, to its innermost secret heart. Here you discover a clearing in the center of which stands an immense cauldron, the Cauldron of Annwn, dark blue and rimmed with pearls. Around the cauldron is a circle of nine standing stones made of white gleaming quartz. You can almost feel the electrical quality that emanates from them and almost hear the ultra-sonic hum of energy they emit.

As if sensing your presence the white stones suddenly begin to move, and the next moment they are no longer stones but have become nine Guardians, hooded and still. You realize they must be the Nine Sisters of Caer Sidi, primordial priestesses as ancient as the moon. Nine faces gaze at you, darkly beautiful, with almond-shaped eyes. The tallest, speaking without words, challenges your right to be here, and you search for the right answer. And it comes, unbidden, as it has always come; the password to ancestral memory:

> *I am a child of Earth and of Starry Heaven;*
> *But my race is of Heaven alone. This ye know yourselves.*
> *And lo, I am parched with thirst and I perish. Give to me*
> *The knowledge flowing forth from the Cauldron of Memory.*[26]

If your request is granted, one of the Ninefold Sisterhood comes forward and dips her hand into the cauldron. She anoints your brow in a spiral pattern, then sprinkles three drops on your eyes and on your lips. This has the effect of a window opening in your mind—as if you can see more clearly with crystalline vision. . . .

And now the Ninefold begin softly to hum an unearthly chant and start to move sinuously in a mesmerizing dance around the cauldron, swirling about like diaphanous strands of mist. Their voices rise higher and the cauldron begins to glow and expand. . . . As they spin more and more swiftly they turn from maidens into crones: nine ancient hags with flying grey hair that stir the whirlpool of the cosmic sea with long and bony fingers turning the mill-wheel of space and time to grind out the stuff of creation from the ceaseless energy of the Void. . . .

Their voices rise in a roaring torrent of sound which rises to crescendo as the cauldron revolves faster and faster, spinning around until it is no longer a vessel but a whirling vortex of effulgent light. . . . In the center two dragons, red and white, writhe in furious combat, as the Two are cast out from the One in the perpetual dance of attraction and repulsion, never-ending until all the worlds shall cease. This is the Cauldron of Annwn, the Cauldron of Rebirth, of the Awen, the Flowing Spirit that surges up from the abyss to be uttered in the sound of creation that is the primal breath of all that lives and dies and is reborn on Earth. . . .

Now up from the cauldron gushes a fountain of light, rising higher and higher in a radiant column reaching to the heavens. And from the bowl of night, the circling constellations pour down an answering river of light that comes streaming down to meet it. You gaze upward to watch these ascending and descending streams of light that spiral up and down in ceaseless motion. Sometimes they seem as great winged Beings of Light ascending and descending a spiral stairway, and sometimes as two luminous serpent shapes weaving a double helix pattern of creation.

Then the dance stops as suddenly as it began, the streams of light subside, and the song of creation is stilled. A tall, graceful woman dressed in midnight blue robes enters into the circle: Morgen, the Lady of Annwn. Smiling, she beckons you forward to gaze into the Cauldron of Creation. Within its depths you see the infinite ocean of probabilities where swirl the etheric waters of potential reality, countless waves of possibilities waiting to be brought to shore by the tides of time. You may become aware of things past that are dissolving away, and many cycles trembling on the verge of becoming. The cauldron is also a mirror of your own subconscious mind, and so you also see swirling within all your dreams, fantasies, and illusions. Some may be negative and fearful, others full of positive energy. The choice is yours as to which dreams to nurture into being and which to let dissolve back into the flowing waters. . . .

And now the surface of the cauldron becomes utterly still and all is profoundly silent and calm like a vast ocean of peace. You know you are witnessing the underlying stillness behind all the turbulent motion of the world of appearances. Stay in this peaceful awareness as long as you like. . . .

Now the Lady dips her hand into the water and brings up something from the depths of the cauldron, which she offers to you as a gift. Take it in your hands and ponder well upon its meaning. . . . She may have words to say to you as well. . . .

When this experience feels complete, the waters within the cauldron start to wrinkle and move like the sea, while the rim of pearls become the white waves about its shores. You fall into its depths and wash up on the shore where first you stood.

Now open your eyes and come fully back to present time and space.

2

The Cup and the Branch

We've now looked at a number of Celtic stories in which a male figure—king or warrior—robs a faery woman of her sacred vessel. However, some tales portray a more harmonious relationship between masculine and feminine, pointing back to a time when the sacred feminine was honored and revered. These tales are centered around a goddess whom the early Celts knew they must respect because she was more powerful than all of their deities. They were utterly dependent upon her for her good will and acceptance of their leader, for she represented the land on which they lived. As noted in the introduction, in early Irish society the High King had to forge a sacred contract with this powerful guardian, otherwise the country would fall into ruin: harvests would fail, the trees would bear no fruit, women would miscarry, and the people sicken and die. For the goddess to grant him sovereignty, the king had to show that he was truly committed to caring for the land, which was her earthly body. Although there are no reliable historical accounts of how this sacred contract was sealed,[1] Irish stories suggest it most likely would have included a ceremonial drink from a vessel of mead or ale.

For example, a ninth-century Irish text, *Baile in Scáil* ("The Phantom's Vision"), tells how the great warrior, Conn of the Hundred Battles, is walking up the ramparts on the royal hill of Tara when he accidentally steps on the Stone of Destiny, which cries out beneath his foot—a sure sign that he is destined to become king of Ireland. A magical mist arises and a ghostly horseman appears and invites Conn into

The Ardagh Chalice from eighth-century Ireland

his Otherworld palace, in front of which stands a golden tree. Inside, a beautiful maiden, wearing a crown of gold, is sitting by a silver vat with gold hoops, which is filled with red ale. The young woman invites Conn to a splendid feast, then takes a gold ladle and fills a gold cup with the ale. She asks, "To whom shall this cup be given?" The horseman—who turns out to be the god Lugh—tells her to offer it first to Conn and then to all of his unborn descendants in the royal line. At the end of the visit, the gold vat, ladle, and cup are entrusted to Conn's care as the regalia of sacred kingship of Ireland. The name of the girl is Flaith Érenn ("Sovereignty of Ireland"). She is also known as Ériu, the goddess who gave her name to Eire: Ireland. As the personification of the land it is fitting that her consort is Lugh, who was originally a god of light and the sun.[2] Elsewhere her husband is named as MacGréine, "Son of the Sun." The fertilization of the Earth by the Sun in summertime is the vital "marriage" that makes life in the Northern Hemisphere possible. As discussed in historian Michael Enright's book, *Lady with a Mead Cup,*[3] this episode is probably based on an actual historical king-making ritual in Celtic society in which a high-born woman initiates a ruler.

GODDESS OF LIFE AND DEATH

A story from eleventh century Ireland illustrates the nature of the goddess of sovereignty as a deity of life and death. In this narrative, she is the guardian of a well, an entrance to the feminine watery deeps and another form of the vessel of the goddess.

Five young brothers are sent out hunting one day to prove their skills. They lose their way in the forest and go in search of water. Before long, they find a clear, bubbling spring, but it is guarded by a monstrously ugly old woman. As each of the brothers in turn approaches the well, she declares she will only give them water in exchange for a kiss. Each of them declines the offer in disgust, although one of the brothers gives her a quick peck. Finally, the young man called Niall gives her a wholehearted embrace, whereupon she changes in his arms to the most beautiful woman in the world, with hair "as gold as Bregon's buttercups and lips as red as the lichens of Leinster."[4] She tells Niall that he will become High King of Ireland, and that all the generations of his descendants will continue the royal line:

> *I am the Sovranty . . . as thou hast seen me loathsome,*
> *bestial, horrible at first and beautiful at last, so is the*
> *   sovranty;*
> *for it is seldom gained without battles and conflicts,*
> *but at last to anyone it is beautiful and goodly.*[5]

And so Niall becomes the greatest of Ireland's High Kings, the ancestor of the Uí Néill family that is destined to rule over Ireland from the sixth to the tenth century.

This story also illustrates the two faces of the Celtic goddess: young and old, beautiful and ugly, symbolizing the ever-changing natural cycles of youth and age, life and death, summer and winter, and so on, in our world of opposites. By appearing in her most repulsive aspect first, the goddess of the land is able to test for a true king, one who is not fooled by appearances, who knows that the most precious treasure is usually hidden in the most unlikely places. He is willing to put aside self-gratification and deal with difficult situations with kindness and compassion. He will be able to be a good leader in harsh winter as well as in easeful summer, in times of war as well as in peace. Above all, he understands the mysteries of life and death as two sides of the same coin, and so has a mature insight into the true nature of things. This sacred alliance between the king and the goddess of the land lies at the heart of the later Grail stories.

THE ADVENTURES OF CORMAC

Many ancient cosmologies, religions, and magical systems recognize a primary unified source—God, Brahman, Kether, and so forth—that divided itself into two polarized forces in order to create the universe as we know it. In Hindu cosmology, for instance, the two primary feminine and masculine forces are personified as Shakti and Shiva. Shakti's symbol is the yoni, represented by a holed stone, basin, and downward pointing triangle. Shiva's symbol is the lingam, which may take the form of an upright stone, pillar of light and upward-pointing triangle. The lingam is often depicted as resting in the yoni symbol to show their natural union and inseparability.

Although no pre-Christian cosmologies survived the advent of Christianity in the British Isles and Ireland, we find traces of these primal symbols paired together in Celtic myth and legend. We have already seen how the symbol of the sacred feminine is the vessel, cup, cauldron, or well; the masculine counterpart to this is the branch, rod, or staff. These two talismans have their origins in the sacred center of the Otherworld where they appear in their primal forms as a Well of Wisdom and Tree of Life. This is illustrated in a fourteenth-century bardic story from Ireland, *The Adventures of Cormac in the Land of Promise*, in which a High King of Ireland is initiated into the mysteries of the Otherworld so that he may learn to become a wise ruler. The story goes as follows:

One Beltaine morning, just before sunrise, Cormac, son of Art, son of Conn the Hundred-Fighter, stood on the high walls of his fortress on the Hill of Tara and saw riding toward him a gray-haired warrior robed in purple and gold. He bore a branch of silver from which hung three golden apples. When he shook the branch, beautiful music rang out. Cormac invited the stranger into his hall where the golden apples chimed out music so sweet that all want, woe, and weariness of the soul melted away, and the sick were lulled to sleep.

He told Cormac that he came from a land where there was only truth, where everyone lived in joy and peace, and never grew old or ill. Cormac longed to possess the magical branch. The warrior told Cormac, "It is yours in exchange for three boons you must grant me when next I return to Tara."

"Whatever you want will be yours!" cried the king.

The warrior bound him to his promise, gave him the branch, and disappeared.

For a year, the silver branch brought solace and delight to all at Tara. But at the end of that time, the gray-haired warrior returned and demanded his first payment—Cormac's young daughter, Ailbe. The king was stunned, but had to hand over the girl. Cormac's wife and the women of Tara were beside themselves with grief until Cormac seized the branch and waved it over them, and they forgot all their sorrow. A month later the warrior returned, and this time he took with him Cormac's young son, Cairbre. Weeping and sorrow filled the halls of Tara, but Cormac shook the branch above them all and once again their sorrow melted away into forgetfulness. Then, one month later, the gray-haired warrior returned for his third boon—Cormac's beloved wife, Ethne. This time Cormac could endure no more. Followed by his entire court, he pursued the warrior with all speed, but a magical mist came down and the king soon found himself separated from his companions, lost in an impenetrable cloak of gray.

When at last the mist unfurled, Cormac found himself in the Otherworld. Many marvels he saw as he wandered through this land seeking his wife and family, and finally he arrived at a stronghold encircled by a wall of bronze. Cormac walked boldly in and saw before him four palaces made of silver and bronze, thatched with the wings of white birds. In the courtyard stood a shining well whose waters bubbled up and overflowed to form five streams of water. A host of people were drinking from it. Around the well grew nine hazel trees whose purple nuts dropped into the well. Five huge gleaming salmon leapt up out of the well and cracked the nuts in their jaws, sending the shells floating down the streams. The music of those streams was more melodious than anything he had ever heard in our world.

The king and queen of this Otherworld court, a couple of radiant beauty, came out to greet Cormac and invited him to feast with them. A huge cauldron hung over a fire in the center of the feasting hall, and a whole pig was cast into it. But the pig would only be cooked when a true tale was told for each quarter of it. Three true tales were told, and when it was Cormac's turn he related the story of the silver branch and his search for his wife and children. The pig was ready to eat, but hungry though he was, Cormac refused to eat without his family and company of men. The King of the Otherworld sang a magical song that put Cormac to sleep, and when he opened his eyes again, there stood before him his wife, with their son and daughter on either side of her, and fifty of his warriors from Tara. After a joyous reunion, they celebrated with a great ale-feast. The Otherworld king drank from a splendid cup of gold, and Cormac remarked on the strange and intricate shapes carved upon it.

"There is something even more strange about it," said the Lord, "Let three falsehoods be spoken under it and it will break into three. Then speak three truths under it, and it will unite again." He placed the cup in Cormac's hands.

"Soon you may return home with your family, and you may take also the cup which will help you discern the true from the false. And you shall also have the silver branch for music and delight. But on the day you die they will disappear once more from the world. I am Manannán son of Lir, King of the Land of Promise. It was I who brought the silver branch to Tara and took your family so that you would follow me here."

That night, Manannán gave Cormac many wise teachings, and the most important concerned the magical well: "Above all, you must remember the well of the five streams. For that is the Well of Wisdom, and the streams are the five senses through which knowledge is attained. But no one will have wisdom unless they drink both from the streams and the wellspring itself. The people of many arts are those that drink from both."

These were the last words Cormac heard before he fell asleep. When he awoke the next morning, he found himself on the green hill of Tara with his wife, son, and daughter, and in his hands were the Silver Branch and Cup of Truth.

THE WELL AND THE TREE

The story of Cormac's journey into the Otherworld is wholly different from those in which the goddess is robbed of her sacred vessel. Manannán (who is often portrayed as a trickster-like character) lures the king into his realm in order to initiate him into the mysteries of the Otherworld. Rather than making off with the sacred totems, Cormac shares in the feast from the Cauldron of Plenty and is given the Cup of Truth to take home along with the Silver Branch, so that he can resume his reign in right relationship with the spirit world. Of course, in this story, which is comparatively late, the totems of the goddess are already in the keeping of a masculine figure. Manannán has a wife, but she remains an unnamed, shadowy figure in this story. Elsewhere, she is named as Fand, and in the folklore of the Isle of Man (Manannán's isle) she is regarded as a faery queen. It's possible that the Cauldron of Plenty and Cup of Truth were once in her keeping, since, as we have seen in chapter 1, these totems traditionally belong to the feminine powers of the Otherworld.

The most important feature of this story in terms of the mythologems underlying the Grail myth is the description of the shining well and nine hazel trees at the center of the Otherworld. These are versions of the primal symbols known as the Well of Wisdom and Tree of Life, which represent the two primary complementary forces which underpin all of creation.

The Well

The Well, as we have seen, is feminine: the watery womb of the Mother. Throughout antiquity water was regarded as the primal element, the very matrix of our world: the ocean out of which all life emerged. A Vedic text proclaims, "Water, thou art the source of all things and of all existence!" Springs and fountains have always been considered sacred because they embody a miraculous outpouring of the spiritual power of water from the depths of the Earth into the everyday world. In many cultures they are associated with female spirits, priestesses, and oracles, the traditional guardians of this gateway to the spirit world, like the well maidens of the Grail story.

The Tree

The Tree is masculine. The old Irish word for a sacred tree, *bile,* comes from the same Indo-European root that gives us "phallus." In Irish bardic tales and magical stories, the Tree of Life may appear as a single tree or in multiples of three and sometimes, as here, to the power of nine. It is portrayed as an apple tree, bearing the fruit of immortality, or as in this story, as hazel trees with wisdom-bestowing nuts. It can appear in full bloom, shedding its blossom, and laden with fruit or nuts all at once, since it is rooted in a world beyond linear time where there are no seasons.

In many cultures, the fruit-bearing tree that provides a shelter and food for birds is regarded as a feminine symbol. But in Northern shamanic traditions the tall, straight tree tends to be perceived as an expression of the masculine principle, thrusting skyward. It becomes the axis mundi, the vertical pillar that bridges the lower, middle, and upper worlds, often symbolized by a pole, ladder, rope, or stairway. This tends to be the case in Celtic myth and folklore in which trees are associated more with men than with women.

Among the Gold Eskimos, the high point of an initiation ceremony occurs when the master shaman climbs a birch tree, circling its trunk nine times.[6] In another Siberian community, the initiate is carried on a felt mat along a row of birch tree nine times, after which he climbs each tree, circling it nine times, calling the spirits from the top. This number nine is also profoundly important in rituals of Nepalese shamanism, where Bhujel initiates climb a pine tree that has been felled and erected in the center of the village. At this point, the shaman-teacher shouts, "Ho!" nine times and with each shout the student slides part way down the tree until he reaches the ground.[7] Perhaps the nine hazels of Celtic tradition recall a lost shamanic tradition of early Ireland.

Wood and Water

So in the Celtic worldview the spiritual source of all life is discovered in the ecology of trees and water. No static image here, the deepest Mystery dances with life and motion, and many interchanges take place: water flows, nuts fall, and salmon leap. Where the waters emanate from hidden depths below the earth, the Tree of Life rises toward the power of the sky. The gushing well and its cluster of hazel trees show that this is a place where the mysteries of earth converge with the heavens to form a dynamic interplay of the opposites. Where water suggests the potential for life on Earth, the tree makes life manifest.

Throughout the ages seekers of truth—poets, philosophers, rulers, and other pilgrims of the spiritual quest—have made the perilous journey to this sanctum. For the sacred nuts dropping from above to meet with the gushing waters below unite heaven and earth. The salmon in the well act as intermediaries by cracking the nuts. In the threefold shamanic universe, they make the knowledge of the upper and lower worlds available to our middle world, which is why "the people of many arts"—the druids, seekers, and artists lining up at the well—desired above all things to eat the sacred salmon and nuts of wisdom.

The sacred ecology of trees and water is enshrined all over the Celtic landscape, where hundreds of holy wells bordered by guardian trees still dot the countryside today—living shrines where people have come for centuries to drink or bathe in the waters and leave a votive offering torn from their clothing on overhanging branches. Even today, the number of ragged cloths and ribbons hanging from trees are testimony that pilgrims still follow the old tracks that lead to that mysterious beckoning water with its magical promise—of healing, of foretelling the future, and of granting a wish. They still come because even the muddiest pool, choked with weeds or trampled by cattle, evokes the half-submerged memory of the Well of Wisdom, while the branches of the most spindly tree still seem to sway to winds that blow in another world.

The archetypal pairing of Tree and Well is universal, found in the earliest of religious texts: the Rig Veda and the Upanishads of Ancient India. In Judeo-Christian traditions also, the same pairing is found in the description of the Garden of Eden:

> And out of the ground made the LORD God to grow every tree that is pleasant to the sight, and good for food; the Tree of Life also in the midst of the garden, and the tree of knowledge of good and evil.
>
> And a river went out of Eden to water the garden; and from thence it was parted, and became into four heads.[8]

Tree and water converge not only at the center of the place where the world has its beginning, but also at its end, for the same image appears in Saint John's vision of the Heavenly City in Revelations: "And he shewed me a pure river of water of life, clear as crystal, proceeding out of the throne of God and of the Lamb. In the midst of the street of it, and on either side of the river, was there the Tree of Life, which bare twelve manner of fruits, and yielded her fruit every month: and the leaves of the tree were for the healing of the nations."[9]

THE SACRED PATTERN

In Cormac's story, the Well and Trees lie within a *temenos* or "sacred space." Celtic audiences would have envisaged the four halls as forming a square around the courtyard, a pattern that clearly corresponds to Caer Sidi (the Faery Castle) or Caer Pedryvan (the Four-Cornered Castle) in *The Plunder of Annwn*. In another poem from the *Book of*

Taliesin we can see that the caers of Annwn and Manannán's castle were patterned from the same archetypal template:

> *Perfect is my seat in Caer Sidi:*
> *Neither plague nor age harms him who dwells*
> *therein.*
> *Manawydan and Pryderi know it;*
> *Three musical instruments round the fire play*
> *before it,*
> *And around its corners are ocean's currents,*
> *And the fruitful spring is above it.*
> *Sweeter than white wine is the drink in it.*[10]

Here Taliesin is describing his bardic chair in the Otherworld realm, whose timelessness ensures that no one grows sick or old. Manawydan is the Welsh equivalent of Manannán, and the "fruitful spring," whose water is "sweeter than white wine," is of course the Well of Wisdom. Pryderi is the son of the Otherworld queen, Rhiannon, who has many of the attributes of the goddess of sovereignty. This design of a four-cornered Otherworld palace with a sacred spring in the center is also used to describe the Grail Castle in some later Grail literature.

The Otherworld castle is clearly a Celtic version of a cosmic pattern of "harmony and wholeness," or *mandala,* to use the Eastern term. The fourfold pattern (pillars, towers, or four-cornered island) delineates the four directions, while the tree and well form the axis mundi, joining the underworld, middleworld, and upperworld, thus completing the seven directions of ancient cosmology. As one would expect, this design also occurs in sacred art and architecture. Many European monasteries have quadrangular cloisters with a fountain playing in the center, while in the Islamic world the court of the mosque has the ritual wash-house in the center. This design can frequently be seen in medieval European art, as the "fountain of youth" in a walled garden. In medieval alchemy, it is the *fons mercurialis,* a

The Alchemical Fount of Life

"fountain of life," within a square of swirling clouds with four stars at the corners, a sacred emblem of wholeness.

THE SILVER BRANCH

The Silver Branch and Cup of Truth are miniature versions of the Tree of Life and Well of Wisdom, small enough to be carried in each hand, like the royal scepter and orb. The Silver Branch appears in a number of Irish Otherworld stories, sometimes laden with apples or covered with shining blossoms, a talisman that gives humans access to the spirit world. It is clearly the Celtic counterpart of the golden bough of the classical world, which the hero must pluck from the tree at the gate of Avernus, the Roman underworld, as described in Virgil's *Aeneid*.

In one of the earliest immrama, the eighth century Irish *Voyage of Bran Mac Febal,* the chieftain Bran is walking by his fortress one day when he hears heavenly strains of music that lull him into a deep sleep. When he awakens he finds an apple branch covered with silvery-white blossoms in his hand. Bran returns home taking the branch with him, and that night, as he and his noblemen are all gathered in the feasting-hall, a beautiful woman dressed in shining raiment appears before him. She sings captivatingly of the wonders and pleasures of the Isle of Women, her country over the sea. This is Emain Ablach, or Emain of the Apple-Trees, the Irish Avalon.

When her song ends, the silver branch springs from Bran's hand to her own and, after daring the chieftain to follow her across the sea, she vanishes. Bran wastes no time; he sets sail with his men the next day, and after many adventures they arrive at Emain Ablach, where they are greeted by the Queen and her three-times-nine companions, recalling the Nine Maidens again, who lead them away to enjoy the many delights of this "wondrous land." In Emain Ablach grows the Tree of Life, a spreading apple-tree, in which live the many magical birds that belong to the Queen. Their glorious song fills the air with sweet sounds and is clearly the source of the exquisite music of the silver branch, as if it has saturated the branch and remains there long after it has been cut from the tree.

The silver branch seems to have served as a magical tool within a lost Celtic initiatory tradition. Graduates of the bardic colleges in early Ireland bore boughs of bronze, silver, and gold with chiming bells, each according to his level of achievement in the arts of poetry and divination. These branches may have been signs of their successful entry into the Otherworld, which we know was part of the training of the *fili,* the Irish "poet-seer." This tradition may have links with Siberian shamanism where the shaman made a spirit journey to the Cosmic Tree at the center of the world for a branch of the Tree. He fashioned it into the hoop of his drum, which he beat in order to return to the tree and make his ascent or descent to the spirit realms.[11] Perhaps these symbolic branches were used in Druid magic for to bear a bough from the Tree of Life is to be a scion of the tree itself, with the ability to gain access to its deeply rooted wisdom.

THE MAGICAL CUP

Cauldron and Cup play a central part in Cormac's adventures in the Otherworld. Manannán's cauldron (which is both a Cauldron of Plenty and of Discernment) is a symbol of the divine feminine, along with the Cup of Truth and the Well of Wisdom. The cup of the goddess carries her protection and blessings, as illustrated in an Irish immram *The Voyage of Teigue mac Cian*. In this story, Teigue and his companions arrive at an Otherworld island where they find a splendid hall laid out in a fourfold pattern. In the center grows the Tree of Life: an apple tree bearing both blossom and fruit together. Here the voyagers meet a beautiful woman of the sídhe, Clíodhna Fair-hair, who presents Teigue with an emerald "cup of virtues," one virtue being that water in it is immediately transformed into wine. She tells him he must not part from the cup or else he will die, for it embodies her protection of his life.

THE DANCE OF LIFE

Well and Tree, Cup and Branch, together represent feminine and masculine in balance, partners in the cosmic dance of life and death. Affirming and maintaining this balanced relationship lies at the heart of Western esoteric tradition, which differs from some Eastern perspectives in which the spiritual goal is to transcend earthly existence, reaching a state of consciousness where the opposites no longer exist and there is only unity. Western esotericism focuses on bringing spiritual influences into human consciousness while still being actively engaged in the world, as reflected in the Hermetic maxim, "as above, so below."

In *Cormac's Adventure* these polarized symbols converge at the heart of the spirit world where the source of all life reveals itself as a sacred dance of water and tree: living patterns of dynamic creation brimming over with life and movement. A central teaching of Western esoteric tradition is that we must learn (drink) both from the source of *numen* at the spiritual source (the well) and also live fully through the five senses of the body (the streams). The "people of many arts" is a translation of the Irish *áes dána,* a name given to the skilled classes of medieval Ireland. Chief of these were the *filid,* members of the druid class who specialized in being able to enter the Otherworld to gain arcane knowledge—figuratively eating the hazelnuts or the salmon of wisdom. This teaching is timeless and relevant to all artists and spiritual seekers in every day and age. To live a conscious and creative life, we must regularly connect back with the source of our inspiration, the wellspring that ever bubbles below the surface of the outer life. If the streams of one's own individual talents and resources are not fed from the source, we risk them drying up all together. Working magically with the Branch and Cup can realign the outer self with the inner soul, and help us live in harmony with the Earth and all beings.

VisionJourney II
The Tree of Stars

The following VisionJourney will enable you to connect with the worlds above and below and to magically empower your body and mind with their influences.

Sit in a comfortable position, relax and quiet your mind. . . . Take some deep breaths and imagine you are breathing in a beautiful silvery and emerald green light. The light fills your body and swirls around you like a mist. . . .

The mist lifts and you find yourself walking down a noisy city street. A foul wind is blowing litter everywhere. There are homeless people squatting in doorways, unnoticed by the people hurrying by. A pair of eyes catches your attention. They belong to an old woman—a bag-lady surrounded by her worldly possessions in plastic bags. For one so old and poor, the eyes are unusually bright, set deep in a brown wrinkled face. She holds out a battered enamel cup for spare change and you drop in a handful of coins with a smile. *As you turn to go, still gazing at her mesmerizing eyes, you trip over the cane of the old blind man next to her. With apologies, you pick it up and hand it back to him. The old man seizes the cane with an astonishingly strong grip, knocking you off balance and jerking you forward with some violence, for you find yourself quite unable to let go of it. The world spins around, you are swept off your feet, and the next moment the street scene has completely vanished into mist. . . .*

Silence. Then you hear the song of a bird. The world is right-side up again, but now you are standing before a gigantic tree with spreading branches, whose topmost ones are hung with shining fruit. It overhangs a well: a pool of clear water. . . .

On one side of the tree stands a man: a muscular warrior clad in royal purple. His face is strong and wise. He holds out his hand. You look down and see that the cane is still in your hand only it has turned into a slender curving branch on which hang three golden apples. You give it to him and he takes it with a smile. On the other side stands a woman. She is tall and stately, a golden circlet about her hair. You realize, by her bright, knowing eyes that you have seen her before, but her face is now young and sparkling with life. She carries a silver chalice instead of an enamel cup.

The Lady offers you the chalice and bids you dip it into the shimmering waters of the Well and drink. . . . It is like drinking light itself. A feeling of deep, quiet well-being spreads through you as the water washes away the residue of the past and purifies your heart and mind. . . .

The Lady takes back the chalice and the Lord invites you to pluck one of the fruits of the tree. You begin to climb up through its lower branches, which is easy at first, but the higher you go, the further the crown of the tree seems to be, receding into deep stellar space above you. The sky is no longer blue, but black as midnight. It seems like you have been climbing forever, and when you finally reach the branches hung with shining fruit, you see they are the stars themselves. . . .

You pluck a star, and the next minute find yourself floating downward then landing softly and unharmed on the mossy ground at the feet of the royal pair. The Lady tells you to take the star home and plant it in a special place so that another Tree of Life may grow. As you are wondering how exactly you can get back home, the Lady bids you look into the Well, where you see the great tree reflected. Surprised, you realize that she means you to dive down to the reflected tree within the pool. You lower yourself into the water, finding that you can breathe quite easily, and clamber down the trunk toward the branches far below. As you reach the crown of the water-reflected tree, you step off and find yourself home again in your own room.

Now cup your hands around the star-seed and plant it in your heart. Immediately a Tree of Light begins to sprout within the soil of your soul, its roots reaching down through the base of your spine, your feet, and into the earth below, connecting you with the wisdom of the deeps. The trunk grows straight and tall up through your spine and emerges like a branchy crown at your head, linking you with the knowledge of the stars. Stay in this place for as long as you want, enjoying your connection with Heaven and Earth. . . .

Now open your eyes and come fully back to present time and space.

Exercise
Harmonizing Earth and Sky

By following the steps below, you can now work with these energies whenever you want to feel connected with these sources of power within the Earth and Stars.

1. *Become aware of the Tree of Stars within you as you did in the above VisionJourney.*
2. *Start a pattern of deep, slow breathing. When you are ready, on the next in-breath let your awareness follow the roots of the tree into the depths of the Earth below you. Become aware of your roots being nourished by the waters of the Well of Wisdom and on the next in-breath, draw these energies up into your lower body through your right foot and leg. You might see this energy as a vibrant shining emerald green color. Let the energy rise as far as your pelvic area, then visualize it streaming across to your left side and flowing*

down your left leg and foot and back down into the Earth, carrying any unwanted energies (e.g., negative thoughts or stressful feelings) as it returns. Some of the pure energy flows up your "trunk" into your whole mind-body system. Feel any energetic shifts and open yourself to receive any images and information from this source.

3. Now let your awareness rise up the trunk of the tree and connect with the stars high above. On the next in-breath, let starry rivers of radiance flow down your branches and trunk and suffuse your mind and body with the silvery light of star-wisdom. Be aware of it flowing down into your "trunk" and mingling with the light from the Well. Feel any energetic shifts and be open to receive any images and information from this source.

4. Each time you work with your Inner Tree, be sure to write down what you learn.

Regular practice of this exercise will help you feel more grounded and centered in your everyday life and also more connected with sources of inner wisdom, beauty, and power.

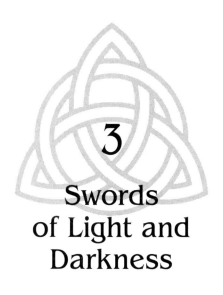

3
Swords of Light and Darkness

Cup and Branch of the early Celts become Grail and Sword in the Arthurian cycle where there is a continual struggle for balance between feminine and masculine. Because this conflict remains unresolved within Western culture both collectively and individually, the stories continue to be told down the centuries. Martin Luther King, Jr. brilliantly articulated the perennial human struggle to balance the Sword (power) with the Cup (love):

> Power properly understood is nothing but the ability to achieve purpose . . . one of the great problems of history is that the concepts of love and power have usually been contrasted as opposites—polar opposites—so that love is identified with a resignation of power, and power with a denial of love. . . . What is needed is a realization that power without love is reckless and abusive, and love without power is sentimental and anemic. Power at its best is love implementing the demands of justice, and justice at its best is power correcting everything that stands against love.[1]

The first part of Arthur's career belongs to the Sword and the second, to the Grail. We will look at each of these themes in this and the following chapter in order to fully understand and work with these two powers within ourselves.

WHO WAS KING ARTHUR?

Arthur is beyond doubt one of the most famous heroes in Western mythology. His legend has a perennial and timeless appeal. But was there ever a living King Arthur? Historians have debated that question for years, and many believe there was, in the form of a sixth-century warrior, who, as the Roman Empire crumbled away, gathered together the remnants of the British tribes and fought back the invading Teutonic tribes from the East. He brought peace and unity to the land for a short but never-to-be-forgotten space of time. Whether Arthur was from Wales, Cornwall, Scotland, or Brittany, we shall never know, but even today, people from all those regions claim him as their own, and the landscape of the northwestern fringe of Europe is rich with places that bear the king's name: Arthur's Seat, Arthur's Hill, Arthur's Cave, Arthur's Footprint, Arthur's Stone—the list goes on, for his spirit endures in the land itself.

But our chief concern is not with the historical Arthur, nor the Arthur of medieval romance. The esoteric Arthur is more than all of these: he is a Son of Light, for every nation must have their storied hero, the sun god, the bringer of light, redeemer from darkness, or savior of the world. Arthur, the "once and future king," is deeply embedded in the folk-soul of Western nations, an archetype of regeneration and renewal, whose memory keeps the dream of a new Golden Age alive in the hearts of all those who are weary with the lack of spiritual vision in today's world.

THE SWORD OF LIGHT

In Celtic tradition the chief symbol of the Son of Light is the Sword, which becomes as a ray of light or flash of lightning in his hand. As the feminine powers of the Celtic Otherworld are associated with magical vessels: cups, cauldrons, vats, and wells, so the masculine powers are bearers of wondrous swords, like the invincible sword of the Irish god, Nuadu: "No one ever escaped from it once it was drawn from its deadly sheath, and no one could resist it."[2] The swords of gods and heroes often blazed with light like a laser beam. The great Ulster hero Cuchullain had a sword known as *in Cruaidín Catutchenn,* the "harsh-headed steely one," which shone at night like a torch. Cormac mac Art, the legendary High King of Ireland, had a sword that shone like a candle, and was so sharp that it could cut a hair on water. One of the Thirteen Treasures of Britain was also a fiery weapon: the sword of Rhydderch the Generous. "If a well-born man drew it himself, it burst into flame from its hilt to its tip."[3]

Excalibur, the sword of King Arthur, derives its name from the Welsh *caledvwlch* which, in turn, comes from the Irish *Caladbolg,* meaning "hard lightning." Excalibur was engraved with two golden snakes from whose jaws two flames flashed when the sword was drawn. The two snakes are equivalent to the pair of dragons who represent the polarized currents of energy within the land. Arthur himself is closely associated with the dragon, since he bears the name of *Pendragon,* meaning "Head" or "Chief Dragon" (a traditional title of a line of British kings). The color gold emphasizes his role as a Son of Light— the rising sun of a new Golden Age. In Sir Thomas Malory's *Le Morte d'Arthur,* when Arthur first uses the sword at a crucial moment during his first battle, "it was so bright in his enemies' eyes, that it gave light like thirty torches."[4]

Excalibur is a gift from the inner feminine power called the Lady of the Lake. Arthur's original sword, which he won after pulling it out from an anvil on a stone—the famous "Sword in the Stone" episode— has broken in battle and the king needs a new one. Merlin, Arthur's druid-like counselor, who acts as mediator between the world of the court and the realm of the Otherworld, takes the young king to meet the Lady:

> So they rode till they came to a lake, that was a fair water and broad, and in the midst of the lake Arthur was ware of an arm clothed in

white samite, that held a fair sword in that hand. Lo! said Merlin, yonder is that sword that I spake of. With that they saw a damosel going upon the lake. What damosel is that? said Arthur. That is the Lady of the Lake, said Merlin; and within that lake is a rock, and therein is as fair a place as any on earth, and richly beseen; and this damosel will come to you anon, and then speak ye fair to her that she will give you that sword.[5]

Arthur rows out onto the lake to receive the sword from the Lady. This is a moment of great significance: up through the deep feminine waters of the lake, a portal to the inner realms, the Lady raises the Sword, the masculine symbol of power for the new Sun King of the outer world. It emerges from the underworld like the first ray of the rising sun from beneath the horizon. So does the goddess bless the king with the gift of Excalibur, a weapon of the Light with which to rule his kingdom. Inner and outer worlds come together to forge a sacred contract of divine kingship with the goddess of the land.

But the young king shows signs of the fatal dominance of masculine over feminine values, which will pervade his reign. Merlin asks him which he prefers: sword or scabbard. Arthur, whom we can imagine brandishing the flashing blade in delight, replies that, of course he likes the sword best. Merlin rebukes him, saying,

Ye are more unwise . . . for the scabbard is worth ten of the swords, for while ye have the scabbard upon you, ye shall never lose no blood, be ye never so sore wounded; therefore keep well the scabbard always with you.[6]

Merlin's point is that the scabbard, clearly a feminine symbol, is more precious than the sword itself, because it magically protects the wearer's life. Merlin's advice comes from experience born of age that recognizes the deeper wisdom of the power that conserves life rather than destroying it. We can almost imagine Arthur brushing off such advice with youth's impatience for action. But the young king's choice of sword over scabbard hints at the imbalance that contains the seeds of destruction for Logres and the end of all hopes for a Golden Age of peace.

THE THREE SWORDS

The Sword has many aspects and functions that can be categorized into three main groups:

> The Sword of Light
> The Sword of Destruction
> The Sword of Spirit

Now let us explore each of the three groups more fully.

The Sword of Light

Like a ray of the rising sun, this Sword brings a new dawn by subduing darkness. It is a symbol of strength and power, an extension of the skill and physical prowess of Arthur and his knights who vanquish the enemies of Logres, inspired by a vision of a unified kingdom. It is a discriminatory weapon that cuts away the false from the true, so that the kingdom may be purged of mutinous and unruly elements. Led by Arthur, a new society emerges based on the ideals of chivalry, valuing justice, loyalty, courage, and courtesy. This Sword belongs to the Warrior archetype, representing the bold new impulse that re-energizes a stagnant status quo. We can see this in action in our own world when a new and energetic visionary leader emerges to overturn a corrupt or stagnant regime and bring hope to the nation's people.

The Sword of Destruction

The Dolorous Stroke

This Sword has the opposite effect of the Sword of Light. It turns good to evil and severs lover from beloved. This is played out in the tale of the dolorous stroke, which provides an alternative explanation of how the Wasteland came about. It concerns two brothers, Balin and Balan. Balin slays an evil knight at a feast in the castle of King Pellam to avenge a damsel he has championed. The damsel's lover has been slain by the evil knight. By killing a guest, Balin breaks a cultural taboo of the highest degree. The outraged king attacks Balin, whose sword breaks. He races through the halls and corridors of the castle in search of another weapon, the king at his heels. At last he comes to a gorgeously arrayed chamber where he sees a golden table on four pillars of silver, and lying upon it, a "marvelous spear strangely wrought." He seizes it, turns, and thrusts it into King Pellam's side. In that moment, the castle crashes down in ruins about them.

When Balin regains consciousness, his first concern is for the damsel he avenged, but she, like many others, is lying dead in the rubble. King Pellam has sustained injuries that can only be healed by a pure spiritual being, for the spear that wounded him was one of the Grail Hallows, which the centurion, Longinus, thrusts into Christ on the cross. He has become the "Wounded King," and his kingdom has become the Wasteland.

Dismally, Balin travels through the wasted land, and after more sorrowful adventures, meets with a knight who kills himself with his own sword because of his lover's betrayal. Balin, worried that people might think he murdered the knight, escapes in the dead man's armor. In this guise, he engages in a battle with a knight completely armored in red, and the two knights fight each other to the point of death. Only then does Balin realize the Red Knight is his beloved brother, Balan, who did not recognize him in the unfamiliar armor.

The brothers are buried in the same tomb, whereupon Merlin appears and puts a new hilt upon the sword. He pronounces that at some future date, Sir Lancelot will also wield it to "slay the man that in the world he loved best"—Sir Gawain. His prophesy comes true when the Round Table is utterly destroyed by the civil war that culminates in Arthur's death and the ruination of Logres.

The Broken Blade

The story of the dolorous stroke makes it clear that the Sword, when not balanced with the protective function of the scabbard, also wounds the masculine principle. King Pellam, wounded by a spear, which carries the same symbolic valence as the Sword, will suffer endless pain and torment as the Wounded King of the Wasteland. Balin loses his beloved brother, Balan, by unwittingly murdering him. What poignant significance there is in that moment when the knights remove their visors and recognize each other as brother! This moment in itself is a perfect vignette of what war-poet Wilfred Owen called, "the pity of war," the ultimate act of the violence of separation in its darkest aspect when we see all too late that "the enemy is us." This is surely the darkest side of the Sword archetype. As Merlin predicts, the evil of the Sword does not end with the brothers' deaths, but spreads and contaminates the lives of others.

Like the perilous sword-bridge that must be crossed in many of the Arthurian knights' adventures, to wield the Sword is to walk a razor's edge between the necessary pruning of perverted growth and evil and the wanton violence that negates life. The hegemony of imperialistic societies both East and West, sanctioned by politics and religions dominated by the imbalanced masculine principle, has been the tragic theme sounding throughout the history of modern civilization and continues unabated today in our war-torn and plundered world.

The Sword of Spirit

Paradoxically, the sword that Balin stole with such catastrophic results plays a large part as an instrument of healing in the quest to redeem the Wasteland. Merlin's appearance at the death of Balin and Balan heralds the sword's transformation into a weapon that can also be wielded to win the Holy Grail itself when in the hands of Galahad, the purest of all knights. First Merlin leaves the scabbard on the island where he foresees that Galahad will find it, then he works his magic on the sword to bring it to Camelot. "Merlin let make by his subtilty that Balin's sword was put in a marble stone standing upright as great as a mill stone, and the stone hoved always above the water and did many years, and so by adventure it swam down the stream to the City of Camelot, that is in English Winchester."[7]

Years later, at a feast of Pentecost,* the sword appears in a stone floating down the river outside the court, and Arthur invites his three best
knights to draw it out. All the best knights of Arthur's court try their
skill at drawing it out, but none is successful. Then Galahad appears for
the first time at Camelot bearing no arms but the scabbard of Balin's
sword that Merlin left for him to find on the island. The young knight
easily draws the sword from the stone and sits in the Siege Perilous, which
is reserved for the Grail Knight alone. These two events clearly proclaim
that Galahad will be the one to succeed in the Grail quest.

This weapon has been transformed into the Sword of Spirit, which
represents the focused aspiration of the seeker toward spiritual enlightenment. It destroys only evil and pierces the veil of illusion. Only the
pure knight, Galahad, manages to pull it easily out of a marble stone in
a parallel scene to Arthur's youthful sword-in-the-stone episode. So, as
Arthur achieves kingship of the outer court by drawing the sword from
the stone, Galahad's equivalent act demonstrates his fitness for ruling
the inner court of Spirit. As a warrior for the Light, the Sword he wins
represents the spiritual will to cut through the world of illusion in order
to facilitate healing, as in the lancing of a poisonous wound. It is the
dividing sword of the stage in the alchemical process known as the *divi-
sio* or *separatio,* which Mercurius wields to help the alchemist extract
the *anima* or *spirito* from the *prima materia.* In other words, it releases
light out of darkness, which, in the human context, means the spirit is
set free from the conditioned self.

ARTHUR AND GUINEVERE

The imbalance between masculine and feminine is also played out in
the drama of Arthur's relationship with Guinevere. Their marriage fails
to produce an heir,† and there is no evidence of love between them—a

---

*Pentecost was the traditional feast-day when coronations and initiations took place in
the Arthuriad.

†In medieval Welsh literature Arthur has three sons, but they were never included in
later Arthurian romance.

situation that leads to the queen's affair with Lancelot, the great champion of the court, and eventually, to civil war, leading to Arthur's death. The failure of the marriage is particularly significant, because although medieval romances depict Guinevere as a weak, flawed, human woman, they cannot hide her original nature as a goddess of sovereignty.

In medieval Welsh texts, which have their origin in an older stream of tradition, Guinevere is called Gwenhwyfar—the Welsh version of the name Finnabair. Finnabair is the daughter of Queen Medb (Maeve), the sovereignty goddess of Connacht in northwestern Ireland. Gwenhwyfar is usually translated as "white spirit," although it can also be read as "Gwenhwy-vawr," *Gwen the Great,* in contrast to her sister, "Gwenhwy-vach," *Gwen the Less,* who is her dark counterpart.[8] The meanings suggest that the two "Gwens" are two faces of the primordial Celtic goddess. Celtic goddesses were also frequently portrayed with a three-fold aspect, and Gwenhwyfar appears in triplicate in one of the Welsh verses from the thirteenth century *Trioedd Ynys Prydein* (Triads of the Island of Britain):

Arthur's Three Great Queens:
Gwennhwyfar daughter of (Cywryd) Gwent,
and Gwenhwyfar daughter of (Gwythyr) son of Greidiawl,
and Gwenhwyfar daughter of (G)ogfran the Giant.[9]

One of the chief symbols of sovereignty associated with Guinevere was the Round Table she brought as her dowry to Arthur on their wedding day. Originally, Merlin had made it for Uther Pendragon, Arthur's father, from whom it passed to King Leodegrance, the father of Guinevere. The table can be seen as representing Guinevere herself, as historian Richard Cavendish explains: "Guinevere is the Round Table's presiding goddess, as it were. Arthur acquires it by marrying her, in something of the same way perhaps as in Celtic tradition he 'married' the land of Britain in her person."[10]

A circular table meant that, unlike the usual long, rectangular ones of a king or nobleman's hall, where each was seated according to rank, all those who sat at the Round Table were acknowledged to be of equal worth, "thus no man could boast that he was exalted above his fellow, for all alike were gathered around the board, and none was alien at the breaking of Arthur's bread."[11]

And so the Fellowship of the Round Table was born, with its allegiance to the ideals of medieval chivalry—to be loyal and true to the king, fair and merciful in battle, to be an advocate for women, and not to start wars for unjust reasons. Yet there is a deeper, esoteric meaning underlying these social ideals. "For in its name it mirrors the roundness of the earth, the concentric spheres of the planets and of the elements in the firmament; and in these heavenly spheres we see the stars and many things besides; whence it follows that the Round Table is a true epitome of the universe."[12]

The Round Table then is a mirror of our solar system, which is presided over by mighty beings whose outer faces are the stars, who keep their eternal vigil over our planet Earth. Esoteric teachings describe them as mediating their influence through the seven stars of Ursa Major, the Great Bear, or Plough. In this view, the Round Table can be seen as the circle in the sky marked by the Bear's rotation around the Pole Star. The earthly Round Table, presided over by a company of the most noble knights and their king, was originally meant to be a reflection of this starry circle. In one version of the Arthurian cycle, the Fellowship of the Round Table is twelve in number, which suggests the chosen knights are meant to be the earthly representatives of the Zodiacal constellations themselves.

RETURN TO AVALON

Guinevere's affair with Lancelot follows a well-known theme in Irish and British mythology in which a beautiful woman, symbol of the sovereignty of the kingdom, rejects its aging king for a younger man who will make a fitter ruler of her territory. This theme propels the famous tragedy of Tristram and Iseult. Behind these stories lie the tenets of sacred kingship, famously explored at length in Fraser's *The Golden*

Bough, whereby the king must be in the prime of his life in order to be a fit consort to the goddess, for the fertility and prosperity of the kingdom depends on their successful union.

In the medieval romances, Guinevere is often described as flagrantly promiscuous; yet in the context of a goddess of sovereignty, it is her responsibility to choose as her partner the man most fit to rule her kingdom. Throughout the Arthurian cycle, Guinevere is continually "abducted" by different men, not because of her beauty, but because she is perceived as the means to seize the throne from Arthur. This theme can be detected in the Irish tales of Queen Medb, who was the wife of nine kings in succession. No king was allowed to rule at Tara without mating with her first. Her promiscuity was not of the human variety, but a symbol of the fecund Earth itself.

Seen in this light, it is easy to understand why the king's evil nephew, Mordred, seizes the queen and tries to force her to marry him when Arthur is absent. He sees Guinevere as his means to becoming king himself. But union with the goddess of sovereignty cannot be forced without the direst of consequences, and as a result, both Mordred and Arthur are killed, the Knights of the Round Table scattered, and the kingdom of Logres falls into utter ruin.

At the end of the Arthurian epic, as the king lies dying on Camlan field, he commands one of his two surviving knights, Bedivere, to cast his sword Excalibur back into the lake from which it appeared. Twice Bedivere hesitates, but finally throws it into the lake, at which a hand reaches up for it, brandishes it three times, and disappears below the waves again. The Lady of the Lake has come to claim her own, now that Arthur is no longer under contract to the goddess of the land.

The return of the Sword to the watery abode of the feminine calls forth the Three Queens, aspects of the old Celtic Triple Goddess. They come to bear Arthur away to Avalon in a barge, that he may be healed by Morgan le Fay, one of the ninefold sisterhood. The king is finally about to be reunited with the goddess in a way that was impossible during his physical life. For, according to some medieval romances, Morgan not only heals Arthur's wounds, but takes him to be her lover or consort. In fact, a number of French *chanson de gestes* ("songs of heroic deeds") include stories of questing knights who come to Avalon and find Arthur and Morgan ruling happily side by side. As an anonymous Latin verse succinctly puts it:

> *Avalon's court see suffering Arthur reach:*
> *His wounds are healed, a royal maid the leech;*
> *His pains assuaged, he now with her must dwell,*
> *If we hold true what ancient legends tell.*[13]

A fourteenth-century Spanish poet, Guillem de Torrella of Majorca, told how he rode on the back of a whale eastwards to an enchanted island where he saw Arthur alive and well. The king told him how Morgan healed his wounds by bathing him in a fountain whose source is the Tigris River, which flows from the Earthly Paradise. His youth was continually restored by frequent visits from the Holy Grail.[14] The Tigris is one of the four rivers that flow out of Eden, so here once again we find ourselves in yet another version of that fourfold paradise with its healing spring and cup that restores health and youth.

The medieval minds that crafted this ending to the story of the king's turbulent and tragic reign were revisiting the Celtic concept of a sacred contract between the king and goddess of the land. On a spiritual level, the royal marriage of Arthur and Morgan is a sacred union of the opposites, and the Sword and the Grail are once more conjoined in harmony—but our world is not yet ready for this event, and so Arthur remains in the Otherworld until we call him back into the world of time.

Exercise

Working with the Three Swords

The Sword is an important symbol of three stages of the human journey of consciousness, and is instrumental at the three seasons of an individual's life: youth, adulthood, and maturity.

Stage 1: The Sword of Separation

The Sword in childhood represents the developmental task of the child to separate out his or her unique identity from the primary caregiver(s). The child's goal is to become an autonomous individual, with a sense of self-determination. At this stage, the sword is an instrument of separation.

When the young Arthur pulls the sword out of the stone—a feminine symbol representing the dense, heavy energy of the Earth—he is playing out the classic struggle of the Young Masculine principle to break free of the Old Feminine. It is worth repeating here that this is a universal dynamic that can be witnessed in the cosmos on many levels, whenever something new struggles to emerge from the old. The Old Feminine might be represented as a circle that constantly treads the same circuit, familiar and comfortable in its predictability, yet ultimately static and non-creative unless it allows the Young Masculine to emerge from its matrix. This upward and outward motion creates the spiral of growth and evolution of all things—from the seed in the ground to the idea in the mind. If it hinders this process, the nourishing womb becomes a devouring tomb. Thus Arthur achieves the "kingship" of his own self, which is the goal of each child.

Stage 2: The Sword of Power

The next initiation of the Sword belongs to adulthood, when it is the task of the hero to undergo the tests and trials of the world, learn how to make the right choices and decisions, and overcome challenges in order to create a relatively stable work and family life; the hero makes a "kingdom" of his or her own. To be successful at this stage, each individual must separate from family and early social conditioning and move into the future confident in his or her unique personhood, able to think and act out of a strong sense of inner authority.

Stage 3: The Sword of Higher Will

The third level is concerned with the mature adult who, having achieved a reasonably integrated sense of self and a measure of social stability, is now concerned with developing the spiritual Self. Here, the Sword becomes an instrument of the higher will, which requires the constant honing of the ego-personality in service to the "Great Work." In Arthurian myth this sword is wielded by Galahad, the embodiment of the spiritually evolved knight who alone is fit to wield the "Sword of Spirit."

Although these "swords" relate to developmental periods in a human life, these are not the only times when they function. For instance, a woman leaving a marriage at mid-life may be wielding the Sword of Separation. An adolescent deciding not to give in to peer pressure by taking drugs is exercising the Sword of Power.

- *Look back at your life and think about three significant times when you have wielded one of these inner Swords.*
- *Which Sword do you need most in your current life situations? Imagine yourself wielding it with focused intent, strength, and power. Visualize clearly what you hope will happen and how your life will change as a result.*
- *Write down how wielding the Sword makes you feel, and what you need to do in your life to make these changes manifest.*

THE ONCE AND FUTURE KING

As one of the primordial Guardians of Britain, King Arthur will never die: he is very much alive within that secret country where time does not exist. Belief in his return has been embedded in the collective unconsciousness of the West for hundreds of years. A Welsh triad lists the graves of other heroes, but concludes, "Not wise the thought a grave for Arthur!" Legends throughout Britain tell how Arthur is living in the underworld, where he presides over abundant feasts along with hundreds of his knights, or holds court in a magnificent palace beneath a hill. Arthur, Merlin's great hope for a new Golden Age, has, like the sun, set below the Earth where he awaits a new dawn.

In many legends Arthur is still believed to be asleep in a cave, awaiting a call to arise again and save his country in her hour of greatest need. Versions of this legend often recount how a traveler stumbles upon a cave in which lie a group of sleeping knights. Here he discovers a sacred object, often a sword or a horn: masculine and feminine symbols. One such story comes from Richmond in North Yorkshire, which is dominated by a magnificent cliff-top castle overlooking the River Swale. A local potter named Thompson discovered a secret cave below the castle and followed it deep underground until he arrived at a large cavern in which lay King Arthur and his knights, asleep around the Round Table. On the table stood an ancient horn and a mighty sword. Thompson reached out and picked up the horn, but the sleepers began to awake and, fearing for his life, the potter fled. As he raced down the tunnel back to daylight and safety, he heard a voice behind him declare:

> *"Potter Thompson, Potter Thompson!*
> *If thou hadst drawn the sword or blown the horn,*
> *Thou hadst been the luckiest man e'er was born."*

Another significant legend comes from Cadbury Hill in southern Somerset, just eleven miles from Glastonbury, which has long been regarded as the original Isle of Avalon. Archaeologists have found evidence that there was a strongly fortified settlement on top of the hill in the sixth century when Arthur, the British warrior and chieftain, may have flourished. For centuries local people called it Camelot, and believed the ramparts to be the remains of his palace; they have long since been covered with grass, yet are clearly visible to this day. They also believed the hill was hollow, and Arthur and his knights lie sleeping inside, waiting to come to the aid of their country in a time of peril. Every seven years on Midsummer's Eve, the king and his cavalcade ride out over the causeway known as King Arthur's Hunting Path to Glastonbury, with light shining from their spears and the horses' silver hooves. A party of antiquarians visiting the site on a field trip in the nineteenth century were accosted by an elderly local man who anxiously enquired, "Have you come to take the king out?"[15]

And so Arthur remains hidden within the land until the time of the Great Awakening—not just of the king, but of *ourselves*—for we are the ones who are really asleep. Arthur and his knights cannot come alive again until we rouse ourselves from spiritual torpor, awaken from the deadly sleep of materialism, and once more take up the challenge of the Sword and the quest for the Grail. This is why, in the legends, a human being must blow the horn to awaken the Sleepers—for only we can rouse them to wakefulness and action; they can't do it on their own. Until that time they are like Christ, unresurrected, Osiris, unfound, and John Barleycorn in perpetual wintertime. Perhaps, lying in the quietness of the cave, they dream of each generation of human souls treading down the centuries, searching among the downturned faces for the ones who will open their eyes and look up to see the substance, not the shadow. Perhaps they silently plead with us, as in Christopher Fry's famous poem from the play, *A Sleep of Prisoners:*

> *It takes*
> *So many thousand years to wake,*
> *But will you wake for pity's sake?*[16]

VisionJourney III
The Sleepers in the Cave

Close your eyes, quiet your mind and take some deep breaths. Every time you breathe out, you exhale a pearl-white mist that soon surrounds you, curling about you, and now gently lifting you off your seat so you feel yourself starting to float upward. . . .

Let the mist carry you in spirit to the ancient county of Somerset, which once was known as the Summerlands. This is where the mighty ones who made this country once walked her highways, forded her streams and strode free as the wind upon her hills . . . where myths and the people who made them never entirely disappear. It is a place where Arthur and his

shining knights can still be seen riding out from the hollow hill of Cadbury on moonlit nights across the marshes to Glastonbury Tor. For all who lived to serve the Light have laid their mark upon the land, and time shall not erase it. They have gone into Avalon and we shall meet them there. . . .

See before you now a steep, green hill, whose lower slopes are covered with beech trees. Although the fortress that once crowned it has crumbled into dust and only banks and ditches remain, it is still called Cadbury Castle, for once it was a stronghold for the dwellers of this land some seven thousand years ago. And 1,500 years ago it was the castle of King Arthur and has ever been known as Camelot. . . . The path is deeply rutted as if only yesterday the wooden horse-drawn carts trundled up with supplies, and cavalcades of warriors rode out to battle. As you walk steadily up this track, avoiding the worst of the ruts and muddy patches, it seems that with every step you take, time slides away. Looking down at yourself, you see you are wearing the clothes of long ago. You sense you are but one of an ancient procession which, for centuries untold, has toiled up this path, returning home to Camelot. . . .

At last you emerge from the tree-lined path where a chill evening breeze whips your hair back from your face and stirs your inner senses into wakefulness. You see before you a long green ridge whose outline is strangely altered by deep ditches and high banks that were once the ramparts of the castle walls. Behind the ridge to the West, the setting sun has painted the sky with amethyst and crimson. To the North, across the Somerset levels, you see in the distance the dim but unmistakable pyramidal shape of Glastonbury Tor. To the South, the gentle wooded hills of Wessex roll away to the sea. Above you, the seven stars of the Great Bear are becoming visible in the rapidly darkening sky, pouring down their celestial light, and you recall that this is the constellation known as Arthur's Wain, the king's chariot that circles through the midnight skies. . . .

Within the hill is a pair of great iron gates. As you approach, you see a tall figure standing motionless before them. It is a Lord of ancient years, shrouded in a dark cloak that sweeps the ground. In his gnarled hand he bears an oaken staff. The staff is very long, and in the dim and wavering half-light, gives the illusion of reaching up to the very stars themselves, like *a tall tree. Although he gives the appearance of great age, the bearded face of this lord is lit from within as if by a smoldering fire. He is looking directly at you with a steady gaze from piercing blue eyes. You are aware that you are being appraised and challenged as to your right of entry into this place. If he is satisfied that you are one who is willing to serve the greater circle of life, he touches the gates with the tip of his staff, and they open with a rumbling sound to reveal a dark cavern within the hill. . . .*

Merlin, for of course it is he, leads you through the gates, and speaks a word that causes a blue light to flare up from his staff. By the light, you see hundreds of armor-clad warriors asleep, each with a white steed lying by their side, all as silent as stone. As you gaze in wonder, the words of an old song seem to go whispering around the cavern, you know not from where:

> *Ah, who among you will wake the Sleepers?*
> *Who will blow the golden horn?*
> *Who will draw the flashing sword*
> *And dare to be reborn?*

> *Who among you will wake the Sleepers?*
> *Who will face the wind and fire*
> *When you have unleashed the force*
> *Of what you most desire?*

> *In the east the dawn is breaking,*
> *The land cries out in pain,*
> *"Who among you will wake the Sleepers*
> *And let me live again?"*

The song fades away with a sighing sound, and all is still once more, as the dust of the ages settles again around the cavern. Merlin leads you past the sleeping knights into a far chamber where stands an oaken table bearing a gleaming, golden horn and a silver sword in a leather sheath, whose forms seem to tremble in the flickering light of the wizard's staff.

Merlin fixes you with an expectant gaze under bushy white brows, and speaks: "Know, seeker, a choice lies before you: if you choose to blow the horn, your note will sound out throughout all the regions of Middle Earth to proclaim the presence of one who is willing to awaken from the sleep of the ages. By the utterance of this sacred sound, your life will resonate henceforth to a new and higher frequency, and many things may change. And if you choose also to draw the sword, you will set the compass of your life to a path that requires you to be pure in purpose, strong in will, and steadfast in spirit. Think carefully now, and act only according to your heart's desire."

Merlin's words pulsate around the chamber, then die away, and he speaks no more, but silently raises his staff aloft. From the tip of the staff streams a light, and the light turns into a silver bridge. . . . You find yourself gliding over this bridge as it shoots up into the air in a great arc. It is the bridge to the future . . . your future . . . and as you cross the bridge of time, you see moving images of your future life, which show you what will happen should you choose to blow the horn, draw the sword, or leave them both untouched. . . . You may also meet ones here who are the people of the future. Talk with them and find out what their lives are like. What are their needs? You are now one of their ancestors. Can you help them?

After a while, you return to the Cave of the Sleepers. . . . You are now ready to make your choice, to blow the horn, draw the sword, or do neither. Do what it is you need to do, and sense the results of your actions or non-action resonating around the cave and rippling out through all the worlds. . . .

And now it is time to return. Merlin leads you back through the cavern of the sleeping knights, who may appear to have changed in some way. The great iron gates close behind you with a thundering crash, and when you turn again, Merlin is no longer there, and the green hillside is simply covered with grass. You make your way back to the path between the beech trees, and as you slowly descend, a pearly mist begins to curl around your legs then covers you completely. . . . You are aware that, within the mist, you are floating back to your own place and your own time.

When you are ready, open your eyes and come back to the room.

4

Women of the Grail

Midway through the Arthurian cycle, the Sword gives way to the Grail. King Arthur and his knights have successfully subdued the warring elements in his land and achieved law and order throughout the realm. In some narratives, Arthur even defeats the Romans and becomes Emperor of Rome. Now the Sword has fulfilled its function in the outer world, it must be balanced by the Grail. For, as we have seen, this sacred vessel is the redemptive principle which will heal the primary wound of Logres, renew the Wasteland, and restore the Courts of Joy. As Anne Baring and Jules Cashford have written in their seminal book, *The Myth of the Goddess:* "The chalice, vessel, cup, dish and stone that are the primary images of the Grail evoke the archetype of the Feminine, which becomes the inspiration, guide and goal of the knights' inner quest."[1]

Having conquered the outer limits of their world, the quest for the Grail has become the only worthwhile adventure remaining to the heroes. The last frontier lies in the country of the soul.

THE GRAIL COMES TO CAMELOT

The Grail first appears in King Arthur's court at Camelot on the Feast of the Pentecost, as described in the fifteenth-century French romance, *Queste del Sant Graal:*

When they were all seated and the noise was hushed, there came a clap of thunder so loud and terrible that they thought the place must fall. Suddenly the hall was lit by a sunbeam which shed a radiance through the palace seven times brighter than had been before. In this moment they were all illumined as it might be by the grace of the Holy Ghost, and they began to look at one another, uncertain and perplexed. But not one of those present could utter a word, for all had been struck dumb, without respect of person. When they had sat a long while thus, unable to speak and gazing at one another like dumb animals, the Holy Grail appeared, covered with a cloth of white samite; and yet no mortal hand was seen to bear it. It entered through the great door, and at once the palace was filled with fragrance as though all the spices of the earth has been spilled abroad. It circled through the hall along the great tables and each place was furnished in its wake with the food its occupants desired. When all were served, the Holy Grail vanished, they knew not how nor whither.[2]

As the light of the Grail fades away, one thing is clear: nothing will ever be the same in Arthur's court. His knights are fired with divine inspiration for a new and different kind of quest and cannot wait to set off, scattering the Fellowship of the Round Table far and wide. No longer do they leave as a band of comrades; instead "they rode out from the castle and separated as they had decided amongst themselves, striking out into the forest one here, one there, wherever they saw it thickest and wherever path or track was absent."[3]

Since the quest for the Grail is a quest of the soul, it can only be followed by each knight as an individual, taking orders from their inner Self rather than an outer authority.

THE LANDSCAPE OF THE GRAIL

This quest takes the knights far from the comforts and comradeship of the court, and out into the trackless forests of the Otherworld in search of the mysterious prize. The knights journey through wild, untamed lands and dense forests. It is a liminal landscape between the worlds: a borderland that abuts onto the civilized milieu of the court at one edge while at the other lies a secret realm of mystery. The wilderness is full of hidden marvels and dangers where the knights encounter uncanny forces: battles with murderous giants in red armor; monstrous, fire-breathing dragons; castles appearing then disappearing, and in which there may be revolving beds and magical chessboards whose pieces are moved by invisible hands. The wonderful vessel for which they seek waits to be discovered at the Castle of the Grail, which, like the faery forts in Irish and Welsh myth, is situated by water. It stands on an island in the middle of a lake or river, on a rock overlooking a river, by the seashore, or even under the sea. To reach it is to undertake an often perilous crossing, for the landscape of the Grail Quest is nothing less than a reworking of the Celtic tales of the Otherworld with all its terrors, beauties, and marvels.

In this dreamlike realm, Arthur's knights encounter a number of female characters who are reflexes of Celtic goddesses or faery women. They discover various "Castles of Maidens," recalling the magical women of Annwn and Avalon. In one of Sir Gawain's adventures, he comes to a city on an island in the middle of a river, where he encounters a woman who shows him a splendid marble building perched high on a rock on the further shore. Gazing up at the castle, Gawain sees many beautiful women and girls, richly dressed in silk, wandering through flowering meadows and gardens. Gawain makes the "crossing by water," typical of the Otherworld journey, in the boat of a mysterious ferryman, who warns him that the Castle of Maidens is enchanted. The castle is as splendid as any Irish Otherworld palace, with doors of ivory and ebony that shine with gold and precious jewels, while the floor is a mosaic of rich colors. After surviving a night of supernatural events in which his courage is tested to the full, Gawain is invited by the queen to become lord of the castle. Like the queen of the Apple Island in the Irish story of Bran mac Febal, she at first refuses to allow him to leave her magical realm, but relents on receiving his promise to return.

However, most of the female personae in the Grail narratives were defamed by misogynistic monks. This is particularly the case in the more heavily Christianized versions, such as the *Queste del Sant Graal,* where the author relentlessly expresses his negative attitude toward women. In one episode, beautiful maidens tempt wandering knights to stay with them forever in their castle by offering them apples. In another, the Grail knight, Galahad, arrives at the Castle of Maidens where seven knights hold captive a number of girls whom they have kidnapped and raped. Galahad kills the knights as they attempt to flee, but regrets their fate because they could have made amends. To quote Celtic scholar, Jean Markale, on this episode:

> What we are dealing with here is the deliberate intention to Christianize a pagan myth. The Castle of the Maidens is the equivalent of the Land of Fairy or the Isle of Avalon, that paradisical island . . . where marvelous and sensually alluring women lull travelers with the shady delights of an ambiguous Eden. But all at once, in the Cistercian perspective, the fairies become diabolical embodiments. . . . The maidens, in the medieval sense of the word unmarried women, are no longer fairies, beings endowed with supernatural powers, but innocent victims of male lust. The Land of Fairy of the ancient myths has been turned into a simple brothel where subjugated women do the will of men, who are themselves regarded as devils.[4]

THE GRAIL CASTLE

The Grail Castle itself is clearly modeled on castles of the Celtic Otherworld. In *Le Conte du Graal,* the Grail Castle and the Castle of Maidens are both "four-cornered." In two other romances, the World Tree and Sacred Well are also to be found within its walls. In the thirteenth-century French romance, *Sone de Nansai,* the castle is on a square island with four towers enclosing a central circular palace. In the center of the palace is a hearth supported by four gilded columns.

Nearby is another island, which can only be reached from the mainland by a sword bridge. It too is square in shape and enclosed by crystal walls like Caer Wydyr, the Glass Fortress in *The Plunder of Annwn,* and has four towers at the corners. In the center of the island is a fountain with waters that well up through a horn of gilded copper.

In *Perlesvaus,* an early thirteenth-century romance from northern France, also known as the "High Book of the Grail," the hero, Perceval, seeks the Grail on a mysterious island of ancient men who appear only half their age:

> Perceval leaves the land behind so that he beholds only the sea. . . .
> The ship has sped so far by day and by night, as it pleased God, that
> they saw a castle on an island of the sea. . . . They came near the
> castle and heard four trumpets sound at the four corners of the walls
> very sweet. . . . They issued from the ship and went by the seaside
> to the castle, and within there were the fairest halls and the fairest
> mansions that one has ever seen. Perceval looks beneath a very fair
> tree, which was tall and broad, and sees the fairest and clearest foun-
> tain that anyone could describe, and it was all set about with rich
> golden pillars, and the gravel seemed to be of precious stones. Above
> this fountain two men were sitting, whiter of hair and beard than
> newly fallen snow, and they seemed young of face. . . .[5]

The landscape of the Grail is clearly based on the timeless Otherworld island where no one ever grows old, transposed from Irish and Welsh mythology.

THE FISHER KING

Only the most worthy knight in Arthur's court can attain the Grail, and this depends on him passing a test that involves asking a ritual ques-tion at the castle of the Fisher King, or Rich Fisherman. This mysteri-ous character is described in *The Elucidation* as a king of great wealth and bounty who withdraws his abundant gifts from Logres when the well maidens are defiled. He is also known as the Wounded King, a central figure in other versions of the Grail legend, who suffers from a terrible injury that will never heal. For the masculine principle suffers equally with the feminine when these two forces are out of balance. His wound is also expressed in sexual terms: he has been struck in the thighs—a euphemism for the genitals—and has been rendered impotent and sterile. As we saw in the last chapter, other versions recount it was a "dolorous blow" from a spear that caused the wasted land. His sorry state is reflected in the barren lands that lie all about him, where the trees bear no fruit, the crops fail, and the women bear no children. The Fisher King himself is representative of the male principle made impotent and infertile due to the severed relationship with the Earth and the feminine.

If the well maidens represent the forces of Mother Nature, then the Fisher King may be the dying and rising god who is both her consort and her son. This god, who appears under many names throughout the ancient world, including Tammuz, Attis, Osiris, and Adonis, is the spirit of the plants and crops that die into the earth each winter, and sprout up again each spring. In the mystery schools of the Near East, fish was the principle food consumed at the ritual meal, as indeed it was in early Christian rituals.[6] But just as the goddess has been violated and become barren as a result, so her lover/son is now impotent and without the power to procreate. In the mystery tales of antiquity, which dealt with the eternal spiral of death, life, and regeneration, the old king must die—sometimes sacrificially, so that a young virile successor can take his place as consort to the goddess. But the Fisher King is unable to die because the natural cycle of things has been disrupted ever since the violation of the well maidens, the fructifying aspect of the feminine earth. He can only suffer and await the coming of the Grail Knight, representing the regenerated masculine principle—noble, fearless, and farsighted—who will renew the sacred contract with the Earth.

The Grail, as the redemptive symbol of the lost feminine, is kept within the hidden castle of the Wounded King, where it is borne by a young woman. In some narratives he is kept alive by a host, or wafer of the Mass, served from the vessel; it comforts and sustains his life, but cannot relieve his pain or cure him. The Wounded King is doomed to suffer this death-in-life existence, awaiting the arrival of the knight who will find the castle, see the Grail, and ask the king a specific ritual question. The question varies throughout the romances, some examples being: "What ails thee?" "Whom does the Grail serve?" and "What is the meaning of the Bleeding Lance?" In other words, the Western wound must be fully brought to consciousness and addressed before the secrets of the Grail can be unlocked and its curative power released. If he fails to ask the question, the knight is sent away in ignominious defeat. In *Perlesvaus,* the failure of the hero to ask the question results in King Arthur becoming weak and feeble, and the lands of Britain falling into waste.

There is also a wealth of meaning in the symbolism of the fish. The wounded king spends his days fishing, and as we have seen, water is a feminine symbol and the abode of goddesses and faery women. He is seeking the healing power of the divine feminine in the depths of the subconscious mind and searching for the vanished well maidens. Perhaps, like the Irish Druids, he is hoping to find the Salmon of Wisdom itself, for the salmon in Ireland was once clearly associated with goddesses. In a country which had no snakes, this fish took the place of the serpent of the Goddess, one of her main totem creatures in the ancient world, whose ability to shed its skin symbolized the power of the feminine to renew all things.

W. B. Yeats explores this theme in "The Song of Wandering Aengus," a poem that encapsulates the deep loss and longing for the beauty and wisdom of the feminine.

> *I went out to the hazelwood,*
> *Because a fire was in my head,*
> *Cut and peeled a hazel wand,*
> *And hooked a berry to a thread;*
> *And when white moths were on the wing,*
> *And moth-like stars were flickering out,*

I dropped the berry in a stream
And caught a little silver trout.

When I had laid it on the floor
And gone to blow the fire aflame.
Something rustled on the floor.
And someone called me by my name:
It had become a glimmering girl
With apple blossoms in her hair
Who called me by my name and ran
And vanished in the brightening air.

Though I am old with wandering
Through hollow lands and hilly lands,
I will find out where she has gone,
And kiss her lips and take her hands;
And walk among long dappled grass,
And pluck till time and times are done
The silver apples of the moon,
The golden apples of the sun.[7]

In Yeats' poem the "fire in my head" refers to *imbas,* the Old Irish equivalent of the Welsh *awen:* the state of inspiration or heightened consciousness experienced by the bard and seer. Hazels are the magical trees that encircle the Well of Wisdom, and the Irish poet's highest attainment was to gather their nuts, which bestowed poetic and mantic vision. Like the Fisher King, he goes fishing—no doubt at one of the streams that flow down from the well, and catches a trout, which represents the Salmon of Wisdom. But when he brings this spiritual prize out of the waters of the subconscious mind into the everyday world, it cannot stay for long. It turns into a faery woman who disappears once more beyond the threshold of dream in an era that does not admit the sacred feminine. The once-powerful immortal figure of the Great Goddess has been demoted to a "glimmering girl." The only reminder of her Tree of Life—or the orchards of Avalon—is the apple-blossom in her hair. Yet her voice continues to echo in our ears, faintly floating across the Wasteland of this modern world, calling us by name, urging us back by long-forgotten ways to the country of the soul.

THE GRAIL MAIDEN

As we have seen, the Grail, the redemptive symbol of the lost feminine, is kept within the hidden castle of the Wounded King. In most versions, the questing knights who manage to find it are invited to a feast at which a mysterious procession passes through the hall, led by a young woman who carries the Grail. The goddess or faery woman with her sacred cauldron or cup becomes the Grail Bearer in medieval romance, with the same supernatural radiance. In the thirteenth century *Lancelot-Grail* (also known as the *Vulgate Cycle*), Sir Gawain visits the Grail Castle:

> Then there came forth from the chamber . . . a damsel, the fairest he had beheld any day of his life. Her hair was cunningly plaited and bound, and her face was fair to look upon. She was beautiful with all the beauty that pertaineth unto a woman, none fairer was ever seen on earth. She came forth from the chamber bearing in her hands the richest vessel that might be beheld by the eye of mortal man. It was made in the semblance of a chalice, and she held it on high above her head, so that all those who were there saw it and bowed.
>
> Sir Gawain looked on the vessel, and esteemed it highly in his heart, yet knew not of what it was wrought; for it was not of wood nor of any manner of metal; nor was it of any wise of stone, not of horn, nor of bone, and therefore he was sore abashed. Then he looked on the maiden, and marveled more at her beauty than at the wonder of the vessel, for never had he seen a damsel with whom she might be compared; and he mused so fixedly upon her that he had no thought for aught beside. But as the damsel passed before the knights, the holy vessel in her hand, all knelt before it; and

forthwith were the tables replenished with the choicest meats in the world, and the hall filled with sweet odors.[8]

The Grail Bearer might be Clíodhna Fair-hair giving Teigue mac Cian the emerald "cup of virtues," or the sovereignty goddess of Ireland offering her cup to a chosen king. She is the epitome of the glory that is the Grail, for indeed she *is* herself the vessel of great price. On the personal level, she is the radiant *anima,* or soul, of the questing knight, and on the spiritual level, the Divine Feminine.

Nowhere is this brought out more clearly than in the grail procession as described in *Parzival.* Before the appearance of the Grail, a series of maidens enter the castle hall: a group of four, followed by a group of eight, then a group of twelve, each more beautiful and exquisitely adorned than the previous ones. The Grail Bearer is the last to enter:

So radiant was her countenance that everyone thought the dawn was breaking. She was clothed in a dress of Arabian silk. Upon a deep green achmardi* she brought the perfection of Paradise, both root and branch. That was a thing called the Grail, which surpasses all earthly perfection. Repanse de Schoye was the name of her whom the Grail permitted to be its bearer. Such was the nature of the Grail that she who watched over it had to preserve her purity and renounce all falsity. . . . Their noblest member they placed in the centre, with twelve on either side, I was told, and the maiden with the crown stood there in all her beauty.[9]

The first group of four maidens, dressed in brown wool, reflect the four elements of the physical world. The second group of eight maidens, dressed in green samite, reflect the eight celestial spheres. The third group of twelve, clad in shining silk shot through with gold, represent the twelve signs of the zodiac. The Grail Bearer, lovelier than the rest, is crowned. The meaning of her name, *Repanse de Schoye,* is uncertain.

---

*An *achmardi* is a green silk cloth with gold threads.

Interpretations include, "knowledge of joy," "remembrance of joy" and "overflow of joy." She is the embodiment of the Goddess herself, who initiates us into the mysteries of the soul's bliss.

THE LOATHLY LADY

When the knight fails to ask the ritual question of the Grail, the bright countenance of the Grail Bearer vanishes, to be replaced by the hideous face of the "Loathly Lady" who mercilessly upbraids him for his lack of compassion and understanding. Her features are described in the romances with extravagant relish, as in this example from *Perceval:*

> They saw a girl coming on a tawny mule, clutching a whip in her right hand. Her hair hung in two tresses, black and twisted, and . . . there was no creature so utterly ugly even in hell. You have never seen iron as black as her neck and hands, but that was little compared to the rest of her ugliness: her eyes were just two holes, tiny as the eyes of a rat; her nose was like a cat's or monkey's; her lips like an ass's or a cow's; her teeth were so discolored that they looked like egg-yolk; and she had a beard like a billy-goat. She had a hump in the middle of her chest, and her back was like a crook. Her loins and shoulders were perfect for leading a dance, for she had a curve in her back and haunches that bent like willow-wands—just right for dancing![10]

Yet this is not all of who she is. In some Grail narratives, the hag is revealed as none other than the beautiful Grail Maiden, and together these women are clearly recognizable as the two faces of the Celtic Earth goddess who personifies both day and night, summer and winter, life and death.

In one sense, the Loathly Lady personifies the Wasteland—infertile and desecrated—who is angry that the ignorance and selfishness of the hero has failed to heal the wounded king and restore his barren domain. In *Perlesvaus,* her unsightly appearance is actually explained as a direct result of the Grail knight's failure to ask the vital question. In this version, she is not so much hideous, as plain and bald—perhaps an image of the land in winter before the sun has fertilized her fields. The Grail knight is a stand-in for the king, who in the Celtic era was the earthly representative of the life-giving sun, but he has shown himself unworthy to be her consort, and so the land remains blighted and infertile due to the tragic disconnect between feminine and masculine, Cup and Sword.

In *Parzival,* the Loathly Lady is called Cundrie, and she is called a "source of sorrow, oppressor of joy." Yet she wears a hood decorated with a flock of doves, which mark her as one of the Company of the Grail. She looks after those in distress, such as Parzival's cousin, Sigune, who is in mourning for her beloved, killed by an evil knight. Once a week, Cundrie brings the young woman food from the Grail, which miraculously keeps her alive. She also compounds healing salves for the Fisher King's wounds. Throughout the poem she plays an active role as the messenger of the Grail, and ultimately is the purveyor of good news: Parzival's name has appeared on the Grail, marking him as the new Grail king. She falls at his feet in joy and blesses him, then accompanies him back to the Grail Castle. Here Parzival asks the question that heals the wounded king, and immediately succeeds him on the throne.

SHEELA-NA-GIG

The Loathly Lady, as an aspect of the destructive aspect of the goddess, is akin to the fearsome Nine Witches of Gloucester in the Welsh Grail romance, *Peredur, Son of Efrawg.* Here the witches are portrayed as evil, yet they are the ones who school the hero, Peredur, in the arts of weaponry and horsemanship as powerful, magical women were wont to do in Celtic myth. The feminine, pagan court of the Nine Witches contrasts strongly with the masculine, Christian milieu of Arthur's Camelot. Glenys Goetinck, a pre-eminent scholar of this work, suggests that the witches are the representatives of the older, matrifocal, pre-Celtic society trying to regain control of the old system.[11] So the Loathly Lady takes us back again to the ninefold sisterhood of creator goddesses of the ancient Northern world, while also reminding us of the Cailleach, the old hag of the Celts.

Images of this formidable feminine force have miraculously survived into modern times in stone carvings known as Sheela-na-gigs, a collective name given to almost 150 figures known to exist in Ireland, Britain, and mainland Europe today. The squatting figure is naked with staring, hypnotic eyes, and she often bares crooked rows of teeth from a gaping mouth. Her body is generally skeletal, with bony ribs protruding beneath minuscule breasts, and she characteristically displays her large and prominent vulva. She appears embedded in Romanesque churches, castle battlements, town walls, on tombstones and pillar-stones, and sometimes overlooks wells or rivers like a protective guardian. The questions—who carved her and why—remain unanswered. Wordlessly, she tells the one story common to all peoples in all times: the mystery of creation—birth and death. In areas of Ireland where traditional ways have altered little over the centuries, there are local people who still make pilgrimages to the Sheela to pay homage to the one that both gives and takes life, is both womb and tomb. Reverently, they touch or rub her vulva for good luck and prosperity, as did their ancestors before them. The sacred generative power of the Goddess is as undimmed as it ever was to those who know who really holds the secrets of life and death.

Sheela-na-gig is a persistent memory of the oldest goddess of all, the Earth herself. As the Cailleach, the old hag, she gave birth to Earth's body, and all bodies, including our own, return to her at the last. Her penetrating gaze is urging us, her youngest and most wayward of children, to remember these truths. As Irish poet Nuala ní Dhomnaill declares, "This is the as yet undifferentiated Mother-of-Life-and-Death. Her self-exhibition has nothing sexual or lascivious about it, rather it is a reminder of something which to us liberated moderns is much more obscene and frightening: 'This is where you came from, and this is where you are going to.'"[12]

Our current global crisis is a result of denying the divine presence of the feminine both in the natural world and within ourselves, of valuing the Sword above the Grail. Today many have seen the wrath of the

The Sheela-na-gig on Kilpeck Church, England.
Photo by David J. Watkins.

Hag Goddess in the natural disasters, which have been increasing in recent years—hurricanes, tornadoes, earthquakes and floods—and the ultimate specter of climate change that may make the majority of our planet uninhabitable. Unless we reconnect with the deeper feminine energy of the universe, and live in alignment with the laws of creation, our species is unlikely to survive. Yet, sad though it may seem, we humans seem to need sorrow and suffering in order to evolve toward wisdom. A comfortable life with all physical needs taken care of does not typically lead to spiritual awakening. In this, the Loathly Lady can be seen as the Wise Woman who holds the sun of daytime consciousness in her Underworld cauldron through the long midnight hours, as in a crucible where we can be transformed and prepared for the dawning of the awakened soul.

THE VANISHING GRAIL

In most of the Grail narratives, the Grail Knight returns to ask the ritual question. In the end, the Fisher King may be healed or else dies a peaceful death, and in some cases the Wasteland is restored to health. Yet the Grail is never brought back into the world of Arthur's court, where, one imagines, it could have been used for the spiritual regeneration of Logres. In the conclusion of the Grail story as told in Sir Thomas Malory's *Le Morte d'Arthur*, Galahad looks into the Holy Grail, views the "spiritual things" within, and dies in ecstasy. His companions, Bors and Perceval, then witness a great marvel: a hand reaches down from above, takes up the Grail and the Spear, and carries them up to heaven, and we are told that since then, the Holy Grail has never been seen again on Earth. Perceval becomes a hermit and dies one year later. Only Bors returns to Camelot to tell the tale to King Arthur's sadly diminished court. We are left with the sense that far from the Grail Quest being the pinnacle of achievement of the Knights of the Round Table, it has left Camelot in a weakened state, with many of its finest heroes scattered or dead. After this, the story shifts to Lancelot and Guinevere's love affair, which intensifies, eventually leading to the downfall and ruin of Logres. It is as if society is not ready to embrace the feminine at the highest level. Guinevere, who, as we saw earlier, was originally an aspect of the sovereignty goddess—represents the chief symbol of the feminine, and, like the Grail, is equally unattainable: by Arthur; by Lancelot, from whom she is forced to part; and by Mordred, who tries unsuccessfully to seize her for himself in an attempt to usurp the throne.

In the end, there was no place for the Grail in mainstream medieval society. The cult of the feminine which flourished briefly in Europe during the twelfth century withered away as the Church gathered its forces to destroy all it considered heretical in the Inquisition. The target consisted mainly of men and women, particularly the Cathars and the Knights Templar, whose spiritual beliefs emphasized a search for God independent from the priestly hierarchy and the rigid dogma of Rome. Also persecuted were the Jewish Kabbalists of Spain, who taught the wisdom of the Shekhinah, the indwelling presence of the living God, whose role as the animating life force of the Earth is to balance the transcendent deity. The Grail could not remain on Earth because according to orthodox Christian belief, Heaven and Earth are utterly separate. God manifested on the physical plane once and once only in the form of Jesus Christ, who after a brief sojourn among humanity was, like the Grail, also borne up to heaven and "never more seen on Earth." The transcendent and the immanent: "masculine" spirit and "feminine" Earth are doomed to be forever apart, as in the Gnostic myth of Sophia, who wanders the Earth forever seeking her lost heavenly beloved.

Each Grail Knight is an initiate who is charged with the task of bringing the vessel of Spirit—the Grail—into the world (Logres), but he never returns because the world is not ready to receive him. Because this circuit cannot be completed, the Grail legends have to be told again and again to each successive generation through the centuries. The legends are forever incomplete because the "below" does not reflect the "above," and the inner cannot become outer, as Hermetic wisdom instructs. Until the polarities of feminine and masculine, Chalice and Sword, are acknowledged as equal powers in a world which welcomes and honors both in equal measure, seekers will continue to set forth in search of the Grail for many years to come.

Exercise
Working with the Three Vessels

The sacred vessels of the feminine—cup, cauldron, and chalice—have a symbolic counterpart in the human psyche, which is an ever-evolving container of consciousness. They can be regarded as three crucibles in which the alchemical transformation will take place. Each one is ultimately a Cup of Life that issues the invitation: "Drink me." On this level, the various quests for the Grail may be understood as psychological processes within the human psyche. However, it must be said at this point that this is *by no means all that they are:* the Otherworld is as real within the invisible worlds as you and I are in the outer world, as hopefully, you are discovering if you are working with the VisionJourneys in these chapters. The archetypal world of the Grail works on many levels, but unfortunately, the modern tendency toward psychological reductionism has led many writers to dismiss the reality of the inner worlds altogether as projections of the human mind.

The three stages on the journey to higher consciousness through the Grail are as follows. Each one is mediated by feminine figures who are the keepers of the vessel of initiation and act as our inner guides and helpers.

Stage 1: The Chalice of Selfhood

The first stage of selfhood takes place from birth to adulthood, as we gradually develop an identity separate from the mother. Some psychologists talk of individuals having a full cup, or pot, when a sense of self-worth and well-being is present, or an empty one when there is ongoing self-doubt and feelings of worthlessness.[13] Without this vessel of the psyche (or with a very leaky vessel), we would have no boundaries and might experience the world as terrifyingly chaotic, as is the case with schizophrenics.

Our initiator is the equivalent of the sovereignty goddess who offers the cup of red ale to the future king, enabling him to rule in peace and prosperity. The king represents the human ego—our sense of individual consciousness, which gives us the feeling of being at the center of our own world. At the psychological level, we experience this goddess as the primary caregiver in our early life—usually, although not always, the mother—who, like the goddess Clíodhna, gives us physical and emotional sustenance and protection from life's harshness. Her positive, nurturing words and deeds fill our cup with self-esteem and affirm we are worthy of love.

Stage 2: The Cauldron of Transformation

Psychological and spiritual growth often only come about when crisis strikes. It seems we humans must be hurled into the cauldron of death and rebirth in order to move from the limited sense of the self as a personality into a deeper awareness of the self as an immortal soul. The cauldron-death helps us remember who we truly are: a spark of divine fire on its long journey back to Source through thousands of incarnations. This dawning awareness of the soul-self is the second stage of consciousness, often occurring at mid-life and beyond; although it may occur earlier in exceptional "older" souls who have been around the "incarnational block" many times.

At this stage the initiator appears as the other face of the nurturer: she is the Dark Goddess who sets out to destroy our identification with the ego-personality in order to release the soul within. She is Ceridwen who throws her baby boy into the ocean so he may be reborn as Taliesin, or the Cailleach who purges and purifies the land in wintertime, bringing death so new life may emerge. As the various Loathly Ladies in the Grail romances, the Dark Goddess forces us, like Perceval, to undergo a harrowing journey through the darkness of the subconscious mind, to face our shortcomings, and to atone for the harm we have done to others. And although we may often feel overwhelmed in times of crisis, she also provides us with the strength to overcome our fears, the courage to endure, and the energy to win through to the other side.

Stage 3: The Grail of the Soul

The third stage occurs when the soul opens to receive transcendental energies from the highest spiritual dimensions. When the Grail of the soul is filled with Spirit, our threefold journey of consciousness is complete, as we can both receive divine influence and pour it out to others in blessing and healing.

- *Look back at your life and identify times in which you have experienced at least two of these stages.*
- *How did you feel at these times? There may have been one or more*

initiators of this experience—who were they? Remember—not all of the initiations of the Grail are pleasant and not all teachers kind and supportive!

- *Which vessel of consciousness is at work in your life right now? What do you hope will be the result of "drinking from" or "being immersed in" this vessel?*

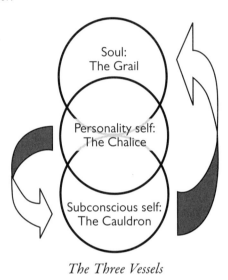

Soul:
The Grail

Personality self:
The Chalice

Subconscious self:
The Cauldron

The Three Vessels

VisionJourney IV
Within the Hill of the Hag

In the following VisionJourney, we encounter the Old Goddess in her aspect as the Cailleach in one of her sacred temples in Ireland: the *Sliabh na Caillighe,* or "Hill of the Hag," in County Meath, a place where her presence is strongly palpable today. This is one of a series of hills she is said to have birthed, and it is covered with the remains of Neolithic passage tombs known as cairns. Although they are considered places of burial, evidence points also to their use as sacred temples and astronomical observatories.

One of the passage tombs, given the name Cairn T by archaeologists, is still intact, having escaped the predations of nineteenth-century treasure hunters who destroyed many of those nearby. It is huge and round like a pregnant belly, and can be entered through a narrow passageway lined with stones carved with spirals. To crawl into the interior is to re-enter the womb of the First Mother. Once inside her "body," one is aware of two small side chambers to the left and right that might represent her arms—or perhaps breasts. At the end of the passageway is the largest chamber with sun-wheels, flower-shapes, chevrons, and other enigmatic petroglyphs carved into the walls. To squat in the darkness and silence of this place is to sit within the mind-womb of the goddess, the place where she dreams the worlds into being. Passage mounds throughout Britain and Ireland were deliberately aligned with the rising sun or moon on special days of the year. At Cairn T, the first beams of the rising sun filter in to the far recesses of the chamber during both the spring and fall equinoxes, illuminating the carved symbols with golden light and fertilizing the goddess with life-giving rays in a sacred marriage of Sun and Earth.

Sit in a comfortable position, relax, and quiet your mind. . . . Take some deep breaths and imagine you are breathing in a soft, silver-gray light. The light fills your body and swirls around you like a mist. . . .

Then the mist lifts, and you find yourself walking up a hill in the gathering dusk of an evening in autumn. As you reach the summit, the mist wreathes about the forlorn shapes of tumbled rocks and shattered cairns, and drifts around the foot of the huge green mound that towers above you. The stones that form its narrow entrance-way are silent, motionless sentinels, but you detect a movement among them. As you draw closer, the shadowy figure of an old woman looms out of the mist. She is dressed in coarse brown and heather-colored garments and is very tall and thin with high cheekbones and a thin mouth. Although she seems very old, her eyes are a piercing blue. As she gazes at you impassively, it feels like she can see right through to your core. . . .

She asks if you are ready to die to your ephemeral self and experience the deeper ground of your Being through entering the Void. If you are ready, she instructs you to remove all of your clothes. Afterward, she lights a small fire and burns them all. Yet when you look down at yourself, you see that you are wearing another set of clothes. The old woman tells you these represent your identity in the world. You must remove these as well, and these, too, she burns. Still you see that you are dressed in another set of clothes. These represent your attachment to your home, family, and personal life. They must also go. Another set of clothes beneath these are revealed, representing all your desires and attachments. You must divest yourself of these as well. And there may be more . . . so let this process continue until you stand there completely naked. . . .

The Old One directs you to the entrance to the mound. You brave the lowering stare of the sentinel stones and stoop to enter through the narrow passageway into Earth's womb. As you take your first steps, your fingers trace an ancient spiral carved in the rock wall—a symbol of the eternal cycling of life, death, and rebirth.

At first the darkness is total and profound, then you gradually become aware of a faint luminescence—this is the Light within the Land, the light of the Underworld that comes not from sun or moon but from the stars buried deep within the stones. By this almost imperceptible glimmer, you come to a central round chamber where you can stand up straight. There are two smaller chambers on either side. You feel as if you are in the heart of the cairn, which is the heart of the goddess herself. Here you curl up and rest for a while in the cradle of the Earth. You drift into a half-sleep in which you are dimly aware of a rhythmic heartbeat and a deep, humming, thrumming sound, as if the Mother is singing a lullaby to you. . . .

After a while, a new sound can be heard above the deep thrumming of the Earth: high, silvery voices of exquisite beauty as if the stars themselves were singing. Long, slender arms and hands reach through the stones to touch you, perhaps to pull you deeper into the Earth. They belong to the Sídhe, the People who Dwell in the Mounds. They are calling you into their world so you may never have to know grief and sorrow again. Their voices weave pictures of Tír na nÓg, the Land of the Ever-Living; Tír fo Thuinn, Land-under-Wave; and Tír-na-Sorcha, the Land of Light, and you are tempted to let them bear you away to their deathless country. . . . Yet you know that cannot be, for you are human, and pledged to life beneath the sun and moon. To leave now would be to break the contract you have made with the Lords of Time. . . . And so the voices fade and the hands are withdrawn, and although your heart aches and longs to follow them to the Land of the Ever-Living, you shake yourself and open your eyes, feeling your feet firmly on the hard earth floor of the chamber. . . .

Now, in the faint shimmering light, you can see the chamber at the far end of the passage. Carved symbols on its walls seem to glow with a light of their own. You crawl into the chamber and feel as if you are entering into the very mind of the Earth Mother, a place that is No-thing and Every-thing at once—infinite space and eternal time. It is the Void and the Pleroma, the point of origin where all comes forth and to which all returns.

You feel as if you are floating in a bottomless lake of darkness, but there is no fear, for you willingly surrender to a process you instinctively feel is benign. As you drift through the dark waters, you are aware of many veils floating away from you: layers of sheaths that were your past thoughts, feelings, patterns, and personalities in this and in previous lifetimes. It feels good to release the cumbersome weight of these old identities. . . . A purification is taking place. Soon you have no awareness of having a body at all. You have only a sense of yourself as a point of consciousness, like a gently glowing light in the darkness of the lake.

Stay in this wordless state for as long as you like . . . for in it you will find "perfect peace profound." . . .

After what seems like eternities have passed, you become aware of a light behind your closed eyelids, which breaks into this peace like an irresistible call to awaken. You open your eyes to see the liquid golden light of the morning sun of the Spring Equinox as it penetrates the chamber and floods it with radiance.

And as your consciousness is still swimming within the mind of the Mother, you experience an explosion of ecstasy of this moment of union of Sun and Earth, for it brings forth a new creation. Continents erupt out of roiling oceans; mountains thrust skyward and volcanic lava streams over the land; roaring rivers cascade over the fiery earth, which cools and becomes green with lush forests and wide flowery plains. The rivers teem with fish; the sky is full of birds' wings and resounding song; creatures of all kinds wander freely over the face of the Earth . . . and you experience yourself as every form, from a sliver of shale on a mountain slope to a whale blowing in the ocean to a snowflake melting on the branch of a tree. . . . Let your consciousness slip through every manifestation of this glorious life force as it crystallizes into form. . . . Become the consciousness of the Earth herself, for indeed that is who you truly are. . . .

And now you gradually become aware of the sun moving on through its daily cycle and that it no longer lights up the deep chamber womb of the Earth Mother. You slowly return to a sense of yourself as an individual and resume everyday consciousness, yet nevertheless aware that, on some level, you are part of the Great Mind of the primordial Mother of all creation, and from now on, you will be able to move back and forth into this deeper awareness at will. The gates of perception have been unbolted and now can open and close freely according to your desire for connection with that greater part of you.

Humbled and awed by what you have been part of, you give thanks to the Mother and return through the passageway into the light of a new morning. The mist has completely gone and you gaze out over a glorious panorama of eighteen counties of Ireland.

Before you leave the Hill of the Hag, you follow the old custom of walking around to the Hag's Chair: a megalithic seat of stone on the far side of the cairn. Here you once more see the Old Woman sitting and smoking a long-stemmed clay pipe and surveying all her lands. You sit beside her and silently pray for a blessing—for yourself and for the fate of the Earth and all her creatures. Then you walk down the hill and back into your own place and time. Open your eyes and come fully back to the present.

5

Trials and Initiations

The Grail quest is a timeless story of initiation, or perhaps many initiations, as there are recognized critical stages within the course of each human life. Separating from our parents, becoming a functional adult, forming relationships and a family, transitioning into retirement—all are passages common to most people's lives, ending inexorably in death: the most mysterious initiation from which no one returns. Those who follow a spiritual path have further to travel on the search for the soul and God. This is the ultimate initiation, when individual consciousness dissolves into the One, and there is no longer any separation between seeker and sought. In this chapter we follow the hero of *Le Conte du Graal* through many of these stages, and we might recognize many of his experiences in our own lives.

Perceval is a simple, untutored Welsh lad who lives alone with his mother in a wild forest. One day he encounters a group of knights from King Arthur's court, and dazzled by their shining armor, believes they must be angels. Deeply impressed, he goes home and tells his mother he wants to be a knight. She is horrified because her husband and two older sons were knights who had met violent deaths in battle. She had been protecting Perceval from the same fate by hiding him away in the woods and bringing him up in ignorance of the outside world. Deaf to his mother's anguished pleas not to follow in their footsteps, the young lad sets off to King Arthur's court, clad in rustic clothes and astride a hunting horse. As he gallops away from his childhood home, he looks back and sees his mother has apparently fainted at the bridge, but presses on regardless.

On his way to the court, Perceval comes upon a pavilion he thinks must be a church—a place his mother told him he should enter to worship the Creator. Inside, he startles a beautiful girl, and misunderstanding his mother's instructions about how to treat a young woman, he kisses her against her will. Then he roughly takes a ring from her finger, helps himself to her food and drink, and in general acts like a boorish lout.

When Perceval arrives at the King's court, he finds everyone in turmoil because a Red Knight has just ridden into the hall, snatched away Arthur's cup of wine and flung its contents over the queen. Although mocked as an ill-clad simpleton by the other knights, Perceval instantly demands that the king make him a knight to avenge this insult, then fearlessly rides away and defeats the Red Knight in a fierce and bloody battle. Afterward, the young knight rides off clad in his victim's red armor, even though he doesn't yet know how to use weapons properly or even how to mount his horse.

Fortunately, he arrives at the castle of a nobleman who takes to Perceval and instructs him in the proper use of weapons and horseback riding in battle. He also teaches him the art of chivalry and the virtues of knighthood, including the importance of not talking too much—advice that leads to serious repercussions later on. Perceval's next adventure concerns his first love affair. He arrives at the castle of a beautiful young woman, Blancheflor (white flower), vanquishes her enemies, and becomes her lover. They spend days of love and nights of sexual bliss together, but Perceval is becoming worried about his mother, and despite Blancheflor's tears and protests, he heads back to his home in Wales.

AT THE CASTLE OF THE FISHER KING

Perceval comes to a deep, fast-flowing river that he cannot cross. He believes if he could only find a way over, he would find his mother alive on the other side, but there is no bridge. He sees two men fishing from a boat in the middle of the water and asks them how he can get across. One tells him that there is no bridge, but offers him lodging for the night in his castle, which stands on a rocky pinnacle nearby, though strange to say, it was not there a short while ago! When Perceval arrives there, he is surprised to see one of the fishermen there before him, only lying on a couch, unable to walk. He turns out to be the king of the castle and he gives Perceval a splendid, richly decorated sword, which was sent by the king's niece, and destined for him alone. As Perceval and his host are conversing in front of a blazing fire, a strange procession enters the hall, walking between the two men and the hearth. First comes a boy bearing a white spear with drops of blood flowing from the tip. He is followed by two more handsome boys bearing ten candles in golden candlesticks. Then comes a beautiful girl, exquisitely dressed, holding the Grail in her hands. This vessel is made of gold, and set with precious jewels, and its light is so brilliant that the candles look dim in comparison:

> *. . . and when she entered with the grail,*
> *the candles suddenly grew pale,*
> *the grail cast such a brilliant light,*
> *as stars grow dimmer in the night*
> *where the sun or moonrise makes them fade.*[1]

She is followed by another young woman holding a silver carving platter, then the little procession disappears into another chamber. Perceval, although marveling at all this, doesn't say a word, because he has taken to heart the nobleman's advice not to talk too much in company. The procession of the Grail is followed by a splendid feast, after which Perceval retires to a well-appointed chamber for the night.

The next morning, the young knight awakens to a deserted castle; all the rooms are locked and the members of the household are nowhere to be seen. Outside he finds his horse already saddled and rides off over the drawbridge, which slams shut behind him. He is puzzling over this mystery when he meets a girl in the forest, lamenting over the body of her lover who has just been slain by an evil knight. She informs Perceval that his adventure took place at the castle of the rich Fisher King, who is crippled from a wound through his thighs. Eagerly she asks him if he saw the Grail procession and whether he asked whom the Grail served and what was the meaning of the bleeding lance. When Perceval tells her he remained silent, she is overcome with grief, for had he asked these questions, the king would have been healed. What is more, she reveals herself as Perceval's cousin and tells him that his mother has died of grief because of his careless abandonment of her.

Bad news is followed by worse as Perceval continues through the forest. He meets a wretched woman clothed in rags, who turns out to be the girl whose pavilion he barged into on the way to King Arthur's court. She is being mistreated by her husband who believed she must have encouraged Perceval's sexual attentions. Perceval fights her abuser and has him make reparation to his wife. Perceval continues to wander in the forest in great sadness. Not only is his mother dead, but he also desperately misses Blancheflor. He returns to Arthur's court, but although he is given a hero's welcome, he is berated by a hunchbacked and crooked hag who taunts him with his failure to ask the vital questions that would have healed the king. Because the king will be unable to rule, his land will fall into ruin and his people despair—all thanks to Perceval's failure.

In deep shame, Perceval sets off again, determined to find the answer to the Grail question. After many adventures, he comes upon a band of pilgrims who reproach him for bearing arms on Good Friday. It has now been five years since he left Arthur's court, and he has wandered far away from God. Finally, he encounters a hermit who turns out to be his uncle and gives him spiritual counsel, including intuition on the meaning of the Grail. Shortly after this incident, the story turns to the adventures of Sir Gawain, and Chrétien's narrative breaks off in mid-sentence, possibly due to his death. It was left to other authors to craft their own endings to the quest in a number of sequels called "continuations," such as *The Elucidation,* which we looked at earlier.

THE INNER MEANING OF THE QUEST

From the esoteric viewpoint, Chrétien's story takes Perceval through the classic stages of the incarnated soul. Like the hero of many a fairy tale, he is the youngest son, completely innocent of worldly ways. His ridiculous dress along with his rash and impulsive actions cast him in the traditional role of "the Fool," setting out on life's adventure for the first time. In archetypal terms, he is the Young Masculine separating from the overly protective Old Feminine, in this case his mother, who has kept him buried in the wild forest, the antithesis of the masculine world of the court. Grail scholar, Glenys Goetinck, points to parallels between the story of the Grail hero's origins and a legend of the Welsh Saint Madrun, another widowed mother who had to flee from her enemies with her youngest son. Just like Perceval's mother, Saint Madrun dies when her last son chooses to leave her to become a knight. Madrun is a thinly disguised version of Modron, the Welsh mother goddess who was originally called Matrona, or, in her triple aspect, the Matrones, in the Roman Celtic era. Her death is symbolic of the passing away of the old matrifocal era at the coming of the new warrior-based society of the Celts.[2]

Another clue to Perceval's symbolic identity is the fact that he is a "son of the widow," a term applied to initiates in Freemasonry. This term derives from the religion of early Egypt where the original widow was Isis, the mother of Horus, whose husband Osiris was killed by an enemy. The same destiny belongs to earlier goddesses of the Near East, such as Inanna and Ishtar, who were also separated from their consorts. Rudolf Steiner had an interesting theory about this expression, believing the Mother refers to soul, the one who conceives, while Father refers to Spirit, the force that fructifies the soul with divine influence. (Soul and Spirit together are the highest syzygy of Grail and Sword—a concept we explore in a later chapter.) According to Steiner, since the fall in Atlantean times, the Father principle has withdrawn, "widowing" the soul. Humanity is thrown back onto itself. We must find the light of truth within our own soul in order to find divine guidance.

Perceval is one of many such heroes of the soul's initiation into higher consciousness.[3]

Too immature to have learned self-direction, Perceval gets into trouble by following the rules of his elders, who are the representatives of conventional society. Slavishly and without understanding, Perceval first forces his attentions on an unknown woman, and later, fails to respond appropriately to the events at the Grail Castle. Yet his later quest for the feminine is prefigured early in the story, for he is the only person willing to be Guinevere's champion when she is rudely assaulted by the Red Knight. In this episode, Guinevere is clearly shown in her role as a goddess of sovereignty with her cup of wine. The seizing and spilling of her cup is tantamount to the gravest insult imaginable, yet only the young and uncouth visitor to Arthur's court is brave enough to avenge her honor.

By defeating the boorish Red Knight, Perceval has overcome his *id,* or instinctual self, and is now ready to be instructed into the ways of the world: first through the manly arts of knighthood, which include how to conduct himself in society, and second in the arts of romantic and sexual love. Under Blancheflor's influence, his heart begins to open, and he feels the first stirrings of remorse for leaving his mother in such a thoughtless fashion. It is significant that he is looking for his mother when he is led, seemingly by chance, to the Grail Castle. Perceval's quest symbolizes the search of the collective Western psyche for the lost feminine, once despised and now deeply desired. At the Grail Castle, the young knight attains a vision of the Grail, but he is not yet mature enough to fully comprehend it. For the next step in the initiatory process is to go beyond the personality, to die to the egoic self in order to attain a greater spiritual prize—the Grail. This requires coming to terms with one's personal shadow and facing the limitations of the ego, an experience often undergone in midlife and termed the dark night of the soul.

THE FOUR HALLOWS

Perceval's journey takes him to a river he cannot cross, where he feels sure he will find his mother safe and well on the other side if he could only get there. Coming to the edge of a dangerous river is a classic motif in initiation stories, so it's clear Perceval is about to be tested. (This river has a resonance with the River of Death, so he was right about his mother being on the other side.) Here he is met by the Fisher King, who directs him to his castle, clearly an Otherworld dwelling that can appear or disappear at will. Unbeknownst to Perceval, it is also the scene of his next initiation. He is shown four talismanic objects of power: the bleeding spear, the silver platter, the Grail vessel in the procession, and the sword, which is given to him as a gift from the king's niece. Once again we are reminded of the old Celtic tradition of an Otherworld woman equipping the hero with a sword, just as the Lady of the Lake presented Arthur with Excalibur.

It has long been recognized that these numinous objects are based originally on the four treasures of the *Túatha Dé Danann,* "the People of the Goddess Danu," the race of gods who brought them to Ireland, as described in verses from the Middle Irish text, the *Yellow Book of Lecan:*

> *Four gifts with them from yonder*
> *Had the nobles of the Túatha Dé Danann:*
> *a sword, a stone, a cauldron of bondmaids,*
> *a spear for the fate of lofty champions.*[4]

These four implements—sword, spear, cauldron, and stone—have become keystones of the Western magical tradition. In the nineteenth century, Irish poet and visionary, W. B. Yeats, who was a member of the Hermetic Order of Golden Dawn, worked extensively with the four gifts in ceremonial magic.[5] Another well-known member of the order was A. E. Waite, who designed the first tarot deck for modern use. Waite developed the system of correspondences between the four treasures and the four suits of the tarot deck, and gave them the name of "Hallows," or holy objects—a term which has now become standard usage in esoteric circles.[6]

The Grail procession and tableau could easily be a description of an elaborate magical ceremony. Jessie Weston, a Grail scholar of the earlier part of the past century, proposed that the Grail legends had their roots in an elaborate ritual from antiquity, based on the myth of the dying and rising god, which had somehow survived into the Middle Ages. This led her to conclude: "The Grail romances repose eventually, not upon a poet's imagination, but upon the ruins of an august and ancient ritual, a ritual which once claimed to be the accredited guardian of the deepest secrets of life."[7]

Although this theory has been discounted due to the lack of any historical evidence and has fallen out of fashion among scholars, the possibility of the Grail ceremony being a description of an actual rite from an unknown historical period cannot be totally dismissed.[8]

In *Le Conte du Graal,* the Grail Hallows form a symbolic double male-female pair: the Grail and Platter are feminine symbols, while Sword and Spear (or Lance) are masculine. In some versions of the Grail procession, the drops of blood that flow from the tip of the spear fall into the Grail itself. The nature of this act as a sacred ritual cannot be underestimated. From antiquity, blood has been viewed as a miraculous substance containing the essence of life itself. In this image, the life force pours from the male into the female, the primal act of creation that can be read on many levels from the purely sexual to the transpersonal uniting of the positive and negative forces that give rise to all the worlds. In the more Christianized Grail romances, the spear is identified as belonging to the Roman centurion Longinus who pierced Christ's side at the crucifixion, and the Grail as the cup in which the blood of Christ was collected by Joseph of Arimathea. Christ's blood, shed in order to give humanity everlasting life, was regarded as a precious life-giving fluid in the Middle Ages.

Yet a similar image is found in Irish mythology, suggesting an earlier Celtic provenance. The saga known as *The Fate of the Children of Turenn* tells of a quest for a magical spear that is eventually found with its head thrust into a cauldron of water, which bubbles and hisses around the burning tip. Like the Irish sword Caladbolg, the original template for Excalibur, the spear is blazing hot because it is akin to a bolt of lightning. What is more, two other Irish narratives describe what is most likely the same spear with its head plunged in a cauldron of blood. The spear belongs to the god, Lugh, who has been associated variously with the sun and with the lightning flash.[9] This theme also explains a line in *The Plunder of Annwn* that describes Llwch Lleminawg (the Welsh Lugh) thrusting his sword into the cauldron of the Nine Maidens. Clearly the early myth-makers were well aware of the primordial symbolism of Cup and Cauldron, Sword and Spear.

This theme of a divine force flowing from above into a sacred vessel also has roots in Hermetic teachings, as found in the *Corpus Hermeticum,* a collection of texts from Hellenic Egypt dating from the first through third centuries CE and attributed to the semi-divine father of alchemy, Hermes Trismegistus (Thrice-Great Hermes). According to scholars Henry and Renée Kahane, this influence can be detected in Wolfram von Eschenbach's *Parzival,* in which the Grail can be compared to a Hermetic vessel called the Krater, which is sent from the stars to Earth and filled with divine wisdom. Souls who immerse themselves in it are able to consciously experience the divine. The Greek word *krater* is the original of the Latin *cratalis,* which may in turn have become *gradalis, graal,* and ultimately, *grail.*[10]

THE RITUAL QUESTION

The question that the Grail Knight must ask differs in each narrative, the most common questions being:

> *What is the purpose of the Grail?*
> *Whom does the Grail serve?*
> *What is the Grail?*
> or, addressing the king: *"What ails you?"*

Arthurian scholar R. S. Loomis has convincingly argued that the origin of this theme lies in the story of *The Phantom's Vision* (see chapter 2) where the sovereignty goddess of Ireland asks, "To whom shall this cup be given?" Others, like Jessie Weston, believe this ritual act could have had its origins in the mystery schools of the Near East, where candidates had to undergo certain trials and tests before they could be initiated into sacred knowledge. We know the tellers of the Grail legends were influenced by ideas brought back by the crusaders from the Holy Land, particularly the Knights Templar, an order known to have performed ceremonies of initiation. Yet it is perhaps not so much the nature of the question that is so important as is the willingness to question the status quo of a world so out of balance that the masculine has become an aggressive force dominating the feminine. To ask the Grail question is to voice a clear intention of one's willingness to redress these matters, to honor the sacred feminine on all levels: the soul within the body; women within society; and the living intelligence of our planet, Mother Earth. To ask the Grail question is to commit to being a *Grail Bearer* on Earth, which means to be "an instrument of healing."

Toward the end of his poem, "The Waste Land," T. S. Eliot explores this theme, and the Grail question becomes:

> *Datta: what have we given?*
> *My friend, blood shaking my heart*
> *The awful daring of a moment's surrender*
> *Which an age of prudence can never retract*
> *By this, and this only, we have existed . . .*[11]

In his version of the ritual question, Eliot conveys the original impulse behind it through precepts taken from the Vedic teachings of the Upanishads: *datta* means "give," specifically referring to the unselfish giving of alms. To give freely and fully of oneself is an existential act, for only through such wholehearted engagement can one be said to be truly human and fully alive.

THE RECKONING

Perceval's first sight of the Grail brings him face-to-face with the spiritual radiance of the feminine. But in his immaturity, he fails to ask the ritual question that would unlock the power of the Grail and heal the wounded king. Failure brings humility, which in turn breeds wisdom. Unceremoniously dismissed from the Grail Castle, Perceval is brought face-to-face with his own shortcomings. He walks the gauntlet through a series of women who, like a Greek chorus, remind him of his offenses against the many aspects of the feminine. They are:

1. Maiden: the young woman who turns out to be Perceval's cousin. As if to emphasize the masculine wound, she is sorrowfully cradling the body of the slain knight whom she loved. Through her, Perceval learns that he has unwittingly condemned the land to ruin.
2. Mother: Perceval's cousin also tells him that his mother has died of grief because of his thoughtless abandonment of her.
3. Wife: the abused woman who is the victim of both Perceval's boorishness and her husband's cruelty.
4. Crone: the Loathly Lady who mercilessly rebukes him for his failures.

Deeply humiliated and tormented with guilt because of his mother's death, Perceval dreams of seeking comfort in the company of his beloved, Blancheflor. On his travels in wintertime, he comes upon three drops of blood in the snow left by a wounded goose, and is filled with a desperate longing for his love: "For the blood and snow together resembled for him the fresh hues of his beloved's face; and he became quite lost in the thought that in her face the red was blended with the white like those three drops of blood in the whiteness of the snow. He was so enraptured as he gazed that he thought he could see the color of his fair love's face."[12]

In medieval alchemy, as we shall see in the next chapter, red and white are the symbolic colors assigned to the polarized energies of the universe. Perceval's longing for his beloved is the desire of the Red King, the solar hero, for the White Queen, the lunar woman. In fact, Perceval's first suit of armor, taken from the Red Knight, is red and symbolizes his persona while Blancheflor's name means "white flower." This passage, then, encodes the universal longing of Two becoming One—the eternal human quest to regain our sense of original created wholeness. As Plato put it in the *Symposium*: "Each of us when separated, having one side only . . . is . . . always looking for his other half."[13]

The absence of his beloved plunges Perceval into loneliness and despair, and brings him to that stage of initiation in which he must face the "Dweller on the Threshold." This is the point where the initiate must face his or her shadow side: all the fears, blind spots, and hidden and unacceptable parts of the self, which must be brought to consciousness and acknowledged before going any further on the spiritual path. In this story the Dweller shows up as the Loathly Lady whom, as we saw in the last chapter, will not let the seeker evolve to higher consciousness until he or she has dealt with the unregenerate side of the psyche.

MENDING THE BROKEN SWORD

Although the quest is for the Grail, the Sword must also be redeemed if balance is to be restored. In some Grail romances, the Sword assumes a central role: unless the hero mends the broken sword that caused the Fisher King's wound, he will fail the quest. In *Le Conte du Graal,* the sword that was sent to Perceval by the Fisher King's niece turns out to be flawed, as he discovers after his ignominious dismissal from the Grail Castle. When Perceval meets his cousin in the forest, she tells him that the sword is treacherous and will break in a careless moment. It can only be repaired by the smith who forged it.

In the *First Continuation* to Chrétien's poem, the story continues with Sir Gawain's arrival at the Grail castle. He witnesses the Grail procession, after which a bier is carried in by four pall-bearers. The bier is covered with a cloth of royal silk on which a sword has been laid. Although the sword looks quite intact, it is in fact broken clean through the middle. Gawain asks the maimed king the identity of the man in the bier, and also the meaning of the Grail and Lance, at which point the king calls for his "good sword" to be brought to him. This weapon, too, is in two pieces. After explaining it was a woman (his niece) who had given him the sword, the king tells Gawain if he can mend the blade, he will answer his questions. Gawain puts the pieces together and they seem to join perfectly, but when the king has him test the strength of the bond, the sword falls apart again. The Wounded King regretfully tells Gawain he is not yet worthy of learning about the mysteries of the Grail Castle. At this, Gawain falls into a sudden, deep sleep. When he awakens, he finds himself lying ignominiously in a marsh, with his horse tethered to a nearby tree.

Gawain fails this test because, in the words of the maimed king: "You have not yet achieved enough as a knight to be able to know the truth about these things; for I promise you the one who will come to know the truth will be esteemed and praised as the finest knight in the world."[14]

From this we can see that the broken sword clearly parallels the Cup of Truth in the Irish story of King Cormac, which falls apart when a lie is told. Cormac was famed for his unwavering dedication to the truth, which was considered the supreme virtue of an Irish king.*[15] Gawain's failure to mend the sword reflects his lack of this quality.

Gawain is later given another opportunity to mend the broken sword when he comes to an island where there is a great hall having all the "fourfold" characteristics of the Celtic Otherworld fortress. He is led into a hall where once again he sees a richly adorned royal bier, this time with the upper half of a broken sword lying on the dead man's breast. A procession of richly dressed monks enters, and they hold a vigil for the dead man while four clerics perfume the air around the bier with the four censers. When the service has ended, the king of this realm arrives and invites Gawain to a feast in which the Grail, followed by the bleeding Lance, makes an appearance. The king tells Gawain the land has been "ravaged and ruined" by the death of the man in the bier, and everyone in this devastated country is awaiting the coming of the finest knight in the world who will mend the sword and restore the land to health. Once again, Gawain tries his hand, but his attempt ends in

---

*In early Ireland this was known as *fir flathemon*, "ruler's truth," a term that also implies the virtues of wisdom and justice.

failure a second time. However, he does ask about the lance. He is told it is the Lance of Longinus, and this results in the recovery of some of the kingdom: "God . . . restored the rivers to their courses in that land and the woods . . . turned green again."[16] So Gawain's partial success at mending the broken sword regenerates at least part of the Wasteland.

In the *Second Continuation* to *Le Conte du Graal,* we return to Perceval, who also tries his hand at repairing the broken sword. He is almost successful; the pieces hold together, but a little notch remains. In the Continuation attributed to thirteenth-century French poet, Gerbert de Montreuil, we learn the notch remains because, although Perceval has made much spiritual progress, he has not yet atoned for having abandoned his mother, leaving her to die of grief. That night he falls asleep in the Grail Castle, but awakens to find himself in a beautiful meadow with a circular enclosure. Through the gate he sees a glorious, radiant light and hears beautiful music and sounds of people rejoicing. The music is so exquisite that for a moment, Perceval forgets all the troubles he has ever known. One half of the wall is white, and the other red—the alchemical colors that betoken the feminine and masculine principles, for behind these walls is a world beyond duality. Longing to be let in, Perceval calls through the gate, but his cries are ignored. In frustration, he hammers on the gate with his sword, which breaks in two. Finally, an old man with snow-white hair arrives and is most displeased at seeing an armored knight making a violent assault upon the gates. He tells Perceval he will not be allowed inside and neither will he achieve the Grail until he has expiated his sins and misdeeds. For this place is the Earthly Paradise and cannot be entered by those who value transient earthly pleasures over eternal spiritual joys.

As Perceval rides away, he glances back, but the walled garden has disappeared. Later he is given counsel by a hermit who tells him his sword can only be mended by the one who forged it, so the knight goes in search of the blacksmith, Trebuchet. The bridge leading to the smith's house is guarded by two fearsome "crested serpents" that Perceval bravely manages to slay. Trebuchet repairs his sword, telling him that, having overcome all his tests and trials, he is now the best knight in the world. At the end of this narrative, Perceval returns to the Grail Castle and heals the notch in the Fisher King's sword so that it is now whole and complete.

In the *Third Continuation,* the story of the broken sword is finally brought to an end when Percival once again visits the Grail Castle and learns the broken sword was the weapon of a treacherous knight who slew the brother of the Fisher King. Perceval sets out on a mission of vengeance and kills the traitor in a duel. On his triumphant return to the Grail Castle, he is once more shown the Holy Grail (although he does not ask the ritual question, as one might expect). The Fisher King discovers that Perceval is his own nephew, to great mutual rejoicing. Not long after, the old king dies and Perceval takes his place. He is crowned at a great feast where the Grail appears at the table and gives the guests all the food and drink they most desire. Perceval reigns at the Grail Castle for seven years, then retires to a hermitage. He spends the rest of his life in prayer and meditation, nourished only by the Grail. When he dies, he is borne up to heaven, and the Grail, lance, and silver platter go with him. No one has since seen the Grail on Earth.

So Perceval has become a fully integrated individual, as symbolized by his "crowning" achievement of kingship. Having mended the broken Sword, the wounded masculine principle, and embraced the feminine Grail, there are no more worldly initiations for him to pursue. When his work in the world is done, he withdraws from the world to focus on spiritual matters, which in many eastern traditions was the proscribed path for the last years of one's life. At his death, the polarized Grail hallows are withdrawn into heaven, symbolizing the end of a life in the world of opposites, as Perceval is subsumed into the One. And so the quest begins again for every seeker down the ages.

THE INNER CASTLE OF THE GRAIL

The four hallows at the Castle of the Fisher King recall the other fourfold symbols we have encountered in the Grail myth, from the four-cornered islands and fortresses of Celtic myth to the castle of the Grail itself. As

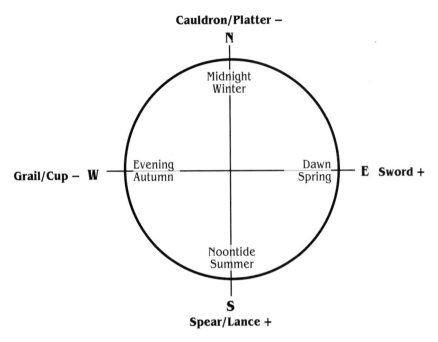

The Four Hallows on the Wheel of Life

we noted earlier, this quality represents wholeness and completion and is a universal sacred symbol of the Center of the World. In Western esoteric tradition, specific qualities are attributed to the four quarters, some of which are shown on the circle-cross diagram above.

This diagram is sometimes known as the Wheel of Life because it illustrates a dynamic process based on the perceived passage of the sun around the Earth, both in its diurnal and seasonal cycles. There are two masculine and two feminine stages on the Wheel of Life and Death, which signify an Ascending Tide (+) and Descending Tide (–). This cycle also corresponds to the human psyche that looks outward at youth and adulthood, symbolized by the action-oriented Sword and Spear; and inward at maturity and old age, symbolized by the receptive Cup and Cauldron. Note how Sword and Grail are opposite each other, forming a masculine-feminine, ascending-descending polarity. In motion, this process becomes a spiral, one of the most ancient glyphs for the dance of polarized energies we call the cosmos, cycling from birth to death to birth again.

We can gain a greater understanding of how these archetypes play out in our lives through the mandala process that follows.

Exercise
The Four Hallows

1. Take a large sheet of drawing paper—black construction paper works well for this exercise—and some pastels, chalks, or other medium.

2. Sit with these materials before you in a comfortable, quiet environment where you will not be disturbed. Take some deep breaths, center yourself, and close your eyes.

3. Imagine you are standing in a circular hall within a stone castle with four unglazed, arched windows at the cardinal directions. Below each window is one of the four Grail Hallows. The eastern window is lit by the morning sun whose rays illuminate a long two-edged Sword resting on a table. Look at it carefully. Is it new and shining or old and rusty? Notched or marked in any way? Straight or bent? Raise it in your strongest hand and let the sun shine upon it. Does this feel good or uncomfortable? If it doesn't feel right, ask yourself why, and let the answer come to you in words or pictures. Think of any situation in your present life in which you must make a decision, choose between two or more courses of action, or separate from someone or something. Feel the power of the two-edged sword, the razor-sharp power of your mind, to think clearly: to discriminate, to separate, to make the right decision. Then replace the Sword on the table.

4. Turn now to the south-facing window, which is lit by the bright golden rays of a midday sun, and look for a long Spear made of wood with a bronze tip. Walk toward it and examine it closely. Is it well-built and sturdy, or damaged in any way? Raise it in your strongest hand and feel its strength. Does it feel good or uncomfortable? Bring to mind a situation where

you must be assertive, exert your will, and move into action, and see yourself doing so with confidence and conviction. Then replace the Spear.

5. Turn now to the western window where the purple afterglow of a sunset illumines a Cup on a table. Notice whether it is plain or decorated, old or new, dull or shiny. Gazing into it, see if there is any liquid inside it or whether it is empty. If it has liquid, look inside and see an image reflected there of something that moves you deeply. Let yourself feel the feelings that bubble up from the chalice of your heart. Then replace the Cup on the table.

6. Turn now to the northern window, which reveals a midnight sky studded with stars. Before you is a large, round Cauldron suspended by a long chain above a fire. Look into the Cauldron and see an image of your greatest challenge in life, the inner demon, dragon, or shadow that you have yet to face and master. Summon up all your courage against this opponent, and see an image of yourself being victorious.

7. Take a deep breath and open your eyes. Draw a large circle on the paper and mark the four cardinal points on the outside, with the North at the top.

8. Set conscious thought aside. Turn your attention to the paper in front of you and draw the Sword in the East, the Spear in the South, the Cup in the West, and the Cauldron in the North. You can add other details: background scenery, people, and more, although this is not necessary. Spend as long as you like making each of these your own with care and attention. You don't have to be a good artist—the mandala is a reflection of your psyche and a useful tool for self-knowledge.

9. Look at the symbol with which you resonate most strongly: how do you express that energy in your life?

10. Now see if there is any image which has no positive meaning for you. How do you experience that in daily life?

11. How balanced are you? Are the feminine symbols more developed than the masculine or vice versa?

Exercise
The Teachers of the Grail

The work of depth psychologist, C. G. Jung, and his followers has added yet another layer of meaning to this ancient fourfold symbol so we can view each quarter of the circle as an expression of four main archetypes, which we may express at different times of our lives.*[17] On our journey through the landscape of the Grail, we have already met these figures—now we can see them in relation to each other and understand their archetypal nature and significance.

THE YOUNG MASCULINE is the young god, the Son of Light, who is born out of the Old Feminine as the sun is born out of night. He appears universally as the young prince, warrior or hero, and his exploits often involve slaying fearsome enemies, thus overcoming the power of death, which rules the North. In Arthurian myth, the Young Masculine is represented by Perceval and other Grail knights as well as King Arthur in his youth. His symbol is the Sword.

THE OLD MASCULINE is the developed masculine principle: mature, experienced, and wise. He is Merlin, Arthur's advisor, and the various Grail hermits who give spiritual counsel to the young hero when he has lost his sense of moral direction; and also the Fisher King, who is ready to relinquish his throne. His symbol is the Rod of authority or Staff of power, which later became the Spear or Lance.

THE YOUNG FEMININE is the beautiful and loving Bright Goddess: Morgan of Avalon, the healer of Arthur, and Queen Guinevere. In

---

*Jungian writer Gareth Hill calls the fourfold archetypal pattern the Static Feminine, the Dynamic Masculine, the Static Masculine, and Dynamic Feminine, and although he discusses these principles in the context of human psychology, he points out that they are ciphers for "the most fundamental patterns in all of life."

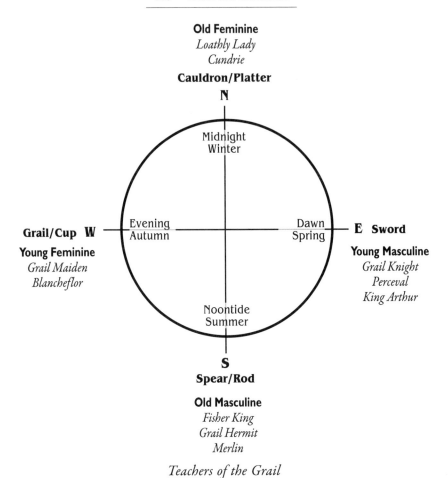

Old Feminine
Loathly Lady
Cundrie
Cauldron/Platter

N

Midnight
Winter

Evening
Autumn

Grail/Cup W

Young Feminine
Grail Maiden
Blancheflor

Dawn
Spring

E Sword

Young Masculine
Grail Knight
Perceval
King Arthur

Noontide
Summer

S

Spear/Rod

Old Masculine
Fisher King
Grail Hermit
Merlin

Teachers of the Grail

the Grail stories, she is Perceval's beloved, Blancheflor, and the Grail Maiden. Her symbol is the Cup of healing—the chalice offered in love, and ultimately, the Holy Grail.

THE OLD FEMININE is the Loathly Lady, who, as we saw in the last chapter, is a medieval reworking of the Dark Goddess. In Celtic mythology and the Grail cycle, the Old Feminine is represented by Ceridwen, the Cailleach, Sheela-na-gig, or Cundrie. Her symbol is the Cauldron, representing both the womb and tomb of life. As we saw in the story of Taliesin, from out of her cauldron-womb the Son of Light is born and the cycle of life begins again.

In our lives, we express:

- The Young Masculine when we are clearly focused on our path, wielding the sword of discrimination to make the right choices and decisions.
- We express the Old Masculine when we are established in our chosen sphere in life, experienced, knowledgeable, and wisely wielding the rod of authority to widen our influence.
- We express the Young Feminine when we approach life from an intuitive, creative, process-oriented perspective, which may include the arts and healing work, finding inspiration within the chalice of the soul that can then be offered to others.
- We express the Old Feminine when experience has taught us inner wisdom and a deeper understanding of life and death, which we can impart to others from our Cauldron of Knowledge.

Each of these archetypes is experienced within the human psyche at one time or another during our lives, depending on the cycles of the soul's growth. Although it might seem obvious that a young man would most likely play out the young masculine archetype and so on, this is not necessarily so. For example, a woman at midlife whose domestic role has become suffocating may take the path of the Warrior by finding independence in a new career. At this time of new beginnings, we might say she is in the East of the Wheel of Life. A young man who is more interested in playing music in a band than going to college is following the way of the Young Feminine, and is in the West of the Wheel of Life.

- *Where do you stand on the Wheel of Life in terms of your life expression today? How has this changed from when you were younger?*
- *Close your eyes and visualize one of the Grail teachers on the Wheel of Life. Using your imagination, see him or her as vividly as you can with your inner eye, along with their particular symbol of power. Greet this being and ask any questions you may have about the aspect of your life he or she represents. You may ask for help and guidance in your search for understanding, resolution, and fulfillment in this matter.*

VisionJourney V
An Initiation of the Grail

The twentieth-century occultist, Margaret Lumley Brown, wrote: "The Grail power represents a great spiritual essence existing in different forms upon every plane and this essence is open to every soul who is going to undertake the Quest, hazardous and dangerous though it may be."[18]

This longer VisionJourney is designed to guide you on such a quest. Readers familiar with the Qabalah will recognize it as a "pathworking" in the tradition of the Tree of Life. Could Chrétien have been familiar with Judaic mysticism? Troyes, in the twelfth century, was the chief center of Jewish religious studies in the world, and, as Professor Urban T. Holmes writes, "It is hard to believe there was little interchange of ideas, stories, and helping hands" among the cultured of that city.[19]

On this inner journey, you progress up the spheres from the Earth to the Moon, aided by guides from the spheres of Mercury or Venus, and arrive at the sphere of the Sun where the Grail is lodged. Since it is a long and complex journey, you may wish to do the parts at different sittings a number of times.

Part One: Earth Temple

Close your eyes, quiet your mind and take some deep breaths. Every time you breathe out, you exhale a pearl-white mist, which soon completely surrounds you. When the mist lifts, you find yourself on a wide green plain gazing up at two huge standing stones, megaliths of a long-forgotten age. The stones have been decorated and carved with two dragons: the one on the left is red, while the one on the right is white. They are so lifelike they seem almost to twist and writhe in the stones. They stand at the head of an avenue of stones that snakes away down a hill toward the seashore. In the distance, you can see the blue-green swell of the sea. A high wind blows back your hair and fills your nostrils with the scent of the salt air. . . .

You feel impelled to follow the stones down to the sea, and so you walk between the two tall pillars, feeling a slight but unmistakable electric shock as you pass through. As you walk down the avenue you are aware that, above the sound of the wind, there can be heard a faint, low hum of voices seeming to emanate from the stones themselves. You pause at one of the stones and notice it is carved with cup-and-ring marks and spirals. When you place your hand on one of these figures, the voices are louder. Placing your ear to it, you can hear men and women talking and the shrieks and laughter of children at play. Sometimes the voices sound even and contented, but at other times there are warlike shouts and cries of distress . . .

Listen now to the voices of the ancestors who set these stones into place, who lived here long ago and who have now gone into the Earth. Perhaps they have a message for you. . . .

They seem so close, yet out of reach. Perhaps they are buried beneath the ground under your feet, and yet the ghosts of these ancient ones still walk the avenue they once raised. . . .

Eventually you find yourself at the shore where the sound of the sea overwhelms the human voices. A little boat is waiting, you climb in and sit in the prow gazing ahead toward a far-distant land. You can just make out a low line of rolling hills and woods, and beyond them, vast mountains with craggy peaks, where the ethereal shape of a distant temple can be seen, glowing like a jewel of great beauty in the light of a setting sun. You are filled with a longing to go there, but the next minute the sun darkens and the temple has gone, leaving you to wonder if you imagined it after all. . . .

Part Two: The Tower of the Moon

The boat sets off of its own accord and bears you over the waves to the distant shore where you alight. You find yourself on a path through an apple orchard, where silver fruit hangs from the trees like little moons in the dusky purple of the gathering twilight. You breathe in their fragrance with deep enjoyment and notice the path is leading you toward a white tower on a low hill that appears to be thatched with the wings of white birds. No one seems to be about, so you enter in through an open door and climb a winding stair to the top. You emerge into a room where stands an altar made from a single piece of white quartz with nine sides. It gleams like ice in the light of the rising moon, which shines through the narrow arched windows of the tower. On it are four artifacts of great beauty: a sword of shining silver; a spear of gleaming grey ash-wood, tipped with bronze; a small silver cauldron, ornamented with intricate knot-work; and a smooth black obsidian stone. Each seems to be surrounded by its own aura of light, as if alive. Mesmerized by their beauty, you bend over them, being particularly drawn to the stone, in whose shining surface you see moving pictures of the most fascinating kind. . . . Gaze at them as long as you like, for there are many wonders here. . . .

The images in the stone are suddenly covered by three faces looking at you. They belong to three female figures standing on the other side of the altar. Standing upright, you confront three women: a young girl, a mature woman of middle years, and an old crone. The mature woman smiles gravely at you and welcomes you to the Castle of Women. Yet, she tells you, you are not to stay long here, for you must reach the Grail Castle by morning. You may choose one of the treasures to take with you on your journey. Ponder well which one you will take.

> The Sword will enable you to cut through barriers.
> The Spear will destroy any attackers.
> The Cauldron will supply you with sustenance.
> The Stone will enhance your inner vision.

When you have made your choice, the maiden takes the inner, astral form out of the treasure on the altar and hands it to you. The original still remains in place. Then the three women circle around you, weaving their hands about your body as they outfit you in an armor of Light; silken filaments of a silvery substance flow from their fingertips and surround you from head to toe. You descend the tower stairs with your chosen gift, feeling light and buoyant; your feet scarcely touch the ground. As you make your way into the deep forest that lies beyond the tower, the *moonlight acts to keep your armor of Light charged, which helps to speed you along. . . .*

Soon you come to a crossroads where the path branches into three. Looking to your left you see that the path leads to a city; to the right, it meanders through a green valley. The path on the left is the Way of Knowledge and the Path on the right is the Way of Nature. You must traverse both these ways before you can take the middle path, which leads upward to the Grail Temple. You go first down the path you feel most drawn to.

Part Three: The Library

The left-hand path leads you to the city, in the center of which is a grand library—an imposing octagonal building of white marble. The library is not an ordinary one, for it holds all the knowledge of humankind from the time our race was first gifted with the spark of consciousness. You enter through huge wooden double doors and find yourself in a hall from which many corridors radiate like the spokes of a wheel. A spiral staircase extends upward into seemingly endless heights and down into the bowels of the Earth. It is clear the building is far bigger than it appeared from the outside. Every now and then, figures bearing armfuls of books or scrolls drift silently in and out of the hall, dressed in clothes of varying nationalities and time periods. A robed librarian is seated at a podium in the center. He is tall with graying hair and sharp, intelligent eyes. He bears a caduceus around which two live serpents, one red and one white, continually entwine. He has been variously known through the ages as Merlin, Thoth, or Hermes Trismegistus. He tells you all the knowledge in the universe is here, even that which has been lost to our world, for this is a place where nothing can ever be destroyed. All history from the dawning of human awareness up to present time is here, and every idea ever conceived exists somewhere in this place. Smiling, he adds that here too are kept the records of the genesis and evolution of every human soul on Earth. He asks you if you would like to see yours, and you nod. . . .

He leads you up the spiral stairway and down several corridors—a walk during which you feel as if you have lost all track of time and space. Eventually you arrive at a door that announces, "Hall of Records." The Librarian touches the door with his serpent rod and you enter into a room so vast that its walls and ceiling are not even visible. The Librarian hands you a book and cautions you that it contains the record of your soul's journey through many lifetimes. Within its pages are catalogued both the negative and positive aspects of your evolution through the centuries. Nervously, you open the first page, but it is completely blank! Only after several minutes do colors and pictures begin to appear, like a developing film, and you begin to see the story of your many lives unfold before your eyes. . . .

After perusing these chronicles for what seems like a timeless time, you come to one you realize with a bit of a shock is your current lifetime. . . . You may learn new things about your life when seeing it from this perspective, but when you reach the present moment, the pages for the future appear blank once again. You find yourself wondering about your future, and as thoughts and images emerge from your mind, you see them form on the new pages. Intrigued, you experiment with this by trying out new and different scenarios and outcomes and watching them play out before your eyes. There is an amused chuckle from the Librarian:

"You are learning," he says, "the power of the creative imagination in the divine play of life."

You may continue to work with your book for as long as you like. It will contain one thing in particular that will be invaluable to you on the quest for the Grail: a piece of wisdom that forms itself into a symbol. You give this to the Librarian who inserts it into a wooden rod which he hands back to you, saying, "Here—take your Staff of Knowledge. It will aid you on your journey."

Part Four: The Green Valley

The right-hand path leads you to the oldest part of the Forest, a dim green valley of infinite beauty and peace where no tree or plant has ever known the bite of axe or knife, and no creature has ever known death from predator's claw or hunter's arrow. Here stands a grove of seven huge trees, which soar skyward like pillars of a vast natural temple, whose dome is of many shades of green or coppery red. Beneath your feet the ground is carpeted with a rich emerald moss. The air is fresh and fragrant with the scent of growing things, and the air resounds with birdsong high up in the leafy canopy. Although you see no creatures here, you get the feeling of being watched by many pairs of eyes from holes in the trunks and shadowy roots of the trees. Then barely perceptible at first, beings emerge from the shadows as if the dim green light itself has taken form. Animals of the wild: badgers, foxes, bears, deer, and many other forest creatures, great and small; and other beings that seem to step out of the trees themselves: dryads and hamadryads, elven creatures all in green—tall and slender with almond-shaped eyes and long silky hair— move noiselessly like sunlight over the forest floor; Woodwives and Moss-women, old and bent, with green skin like lichen; gnomes with bark-like skin, gnarled and knotty as tree-roots . . .

They do not seem to have noticed you, for they are all turning in the direction where someone is now approaching: a Lady of great beauty with a radiant countenance and long coppery-gold hair which trails down behind and all around her. Wherever it touches the mossy ground, red and white thornless roses spring forth. In one hand she holds aloft a shining emerald stone like a lamp which suffuses the forest grove with a warm gold-green light. She is the Queen of Elphame, the goddess Venus, who is known as the Empress in the Grail legend of Peredur, or Repanse de Schoye in Parzival. All beauty and harmony are hers, and as she walks, she sings the worlds into being, for her song is a song of love that is the purest creative force in the cosmos. . . .

You are so overcome by her wordless song and wish for nothing more than to bask in the streams of love and harmony and joy that her voice pours forth. The beauty of her song fills you with heartbreaking pain for all you have suffered in this and many other lifetimes. Seeing this, the Lady reaches down to you and touches the pain in your heart, which takes the form of a symbol. Bring this symbol out of yourself and hold it in your hands as an offering to the goddess. She sings over this symbol and fills it with light which transforms your pain into pure love. The symbol changes into a flower—note it well—that she places in your heart. You feel yourself strengthened and renewed. The pain begins to subside, then totally disappears. You begin to breathe deeply. Pure, unconditional love flows through you. As you continue to breathe deeply, a great sense of calm and inner peace washes over you. You sense that all is well and are ready to continue your journey. . . .

Part Five: The Challenge

On your return to the crossroads a challenge awaits you, preventing you from going any further. This may be in the shape of a dark knight, a monstrous beast, a churlish giant—only you will know—and you will also know what it represents, for this fearful manifestation is the Dweller on the Threshold, your own shadow-self that lies within your unconscious mind and is the thing you fear most in the world. The fear may make you feel weak, helpless, and despairing, which will make your opponent seem even stronger and more terrible. It is at this point that you will need to use the gift you brought from the Castle of Women.

Do what you must do to overcome this opponent.

Afterward, take some time to reflect on what you have learned from this experience and perhaps rest a while. When you are ready to resume your journey, take the path that leads upward and out of the forest. . . .

Part Six: The Mountain

Soon the trees thin out and you see before you the steep slopes of a mountain, and at its summit, the shining circular wall of the temple you saw from afar—the Temple of the Grail.

At first you make good progress, striding upward, the Staff of Knowledge in your hand, pausing now and then to enjoy the magnificent views opening up all around you. But the higher you go, the steeper the path, which has now become a series of ledges like great steps. You have to drag yourself up with great effort, for here the air is much thinner. A fierce wind starts to blow down from the icy heights and you are again grateful for the armor of Light, which is the only thing saving you from freezing to death. . . .

The sky has been growing gradually darker and it feels as if you have been climbing for hundreds of miles and hundreds of years. What is more, the path has now become so narrow that it is scarcely wide enough for both your feet and you have to lean into the cliff-face on one side for fear of falling into the depths below. . . . And now the path peters out all together, and the only way forward is across a narrow bridge of stone that curves in a steep arc over the darkness of an abyss through which you can hear the whistling of mighty winds. You can no longer see the summit of the mountain—there is only a dark and interminable void below, an endless nothingness. . . . As you contemplate this terrifying prospect, you may once again find your gift from the Moon Tower to be of assistance. . . .

Part Seven: The Grail Temple

Once over the Sword Bridge, slowly and gradually, something appears before you: a tall, gleaming tower high up in the darkness. . . . The climb becomes easier now as if it is pulling you toward its light. But when finally you reach it, it is not a tower at all, but a great door glowing from the intensely bright light behind it.

The door is firmly shut, and you see no handle. Exhausted, you collapse on the doorstep in despair. Have you come all this way only to be shut out? Tears trickle down onto your chest and fall upon the flower that the goddess placed in your heart. Its petals open, filled with light, and this bright thing in the darkness fills you with courage, strength and hope. You leap to your feet with renewed vigor and knock boldly on the door. After a terrible pause in which nothing happens, it slowly begins to open and you enter in.

When your eyes have adjusted to the intensity of the light, you see that you are in the circular courtyard of a great temple where a beautiful garden grows. . . . Pilgrims from all times, clothed in shining garments, are walking or sitting here, their faces either rapt with ecstasy or deep in contemplation. In the center is the Temple of the Grail, golden in the rays of the sun, which is pouring down beams of supernal light, ten times brighter than the sun in our world, upon this holy place. . . . As you approach its doors, you see the way is guarded by two terrifying angels with huge wings bearing fiery swords. Their eyes are green like emeralds and can see right inside of you. They may either allow you into the inner sanctuary or else tell you that you must stay in the garden. . . .

If you stay in the garden, one of the Grail pilgrims will approach you and spend time with you in conversation in which you will learn many things. If you are allowed into the Grail Temple, the door will open and you will enter into a vast dimension with a backdrop of stars, galaxies, and limitless space. A smiling Being comes toward you: one whom you recognize with a leap of joy as someone who is very dear to you, for you *have loved each other throughout the ages . . . This loving Companion leads you to an altar on which the Holy of Holies stands behind a veil. You are unable to see his or her form, but you are aware of the divine presence that is in this place. . . . You kneel before the Grail and enter into a profound stillness in which all movement stops and there is utter silence as you enter into an awareness of eternity. . . . What happens next, only you can know. . . .*

And now the voice of your Companion is calling your name. Listen with all your heart to what is said. . . .

When it is time to leave, you pass out of the Grail Temple back into the garden, where you take the blossom from the Green Valley out of your heart and plant it as a divine offering among the flowers here. You may spend some time with your Companion or others present in the garden, then you bid farewell and return down the mountainside with light, sure steps and a joyful heart. You drop below the tree-line and once more enter the forest where the path leads you straight toward the Tower of the Moon. As you reach the tower, the treasure that you were given floats away to melt into its counterpart on the altar. . . .

You pass through the orchard and reach the shore where the boat awaits you and bears you back to the mainland. You are aware that your armor of Light is fading away, leaving you feeling more solid as you step onto dry ground. . . . You turn around just once to see if you can catch a glimpse of the Grail Temple on the far mountains, but it is hidden behind a cloud. So you set your sights steadfastly toward home and make your way up the hill through the avenue of stones. . . . The voices of the ancestors are hushed and at peace. When you arrive at the top, you plant your staff firmly into the ground where its knowledge can seep into the earth to be used by future generations that may pass this way. . . . Then you walk back through the two dragon stones and return to your own time and place.

Now open your eyes and come fully back to present time and space.

6

The Grail Comes to Glastonbury

From their source in the Otherworld, the streams of the Grail legend flowed into the physical world and became part of the geomythical landscape of the British Isles. Yet in truth, the Grail was always present within the landscape. Ceridwen continued to stir the Cauldron of Inspiration below the waters of Bala Lake in North Wales. In Ireland the sovereignty goddess still waited beneath the Hill of Tara for a true king to whom she could offer a drink from her sacred cup. In England, the Grail legends clustered around many places of power in the landscape, and none more so than in the small town of Glastonbury.

Intimations of the Otherworld weave like the mists around Glastonbury's somewhat surreal landscape. In the days before the Romans reclaimed the low-lying fields known as the Somerset levels from the sea, it was an island, believed to be a portal to the faery realm and the land of the dead, both of which were regarded as one and the same location in Celtic tradition. The fourteenth-century *Prophecy of Melkin* identified Glastonbury as "the Isle of Avalon, eager for the death of pagans."[1] It was once called *Ynys-witrin,* a Welsh name meaning the "Isle of Glass," an echo of Caer Wydyr, the Glass Castle of Annwn, where the Nine Maidens kindled the magical cauldron. With its fruitful orchards, it became the Apple Isle, where King Arthur rested in the arms of Morgan le Fay. Even today, prominent council road signs announce to twenty-first-century drivers that they are approaching the "the Ancient Isle of Avalon."

In his novel, *A Glastonbury Romance,* John Cooper Powys wrote: "There are only about half a dozen reservoirs of world-magic on the surface of the globe: Jerusalem . . . Mecca . . . Lhasa—and of these Glastonbury has the largest residue of unused power. Generations of mankind, aeons of past races, have—by their concentrated will—made Glastonbury miraculous."[2]

A SACRED CENTER

In many ancient civilizations and tribal societies, the Glastonbury landscape would have been instantly recognizable as a sacred center. This universal religious symbol refers to a numinous place at the designated center of a land: a point where spiritual forces irrupt into the physical world. The Greeks called the sacred center the *omphalos,* or "navel." Just as the navel is found at the center of the human body where it once joined us to our maternal source of life and nourishment through the umbilical cord, so too is the navel of the Earth attached to a universal supply of cosmic energy via the vertical channel that passes through it. This is the axis mundi, the universal axis that joins the Earth to the worlds above and below, variously pictured as a giant tree, pillar stone, pyramid, or mountain.

Glastonbury's sacred center is the Tor, a hill topped by the ruined tower of a medieval church dedicated to Saint Michael, the archangel who guards the high places of England. Most likely, Michael took over the job from a pagan sun-god, perhaps Belenos, whose name means "bright," or "shining," and comes from the same root as the Celtic festival of Beltaine (the Bright Fire), which celebrates the beginning of summer. While not much more than five hundred feet high, the Tor can be seen in the distance for miles around, an unforgettable landmark that has an uncanny knack of shape-shifting—appearing conical, whale-backed or pudding-basin round, depending on your vantage point. Standing on top of the windy summit, it is not hard to imagine

Glastonbury Tor. Photo by Nicholas Mann.

that Glastonbury was once an island. In fact, if you have come just after the winter rains, the land around the Tor looks like a shining sheet of water, as it was thousands of years ago. The locals are fond of saying that when Glastonbury becomes an island once again, Avalon will be restored and the golden age will return once more to the land.

The Tor seems to have been a place of great importance from the earliest times. Archeologists have found traces of prehistoric settlement on its summit, indicating its significance in the age of the megalith builders. Footings of a building dating from the Romano-British era have also been discovered, together with over four hundred ammonites, objects known to have been used as votive offerings in Gaulish temples of that period. A three-dimensional spiral path of unknown origin winds all the way to the top in seven circuits. Long ago, the pyramid-shaped Tor, surrounded by water and encircled by a sevenfold spiral trackway, may have been used for ritual ascensions to a hilltop temple, like the seven-stepped pyramids and ziggurats of the Near East, which were constructed as microcosms of the sacred mountain. This was not unknown in Neolithic England, as archaeologists have discovered at Silbury Hill in Wiltshire: an artificial, pyramid-shaped mound with a spiral path of seven circuits winding up to a broad, flattened summit.

Long considered an entrance to the Otherworld, when the Tor was surrounded by water, it may have resembled one of the caers of Annwn in *The Plunder of Annwn*. Local tradition claims it is honeycombed with caves, like the "hollow hills" of the sídhe, and a legend describes it as the home of the King of the Faeries and Lord of Annwn, Gwyn ap Nudd (pronounced *gwin ap nith*). Gwyn's name comes from the same Celtic root (*vindo*, meaning "white," "bright," or "shining") as "Gwion" and the Irish "Fionn," and was invoked by Welsh seers when they wanted to enter the realms of Annwn to consult the spirits for prophecy.[3] They saw him as a hunter with a pack of spectral hounds known as the *Cwn Annwn* or the "Dogs of Annwn." On stormy winter nights, Gwyn is said to ride at the head of the Wild Hunt, the great cavalcade of spirits that sweep through the skies in pursuit of the wandering souls of the dead, whom he leads to their home beyond this world. It is a role he shares with other northern heroes, including Woden, Herne the Hunter, Sir Francis Drake, and even King Arthur himself.

And so Glastonbury became both Annwn and Avalon, a sunset island in the magical West where the souls of the dead voyaged on their last journey, a "thin place" where inner and outer, above and below intersect. Today the area is acknowledged by many as the spiritual hub of England, and it continues to be a place where many report inexplicable experiences of the supernatural, from faery sightings to UFOs, spirits on the Tor, ghostly monks in the grounds of its abbey, and the White Lady who haunts the Chalice Well, the sacred spring below the Tor. Visitors and local residents remark upon the "Glastonbury experience" of unaccountable synchronicities and strange phenomena that often have life-changing consequences. Each year, thousands of pilgrims and seekers make Glastonbury their destination, for the light of Avalon still gleams fitfully, yet unmistakably, even through the materialistic veil of the twenty-first century.

THE OLD CHURCH

If the Tor enshrines Glastonbury's pagan past, its claims to being the spiritual heartland of Christian England rest on its famous abbey, which, in the Middle Ages, was believed to be the first church in Britain and home to the Holy Grail. Today Glastonbury Abbey lies in ruins, the legacy of Henry VIII's dissolution of the monasteries during the Reformation. A tragic hulk of a wrecked ship of stone, it lies beached forever on the shores of time, yet was once the richest and most powerful church in medieval England. The early history of Glastonbury, as set down by the monks in the Middle Ages, is a tapestry of myth interwoven with history, with neither strands being clearly identifiable. The recent fashion in scholarly circles is that most of Glastonbury's legends were forgeries concocted by the monks, and historians are justifiably skeptical about some of their more extravagant claims. Yet there is evidence that Glastonbury's foundation legends may have had their origins in a long-standing oral tradition before being committed to writing, which only became a social necessity in the eleventh and twelfth centuries.[4]

While these pseudo-histories fail to convince in the realm of actuality, they are nevertheless living legends and traditions that embody mythopoetic truths. In other words, they may be untrue in Glastonbury but true in Avalon, which is, after all, an inner dimension. Avalon is the land the poet and mystic see in vision; where the artist and musician find inspiration; where the soul goes for healing and spiritual refreshment—a timeless land of power and mystery that offers initiation and enlightenment to all those that dare make the voyage. On this level, history and legend flow into each other to create the potent mythic reality of Glastonbury as Avalon. Dion Fortune, the twentieth-century occultist who founded her magical order in Glastonbury, puts it this way:

> There are many different roads leading to our English Jerusalem, "the holyest erthe in Englande." We can approach it by the high-road of history. . . . Or we can come to Glastonbury by the upland path of legend. . . . And there is a third way to Glastonbury, one of the secret green roads of the soul—the Mystic Way that leads through the Hidden Door into a land known only to the eye of vision. This is Avalon of the Heart to those who love her.[5]

THE HOLYEST ERTH

The story of how the Holy Grail came to Avalon is one of Glastonbury's most enduring legends. The connecting link between Glastonbury and the Grail is Joseph of Arimathea, the uncle of Christ. According to varying versions of the legend, Joseph of Arimathea, after burying his nephew's body in a sepulcher in his own garden, left Palestine in 63 CE. He brought with him the Cup of Christ from the Last Supper, and sailed to France to join the apostle Philip, who had converted that country to Christianity. Philip sent Joseph together with his son, Josephes, and ten companions on a mission to Britain. Borne swiftly northward by a miraculous wind, they sailed first to Wales, but being met with an inhospitable reception, they journeyed southward to the lands of Arviragus, a pagan British king.

Joseph and his companions trekked across the marshes for Glastonbury, and when they reached a hill just south of the Tor, they rested a while for very weariness, thus giving it the name Wearyall Hill.*

---

*Although officially known as Wirral Hill, it is still called "Wearyall Hill" by many locals today.

To raise the spirits of his exhausted companions, Joseph planted his staff in the earth and knelt to pray. Miraculously, the staff burst into blossom and grew roots, an act of great mythic significance, for now a Tree of Life was set to flourish in a new sacred center along with the Grail, just as the Celtic cup or cauldron was paired with the sacred Tree in the Otherworld.

Rejoicing, the little company made its way to the Isle of Avalon where Arviragus, although not interested in their Christian mission, was impressed by the bearing and manner of these foreign travelers, and gave them land on which to settle.

As a Latin verse puts it:

> *Avallon is entered by a band of Twelve:*
> *Joseph, Arimathea's flower, is chief of them:*
> *And with his father cometh Josephes.*
> *So to these Twelve Glastonia's rights are given.*[6]

Here Joseph received a vision from the Angel Gabriel that he was to build a church dedicated to Mary, the mother of Christ. With woven willow saplings and reeds, plastered together with mud, the little hermit band built a simple chapel, perhaps in the style of the houses in the nearby lake villages. Their lives were simple, devoted to fasting, vigil and prayer, sustained by frequent visions of the Virgin Mary. After King Arviragus died, his sons granted the twelve hermits twelve hides of land adjoining the church. A hide was as much as a man could cultivate in a year with an ox-drawn plough—about 120 acres. For centuries, local maps showed the land around the Tor as the "twelve hides." Some historians believe it is not beyond the bounds of possibility that Glastonbury was, as claimed, the location of the oldest ecclesiastical site in Britain. In those days it was on the old Mediterranean trade route on the Severn estuary and could easily have been its chief port and the first to receive the news of Christianity from traders from the Middle East.[7]

In his earlier life, Joseph was said to have been a wealthy merchant who sailed to England in search of tin in Cornwall and lead and other minerals in the Mendip Hills of Somerset. As late as the early twentieth century, this rumor could be heard in the tin-mining communities of the Mendip Hills or further west in Cornwall where tin had been sold to merchants from Phoenicia and the Mediterranean since the Bronze Age. According to some reports, tin-miners would chant: "Joseph was in the tin trade!" to bring good luck to their work. Enduring local legends in Cornwall and Glastonbury also declare that Joseph may even have brought with him his nephew, Jesus, as a young man, perhaps to spend his formative years learning from the Druids who had a college at Ynys Witrin. The village of Priddy in the Mendips had an old proverb: "As sure as Our Lord was at Priddy."[8] The visionary poet William Blake was probably thinking of this legend when he wrote the famous opening lines of the stirring poem "Jerusalem," which has come to be something of an unofficial national anthem in England:

> *And did those feet in ancient times*
> *Walk upon England's mountains green?*
> *And was the Holy Lamb of God*
> *In England's pleasant pastures seen?*

This may have been behind the mysterious allusion in the tenth-century biography of Saint Dunstan, Glastonbury's greatest abbot, which claimed that the first preachers of Christ in Britain found at Glastonbury a church built by "no art of man," but by Jesus himself, who dedicated it to his mother, Mary:

There is on the confines of western Britain a certain royal island, called in the ancient speech Glastonia. . . . In it the earliest neophytes of the Catholic rule, God guiding them, found a church, not built by the art of man, they say, but prepared by God himself for the salvation of mankind, which church the heavenly Builder himself declared—by many miracles and many mysteries of healing—he had consecrated to himself and to holy Mary, Mother of God.[9]

It also accounts for Glastonbury's reputation as "the holyest erth of England."[10]

SACRED BLOOD

Another version of Joseph's coming to Glastonbury was told by Robert de Boron, a poet of the late twelfth century from Burgundy. His book, *Joseph d'Arimathie,* is the first to describe the Grail as an explicitly Christian symbol. It tells how Joseph was a paid soldier of Pontius Pilate and a secret follower of Christ to whom Pilate gave the cup used at the Last Supper. When Joseph took down Christ's body from the cross to prepare for burial, he collected drops of the blood in the cup. When the body disappeared from the tomb, Joseph was thrown into prison and left to starve to death. But Christ appeared to Joseph, bearing the sacred cup, and taught him how to use it in the sacrament of the Eucharist. He also instructed him in the secret mysteries of the Grail, which, the author says, he "dare not tell." From then on, a dove appeared each day and dropped a single wafer into the cup, miraculously keeping Joseph alive until he was released. Together with a small band of followers, Joseph fled to the desert where Christ instructed him to set a table like the one at the Last Supper and place the Grail upon it. Joseph's brother-in-law, Bron, was told to catch a fish and lay it by the holy vessel. Bron became the new guardian of the Grail, and was sent westward to "the vales of Avalon" (here spelled Avaron), where he became known as the "Rich Fisher King," in honor of his catch. A local belief names this as the reason why the eastern end of Wearyall Hill is called Fisher's Hill.

There are strong reasons to see Bron's origins in the figure of Brân, the Welsh god who is brother to Manawydan, son of Llŷr, the counterpart of the Irish Otherworld king, Manannán mac Lir. As you will recall from chapter 2, Manannán is keeper of two sacred vessels: a Cauldron of Plenty and the Cup of Truth, whose magical attributes clearly mark them out as prototypes of the Grail. In the Mabinogi, Brân is king of Britain, and owns a Cauldron of Rebirth.[11] In a battle against the Irish, Brân sustains a fatal wound to his leg or foot like the "lamed" Fisher King of the Grail romances.

Just as the Celtic Grail encodes the mysteries of rebirth, this symbolism is carried forward in the Christian era by the Cup of Christ. Within this container is the sacrificial blood that is also the blood of redemption, which promises a new birth for the human race. As the chalice of the Eucharist, the Grail acts as the womb in which the miracle of transubstantiation takes place: sacramental wine turns into the life-giving blood, which is ceremonially ingested by the communicant who believes that in so doing, Jesus "will raise him up on the last day."[12]

THE HOLY THORN

A legend familiar to every resident in Glastonbury today centers around Joseph's holy thorn, a famous local landmark of a tree with branches reaching out of the mythopoetic dimension into the outer world. The story is that when Joseph's staff was miraculously transformed into a hawthorn tree on Wearyall Hill, it ever after flowered at Christmastide as well as in May. The tree was indeed not the common British hawthorn but a Middle Eastern species, *crataegus monogyna praecox,* or Levantine thorn. It did indeed bloom around the time of Christmas Day in the Old Style calendar, which was on January 5.* In the sixteenth century, a fanatical Puritan took an axe to it, considering it to be a heathen relic. He seemed to have paid for his sacrilege by wounding himself in the leg and becoming partially blinded when a splinter of wood flew into his eye.[13] The tree survived for another hundred years or so, only to be hacked down by a Roundhead soldier in Cromwell's time.

Fortunately, cuttings were taken which ensured descendants of the original tree continued to flourish. One was planted in its original place on Wearyall Hill, another in the grounds of Glastonbury Abbey, and a third in front of Saint John's Church in the High Street. Since 1929, a custom has taken root in Glastonbury, initiated by the Rev. Smithett

---

*The Old Style, or Julian, calendar was retained in England until 1752.

Lewis, and based on a historical tradition that may date from the time of Charles I: before Christmas each year, the vicar cuts a budded branch from the tree in the ground of St. John's Church in a popular ceremony attended by townspeople and schoolchildren, after which it is sent as a gift to the Queen of England to grace her Christmas breakfast table. The hawthorn is a tree sacred to the feminine: in the British Isles and Ireland, it is a faery tree, and its five-petaled white flowers, with their musky scent are sacred to the Queen of the Faeries, who is an aspect of the Earth Goddess. The midwinter flowers of the Glastonbury thorn are living symbols of Nature's renewed covenant with humankind.

ARTHUR IN AVALON

Perhaps the major reason that the Grail legends found a home in Glastonbury was due to the startling events of 1191. By this time, Joseph's church had risen from its humble wattle-and-daub beginnings and had become a magnificent stone abbey set like a jewel in the surrounding marshland. According to one account, a Welsh bard whispered an astonishing secret to King Henry II: none other than King Arthur himself was buried, together with Queen Guinevere, at Glastonbury Abbey. Henry passed the word to the abbey monks who lost no time in their excavations. A full sixteen feet down, between two stone pillars, they uncovered a coffin made from the hollowed trunk of an oak, containing the bones of an exceptionally tall man and woman. A large hole in the skull was evidence of the violent blow that apparently caused his death. The woman had a lock of bright golden hair, and one of the young monks impetuously jumped into the hole to grasp it—but it turned to dust at his touch. The monks reburied the bones in a black marble tomb set before the high altar in royal state where it remained until the Reformation, when like most of the abbey, it was smashed to pieces. A prosaic sign in the abbey grounds today marks the spot.

The discovery of Arthur's tomb was highly fortuitous, because seven years earlier a great fire had all but razed the abbey to the ground, and funds were desperately needed for rebuilding. According to some historians, the "discovery" of Arthur and Guinevere was an ingenious publicity stunt to attract flocks of pilgrims with full purses and so boost the medieval tourist trade. Others argue that the whole affair was engineered by Henry II as a propaganda exercise to demoralize the Welsh, who were continually fomenting rebellion against England. Proof that Arthur was dead and buried in English soil was designed to dash the hopes of those descendants of the ancient Britons, who fervently believed that one day their king would return from Avalon and defeat their old enemies. As the old Welsh triad says, "Not wise the thought a grave for Arthur." Was he not supposed to be the "once and future king" who would return to aid his people in their hour of greatest need?

While these and other pragmatic reasons, analyzed in much detail by modern scholars, seem convincing, Arthur's appearance in Glastonbury has a certain mythic inevitability about it, as if he were a traditional character whose entrance everyone is waiting expectantly for at a medieval mumming play. Gerald of Wales, writing shortly after the discovery of the grave, was among the first chroniclers to clearly identify Glastonbury with Avalon as Arthur's final resting place: "The place which is now called Glaston was in ancient times called the Isle of Avalon. . . . Morgan, a noble matron and the ruler and lady of those parts, who was, moreover, kin by blood to King Arthur, carried him away after the battle of Camlann to the island that is now called Glaston, that she might heal his wounds."[14]

Yet Arthur's name was linked with Glastonbury even before the excavations at Glastonbury Abbey, as we know from a story told in Caradog of Llancarfan's *Life of Gildas,* written forty to fifty years before this event. Caradog was a contemporary of Geoffrey of Monmouth, who had popularized the story of Arthur's final departure for Avalon, which Caradoc clearly identifies as Glastonbury in his account. It tells how Melwas, the "King of the Summer Country," abducted Arthur's wife, "Guennuvar," and kept her captive in his stronghold on Glastonbury Tor. Gildas, a renowned monk of Glastonbury Abbey, brought the protagonists to the abbey where he helped resolve the conflict. In their gratitude, the two kings donated lands to the Abbey, where they often returned to offer their prayers at the "temple of St. Mary."[15]

Historian James Carley believes that more stories linking Arthur with Glastonbury, long since lost, were most probably in common currency before this time:

> Nor is there any reason to doubt that stories concerning Arthur, who appears early to have been associated with the south west, would have circulated orally at Glastonbury even before Caradog wrote about his sojourn at Glastonbury. If Glastonbury could be identified as Avalon as well as the Isle of Glass, moreover, then the logical consequence would be that Arthur's mortal remains (known to be at Avalon) must be found in the cemetery, itself revered as a magically resonant and holy place. From the viewpoint of the medieval Glastonbury community it would seem altogether logical that this great Christian leader would have venerated the oldest church in his kingdom and wished to be buried there.[16]

Rather than being a quick "PR job" fabricated by the monks for their dubious "discovery" in the abbey grounds, there may have been a genuine longstanding tradition of King Arthur's presence at Glastonbury: a mythic mycelium biding its time beneath the fertile soil of Avalon for the right conditions in which to send up spores of story.

GRAIL QUEST IN GLASTONBURY

With Glastonbury firmly established as Avalon, its landscape proved to be a fruitful setting for the Grail romances. The first of these was *Perlesvaus,* or *The High Book of the Grail,* composed in the early thirteenth century by an anonymous author who may have actually written it at Glastonbury Abbey. He claims he got the story from a manuscript from "the Isle of Avalon, in a holy house of religion that standeth at the head of the Moors Adventurous, there where King Arthur and Queen

Guinevere lie, according to the witness of the good men religious that are therein, that have the whole story thereof."[17]

In one passage, the author describes Lancelot approaching "Avalon" via what can only be Glastonbury Tor, topped by its church:

He rideth until he is come toward evening to a great valley where was forest on the one side and the other, and the valley stretched onward half a score great leagues Welsh. He looketh to the right, and on the top of the mountain beside the valley he seeth a chapel newly builded that was right fair and rich, and it was covered of lead, and had at the back two quoins that seemed to be of gold. By the side of this chapel were three houses dight right richly, each standing by itself facing the chapel. There was a right fair grave-yard round about the chapel, that was enclosed at the compass of the forest, and a spring came down, full clear, from the heights of the forest before the chapel and ran into the valley with a great rushing; and each of the houses had its own orchard, and the orchard an enclosure. Lancelot heareth vespers being chanted in the chapel, and seeth the path that turned thitherward, but the mountain is so rugged that he could not go along it on horseback. So he alighteth and leadeth his horse after him by the reins until he cometh nigh the chapel. . . . There were three hermits there within that had sung their vespers, and came over against Lancelot. They bowed their heads to him and he saluted them, and then asked of them what place was this? And they told him that the place there was Avalon.[18]

Another well-known Glastonbury landmark that features in the Grail stories is Pomparles Bridge, not far from Wearyall Hill. This is an anglicized version of Pont Perileux, the Perilous Bridge, from the French romances. Now made of concrete and steel and barely noticeable as a part of the busy main road that runs over the River Brue between Glastonbury and the town of Street, it was once believed to be the Sword Bridge, which led the way to the Grail Castle. Here too, according to legend, was where Arthur's sword Excalibur was cast back into the waters after his final, fatal battle, and where the Lady of the Lake came to bear him away in her barge to Avalon.

In *Le Morte d'Arthur,* Sir Thomas Malory set the denouement of his epic tale in Glastonbury. After the last battle when the Round Table is finally broken up, Sir Bedevere rides all night and discovers a hermit digging what appears to be a grave for Arthur at a chapel between two wooded hills "beside Glastonbury." This would seem to be the little vale between the Tor and Chalice Hill, and there is some evidence of footings, possibly for monks' cells, near this spot. Bedevere stays here, becomes a hermit, and is later joined by Lancelot, the defeated knights both spending their last days in holiness near the grave of their beloved king.

OUR LADY OF GLASTONBURY

In medieval Glastonbury, the Grail as a symbol of the feminine is figured forth in the cult of the Virgin Mary, in whose honor Joseph of Arimathea was directed to build the abbey. The unusual importance granted to "Our Lady, Mary of Glastonbury" has given some to wonder whether her cult replaced that of an earlier aspect of the divine feminine—a Celtic, or pre-Celtic goddess of these parts. It is well documented that, with the rise of Christianity, the Virgin Mary filled the slot vacated by deposed pagan goddesses in Western religion. Mary's role in the Christian narrative was marginalized in the early development of the Roman Church, but in 431 CE, she was officially proclaimed *Theotokos,* meaning "Mother of God" at Ephesus, Turkey. Ephesus was a center of worship of the pagan mother-goddess Artemis, one of whose titles was Queen of Heaven, a title subsequently given to Mary.

A host of churches dedicated to her sprang up in quick succession, many of them built on top of shrines dedicated to earlier divinities. In Rome itself, the church of Santa Maria Maggiore arose over the old temple to Cybele, while *Santa Maria sopra Minerva* (literally "Saint Mary over Minerva") replaced the shrine of the classical goddess of wisdom. In Athens, she took over the temple of the goddess Eireithya, who aided women in childbirth, and continued to be a source of comfort to pregnant women who were probably not in any way taken in by the name change. In Cyprus, Mary appropriated the shrines of her predecessor, Aphrodite, and is revered down to this day as *Panaghia Aphroditessa,* meaning "All-Holy Aphrodite." At Soissons in France, the Temple of Isis was rededicated to the Blessed Virgin Mary. She even assumed the names of her pagan antecedents, such as "Star of the Sea," one of the aspects of Isis in her role as guardian of sea-farers. Many images of Mary enthroned with the Holy Child bear a striking resemblance to Egyptian icons of Isis and her son, Horus.

In the twelfth century, the influential French abbot Saint Bernard of Clairvaux raised Mary to towering heights in Europe, even going so far as identifying her as the bride of the *Song of Songs* in the Old Testament. Throughout France, great cathedrals—glorious symphonies in stone, light and rainbow-colored glass—sprang up as "palaces of the Queen of Heaven."[19] The most famous of these at Chartres arose on the site of a great pagan center where the Druids worshipped a *Virgo Partitura,* or "a virgin about to give birth."[20] The huge number of statues and images of the "Black Madonna" in cathedrals and churches throughout Europe are also clues to Mary's links with several goddesses of the Near East who were depicted as dark-skinned. Some of these mysterious icons were found by chance in a grove of trees or by a sacred spring, suggesting that the worship of a pagan goddess continued for centuries as a well-kept secret from the Church. Now the divine feminine was once more exalted and revered throughout Europe, a great goddess in all but name, as theologian Rosemary Ruether points out in her book, *Goddesses and the Divine Feminine:* "Never touched by sin, incorruptible, ascending to the celestial realm immediately after death to be crowned as queen of heaven, appearing in endless visions, and celebrated in tens of thousands of pieces of art, she is functionally the Christian Goddess, although officially she is simply the representative of our original nature, our best human potential."[21]

JESUS-MARIA

According to Glastonbury legend, Joseph of Arimathea brought Christ's mother with him to Ynys Witrin and lies buried with her beneath the original "church of boughs," a theme we shall look at more closely in the next chapter. Another tradition, even more mysterious, hints that the first church was "constructed by no human art," but built by Jesus himself who dedicated it to his own mother. When the original building showed signs of collapsing with age, its remains were carefully preserved by being enclosed in a small rectangular structure, roofed with lead, and rededicated to Mary. By the Middle Ages, this was known as the "Ealde Chirche," the Old Church. To the east of this simple shrine, the great stone abbey was soon to rise to magnificent heights. Around 700 CE, the Saxon King Ine, himself a Christian, built a new stone church and dedicated it to the Apostles, Peter and Paul. The new buildings in no way detracted from the veneration accorded the original church, which Ine praised as "the first in the kingdom of Britain and the source and the fountain of all religion."[22] A steady stream of pilgrims came from all over England to visit Glastonbury, and a great annual pilgrimage was held on September 8, Mary's birthday in the astrological sign of the Virgin.

Sad to say, in the great fire of 1184 the Old Church was burnt to the ground. Yet it was so important to the monks that it was the first building to be reconstructed, this time in stone, and named the Chapel of Saint Mary, or Lady Chapel. Before the fire, the old wattle church would have been filled with icons of Mary. In fact, the chronicles of Glastonbury Abbey tell how the only thing salvaged from the Old Church was an old and venerated wooden statue of Mary that had been on the altar. The wood was scarcely blistered at all, which was regarded as a miracle and a blessing from the Virgin herself.

Today, visitors to the Abbey can see a thirteenth-century stone in the south wall of the ruined Lady Chapel carved with the words "JESUS MARIA." It is a curiously moving inscription. Lionel Smithett Lewis, a mystically inclined Glastonbury vicar of the early twentieth century, pondered this mystery:

Why suddenly in that wall do those two names appear? The monks evidently attached a great veneration to that stone. Did the feet of

The Jesus-Maria Stone on the wall of Glastonbury Abbey.
Courtesy of Glastonbury Abbey.

the holy beings named ever tread this spot? I instinctively take off my hat when I approach it. It is a hallowed spot. The very possibility sanctifies beyond all words. One hopes it is true. And those who seek may find. It makes Our Lord seem very near.[23]

W. G. Gray, the esoteric magician who was partial to word puzzles, proposed that it may have been a "monastic cipher"[24] (see page 145).

Mary's presence in Glastonbury is kept alive today by the Church of Our Lady in Glastonbury, which replaced the abbey as the town's center of worship in the Roman Catholic faith. In this very modern looking church is a shrine to Mary, with a statue of her holding her Son in her left hand and a flowering bush in her right—perhaps meant to represent the Glastonbury thorn. As a reminder of the simple wooden shrine where all this began, the statue is placed in front of a wattle hurdle (a woven willow fence) and stands on a pillar carved with the same two names.

```
I   E   S   V   S
n   c   e   i   a
i   c   p   r   n
t   l   u   g   c
i   e   l   i   t
u   s   t   n
    i   u
M   A   R   I   A
```

InitiuM EcclesiA SepultuR VirginI SanctA:
"The First Church was of the Sepulchre of the Holy Virgin."

ARTHUR AND THE BLESSED VIRGIN

One of the most vivid and powerful stories of Arthur at Glastonbury tells of the king's vision of the Blessed Virgin Mary. John of Glastonbury (fl. ca. 1400), a monk and scribe, tells how Arthur was staying at "a monastery of holy virgins," which is located "in Wirral within the island of Avallonia." One night an Angel spoke to him in a dream, telling him to "go to the hermitage of St. Mary Magdalen of Bekeri in this island." Beckery, as we shall see later, was associated with Saint Bridget (Brighid) and was supposedly the site of an even earlier oratory dedicated to Mary Magdalene.[25]

Arthur entered the chapel where he saw a vision of the "glorious Mother of the Lord, bearing her Son in her arms." Then followed a mystical Mass, presided over by the Child himself. The story was adapted from *Perlesvaus: Branch One,* wherein Arthur's vision of Mary is described in deeply mystical language:

> And he looketh at the holy hermit that was robed to sing mass and said his Confiteor and seeth at his right hand the fairest Child that ever he had seen, and He was clad in an alb and had a golden crown on his head loaded with precious stones that gave out a full great brightness of light. On the left hand side was a Lady so fair that all the beauties of the world might not compare them with her beauty. "Sir," said she, "You are my Father and my Son and my Lord, and guardian of me and of all the world." King Arthur looketh at a window behind the altar and seeth a flame come through at the very instant that mass was begun, clearer than any ray of sun nor moon nor star, and evermore it threw forth a brightness of light such that and all the lights in the world had been together it would not have been the like.[26]

Afterward, Mary gave Arthur a crystal cross as a gift and a testimony to this miracle. In response, King Arthur changed his coat of arms, so that from this time forth his shield was emblazoned with three green lions and a silver cross with the Mother and Son in one of the quadrants. This description of Arthur's shield is found in an even earlier source: the ninth-century Welsh historian, Nennius, writing about Arthur as the historical British chieftain, describes him going into battle "with the image of the holy Virgin Mary on his shield." The image on Arthur's shield was later adopted as the arms of Glastonbury Abbey.

MARY AS THE GRAIL

Perhaps it was only natural that the deep reverence inspired by the Blessed Virgin at Glastonbury led to her becoming identified with the Grail itself: a symbol of the divine feminine as the life-giving womb of God's only Son. Like Ceridwen and Taliesin, Isis and Horus, and all primordial goddesses of antiquity, Mary is the Great Mother, the living matrix from which the Son of Light is eternally reborn and whom she nourishes at her breast—

King Arthur's Shield

another symbolic meaning of the Grail. Her name may have its root in the word for the sea, for she is the Great Sea of Space, the Void from which springs forth all creation and whose tides set the worlds into motion.

This unorthodox undercurrent of mystery and beauty found expression in poetry and song throughout the Middle Ages. In the Welsh language, the word for cauldron, *pair,* has a secondary form, *Mair,* meaning Mary. Daffid Benfras, a Welsh poet of the thirteenth century, who was perhaps familiar with Ceridwen's Cauldron of Inspiration, addressed Mary as *Pair pur vonhedd,* "My cauldron of pure descent," and no less than three German poets of the time addressed Mary with the words: "Thou Art the Grail."[27] The twelfth-century Litany of Loreto, a prayer recited after the rosary, calls her:

> *Spiritual vessel*
> *Vessel of honor*
> *Singular vessel of devotion . . .*[28]

In a fifteenth-century song of praise to the Black Madonna she is addressed as:

. . . mother and maid,
vessel of purity . . .[29]

Arthurian scholar John Matthews writes lyrically of Mary's identification with the Grail:

> From the beginning, the Grail was a vessel which contained some of
> the divinity of God. . . . In the intensity of the Christian interpreta-
> tion, it is also the womb of Mary, in which the divine seed is trans-
> muted into the body of the infant Christ. . . . In effect, Mary has
> become a *living* Grail, a vessel in which the blood and the essence of
> Christ are both contained.[30]

*A Russian icon shows
Mary carrying the
Christ Child in a
Grail-like Vessel.*

In this beautiful expression of the sacred marriage between Heaven and Earth. Mary, the human woman, is impregnated with the divine, who through this miraculous birth, becomes God incarnate, Savior of the World. In esoteric Christianity, the Virgin Mother is the human soul that, through years of being perfected through spiritual practices, can receive, like a chalice, the divine force known as the Cosmic Christ. In this sense, Christ is not an individual human being located in a specific historical context, but the alchemical "philosopher's child" born of the sacred marriage of soul and Spirit: the supernal, creative power of the divine through whom each human being can awaken to full self-realization.

Historian Geoffrey Ashe has even suggested in *King Arthur's Avalon,* his seminal book on Glastonbury, that the Grail stories only thinly disguise what was possibly a hidden heretical cult of the Virgin involving a special "Mass of the Mother of God."[31] More recently, Professor Joseph Goering, in his book, *The Virgin and the Grail,* hints at something similar with the discovery of frescos in a number of churches in the High Pyrenees that may predate the first Grail romance of Chrétien de Troyes, depicting Mary holding what has been called a "fiery grail."[32]

Mary is completely at home in Glastonbury where she has carried forward the power of the divine feminine just as goddesses have done in previous times, with Joseph of Arimathea acting as priest of her mysteries. Through them, the symbolic pairing of Sacred Branch and Cup of Truth of an earlier age become the Flowering Staff and the Holy Grail.

VisionJourney VI
The Lady Chapel

Through the *Mater* all *matter* comes forth. Like Ceridwen and Isis, too, Mary is the Grail, the great Initiator, and the Mother through whom we may give birth to the divine spirit within each of us.

To prepare for this VisionJourney, it is helpful, though not essential, to place on your altar an image or statue depicting the Mother Goddess and her Child. This might be a traditional icon of Mary and the Christ Child, or a statue of Isis holding Horus.

Place two candles on either side.

Light incense.

Light the candles.

Strike a chime or bell, then reciting the following traditional prayer:

> *Praise of Mary*
> *Thou shining Mother of gentleness,*
> *Thou glorious Mother of the stars,*
> *Blessed hast thou been of every race*
> *And people.*
>
> *Thou art the Queen—maiden of the sea,*
> *Thou art the Queen—maiden of the kingdom,*
> *Thou art the Queen—maiden of the angels*
> *In radiance.*
>
> *Thou art the star of the earth,*
> *Thou art the star of the kingdom,*
> *Thou art the star of the Son of the Father*
> *Of Glory.*
>
> *Thou art the corn of the land,*
> *Thou art the treasury of the sea,*
> *The wished-for visitant of the homes*
> *Of the world.*
>
> *Thou art the vessel of fullness,*
> *Thou art the cup of wisdom,*
> *Thou art the well-spring of health*
> *Of humankind.*
>
> *Thou art the garden of apples,*
> *Thou art the lull-song of the great folks,*
> *Thou art the fulfillment of the world's desire*
> *In loveliness.*

Thou art the sun of the heavens,
Thou art the moon of the skies,
Thou art the star and the path
Of the wanderers.

Since thou art the full ocean,
Pilot me at sea;
Since thou art the dry shore,
Save me upon land.

There is none who utters my song
Or puts it into use,
But Mary will reveal herself
Three times before his or her death.[33]

Pause to experience the presence of the Mother and Son.
Ring bell or chime. Sit.

Relax and quiet your mind. . . . Take some deep breaths and imagine you
are breathing in a beautiful, silver-blue light. The light fills your body and
swirls around you like a mist. . . .

When the mist lifts, you are walking over meadowland toward a little
settlement of circular buildings, surrounded by a protective wall of stone.
All is still; no breath of wind in the chill air. The sky is a dusky purple
streaked with a dark red glow marking the sun's descent in the West, while
far above, the first stars come glittering out. . . . You approach a wooden
gate built of sharp palisades, and see within a circle of huts, each built of
woven willow branches packed with river mud and topped with thatched
roofs that rise to a point in the middle. There are twelve of them; from the
door of each a path leads out, like the spoke of a wheel, to a central round
building, larger than the rest. It seems to crouch low as if guarding a secret
that it holds close to itself. . . . This simple edifice is nothing less than the
Old Church of Glastonbury, the first church built by Joseph of Arimathea,
dedicated to the divine Mother . . .

You are aware of the presence of others inside each of the surrounding huts, for the soft glow of candlelight can be seen within each one and the low singing of men's harmonious voices rings clearly through the still evening air. . . . A figure appears from one of the huts—a monk in a rough brown robe—walking toward you. It is one of the Company of Avalon, the original guardians of the Old Church, companion to Joseph himself. Note him well. . . .

He greets you and asks you your business, and you answer from your heart. If your response is met with approval, he leads you toward the central chapel and holds aside the heavy door-covering for you to enter inside. . . .

You feel as if you are walking into a cave, it is so dark inside—a velvety midnight darkness that is strangely warm. Only the soft glow of two tapers reveals a plain stone altar on which stands the carved likeness of the Lady and her Child. . . .

As you approach the altar, the two tapers flare up into tall flames so bright you momentarily close your eyes. When you open them again, the oratory is filled with radiance, and you see before you a wondrous sight: the Lady has grown as tall as the ceiling and her mantle of midnight blue seems to swirl about her as if in a wind. Her feet rest upon a crescent moon, and upon her head is a sparkling crown of twelve stars. The Child in her arms shines with the dazzling light of the sun. . . .

You are also aware of the singing of the monks in their cells, which has grown louder and more resonant. It sounds, in fact, like a heavenly choir encircling the oratory, and the harmonies are becoming more exquisite and heartrendingly beautiful than anything you have heard before. . . .

As the music soars about you, you realize you are no longer in a small dark chapel, but are standing far above the world in the dome of the midnight sky. . . . The Lady's mantle is spangled with stars and spread out over the vast reaches of space, curved protectively over the universe.

At her heart, the folds of her mantle reveal the Child of Light who shines forth with the supernal glory of the Solar Logos, the great Spiritual Sun that is the Source of our solar system. . . .

Around this Being of Light circle the twelve constellations, singing the symphony of the stars in mighty chords, which roll and vibrate in vast waves of heavenly sound all about you. As you listen, the notes of their song become filaments of light that shimmer throughout the universe forming a vast network of brilliant light in an exquisite pattern of harmony and beauty. . . .

And now you see that within the Light Body of the Solar Logos are seven planets, each one a whirling vortex of radiant color. They too are singing, adding a counterpoint to the melodies of the stars, clear pure notes that become rippling colors of rainbow light washing over you, drenching you with their heavenly influences. . . .

You are aware that the seven chakras within your body are resonating, too, each singing their own note, echoing the harmony of the spheres. Then suddenly you realize your chakras are reflections of the seven planets themselves; they are within you as well as outside of you. You realize that the infinite reaches of the sea of space about you are also within your body, where every one of your atoms is surrounded by vast distances of inner space. For you too are a solar system, and within you there is a Child of Light waiting to be born from deep inside the dark womb of your inner space. Be aware now of the nurturing mother of darkness within yourself, and let the Child of Light be born within your own heart. . . . Welcome the Child of Light into your world. . . .

And now gradually become aware of your surroundings and open your eyes. Gaze upon the image of the Lady and the Child upon your altar with new understanding and give thanks for their blessings. . . .

When you are ready, extinguish the tapers and come fully back to present time and space.

7

The Alchemical Grail

From the cauldron of the goddess to the cup of Christ, the Grail has had many shapes throughout its long history. It was to undergo a further transformation in the crucible of mystical Christianity that was Glastonbury in the Middle Ages. For by the fourteenth century, the holy cup that Joseph of Arimathea brought to Avalon became not one vessel, but *two*. A description of this is given in a mysterious passage known as *The Prophecy of Melkin* in the chronicle of the abbey written by John of Glastonbury:

> The Island of Avalon, eager for the death of pagans, at the burial of them all will be decorated beyond the others in the world with the soothsaying spheres of the prophecy, and in the future will be adorned with those who praise the Most High. Abbadare, powerful in Saphat, most noble of the pagans, took his sleep there with 104,000 men. Among these, Joseph of Arimathea received eternal slumber in a marble tomb, and he lies on a divided line next to the oratory's southern corner where the wickerwork is constructed above the mighty and venerable Maiden, and where the aforesaid thirteen spheres rest. Joseph has with him in the sarcophagus two white and silver vessels full of the blood and sweat of the prophet Jesus. Once his sarcophagus is discovered, it will be visible, whole and undecayed, and open to the whole world. From then on, those who dwell in that noble island will lack neither water nor the dew

of Heaven. For a long time before the Day of Judgment in Josaphat these things will be openly declared to the living.[1]

A PROPHECY OF MYSTERY

The only thing we know about Melkin is that he was born "before Merlin." Some scholars have associated him with the fifth-century King Maelgwn of Gwynedd, but he was neither a bard nor a prophet. As historian James Carley, editor of the *Chronicle of Glastonbury Abbey*, points out, Eastern and Islamic references in the text show the influence of the Crusades. This suggests a much later origin for this text. Jesus is called a prophet, and "saphat" is probably a reference to Safed, a holy city in Acre associated with the Knights Templar and later a center for Kabbalistic mysticism.

This strange text is the only existing written reference to Glastonbury before the coming of Christianity in which Avalon is described as an Isle of the Dead where thousands of pagans were buried. It claims Joseph of Arimathea lies among them in the "Old Church," which he founded, and with him the most prized and potent holy relic of that age: the blood and sweat that flowed from Christ's sides at the Crucifixion: the precious life force that was shed to give humanity eternal life. But rather than a single cup, Joseph bears the holy fluids in two vessels (sometimes called "cruets"), the significance of which will be discussed below.

Joseph does not lie alone in the Abbey, but "above the mighty and venerable Maiden." Could this refer to the legend that Mary, Christ's Mother, accompanied Joseph to Glastonbury and was buried in the church dedicated to her? And what about the mysterious thirteen "soothsaying spheres" nearby the tombs? Perhaps these were the designs alluded to by William of Malmesbury when he wrote: "In the pavement may be remarked on every side stones designedly interlaid in triangles and squares, and figured with lead, under which if I believe some sacred enigma to be contained, I do no injustice to religion."[2]

If so, these designs may have been the twelve signs of the zodiac with the sun in the center.[3] The presence of the zodiac in Christian churches may seem odd to us today, given that the Church, along with the modern world, has long divorced itself from the ancient art of astrology. Yet the association of Christ the Son/Sun surrounded by his twelve disciples on whom He bestows His light, did not go unnoticed by medieval church architects, and indeed, many fine examples of church zodiacs can still be seen today as mosaic tiles in the floor, or carved in stone around arched doorways in medieval churches and cathedrals throughout England.

The tradition of the sun representing the physical face of the supreme deity goes back to the time of the Chaldeans, and was applied to the gods Mithras, Apollo, and Helios in the Classical era. Mithras was portrayed at the center of the twelve signs of the zodiac. Jesus Christ became the new earthly representative of the Solar Logos with his birthday assigned to the Winter Solstice, when the sun is reborn. The early Christians assigned the twelve apostles of Jesus to the solar months of the year or to the twelve constellations of the zodiac. This cosmic pattern was incorporated in the architecture of the shrines and temples of antiquity, which were designed to be the dwelling-place of divinity on Earth. Although no visual evidence survives of a zodiac design at Glastonbury Abbey, the Reverend Richard Warner, a visitor to the ruins of the Lady Chapel in the 1820s, mentioned that he had seen "traces of the suns, and moons, and stars, that covered the intervals."[4]

Historian James Carley also notices that the text is full of allusions to alchemy, a highly fashionable field of study at the time, which leads him to conclude "Melkin's Prophesy is an example of a highly esoteric text laced with occult information and . . . contains hints of a consciously coded secret which by the time of John of Glastonbury had become altogether garbled."[5]

It is time we took a look at the connection between alchemy and the Grail.

THE YOGA OF THE WEST

Alchemy is an ancient art that originated in Egypt and spread throughout Europe due to Arab influences in the twelfth century. Alchemists wrote about their work using a special language of symbol, metaphor, and allegory, partly because it was the best way to convey these profound and multi-layered teachings, and partly to keep their knowledge hidden from the profane—and probably the Inquisition. Although it is popularly believed that the alchemists' goal was to transmute base metal into gold for material gain, the art of alchemy was in fact a serious study of the nature of reality on many levels: physical, psychological, and spiritual.

Transformations that occurred in the laboratory had to also take place in the personality and soul of the alchemist, otherwise the work was deemed useless. As the sixteenth-century alchemist, Paracelsus, proclaimed in the *Alchemical Catechism:*

Q. When the Philosophers speak of gold and silver, from which they extract their matter, are we to suppose that they refer to the vulgar gold and silver?

A. By no means; vulgar silver and gold are dead, while those of the Philosophers are full of life.[6]

Changing lead into gold was therefore a metaphor for a spiritual process, which involved rejuvenating the body, integrating the personality, and uniting the soul with God. The seven metals corresponded to the stages toward this goal of "leading out the gold within." Lead, heavy and dull, is the unregenerate human, whose evolution proceeds through the stages of iron, tin, mercury, copper, and silver to reach perfection in gold, the radiant solar spirit. These seven metals correspond to the seven planets of medieval astrology, which influence and shape the human body and personality. As esotericist A. E. Waite put it: "the experiment of spiritual Alchemy was the Yoga . . . of the West."[7] This was the *magnum opus,* or "Great Work," of the alchemist, and it could only be achieved through the *lapis philosophorum,* or "Philosopher's Stone," a substance that could transmute imperfect matter into the purity and perfection of gold. Like the Grail, to which it has often been compared, the stone was believed to be an elixir of life, capable of curing all diseases, restoring youth, and even bestowing immortality.

There is little agreement among alchemists on the nature of the Philosopher's Stone. Instructions for making it also vary considerably, but two chemicals were consistently fundamental to the process: sulfur and mercury, which in themselves came to be known as the red and white "stones" of the alchemical art. It is generally agreed (although with some exceptions): sulfur = red = soul and mercury = white = spirit.

In alchemical texts, these two substances are often represented as The Red King and The White Queen, or *sol* and *luna*—"sun" and "moon," whose "chymical wedding" produces the miraculous child, the *filius philosophorum,* which is another name for the "Philosopher's Stone." As Jungian writer, Anne Baring, puts it:

Alchemy is the science of bringing the two great feminine and masculine principles and mythological traditions into relationship—into a state of marriage. There is a beautiful Hasidic saying from the Jewish mystical tradition: "When the moon shines as brightly as the sun, the messiah will come." (Baal Shem Tov) The moon is an age-old image of the feminine principle, as the sun is of the masculine one. So when these two shine as brightly as each other, when each is fully honored in human consciousness, when solar mythology is softened and tempered by lunar mythology, the Messiah will come—not as an individual but as the raising of the consciousness of the whole of humanity. When this happens the Wasteland will be healed.[8]

The creation of the Philosopher's Stone is a threefold process. The first stage is called the *nigredo,* or "blackening," which refers to the "death" of the original metal—the *prima materia*—in order to remove its impurities. This takes place during the second stage, the *albedo,* or "whitening." At the third and final stage, *rubedo,* or "reddening," the material takes on a red tint, which signals its transformation to gold. Although these colors refer to physically observable changes in the metals within the alchemist's laboratory, they also outline a threefold path to spiritual awakening.

The prima materia is the unawakened individual, heavily identified with the egoic self and the body. The first stage, or blackening, comes about when living an ego-centered life is no longer satisfying: there may be a crisis of confidence, traumatic loss, deep depression, or debilitating illness—a "dark night of the soul." This passage often occurs at mid-life, as the poet Dante well knew when he wrote his famous lines: "Midway in the journey of our life I found myself in a dark wood, for the straight way was lost."[9]

In the next stage, the whitening, we gain an awareness of our deeper identity as a soul. The experience of the soul-self is one of being guided by a luminous, gentle light, which, like the moon, conveys a sense of serenity from a higher plane, transforming the stresses of earthly life by showing them to be evanescent and illusory. In Western tradition, the soul is feminine and lunar. Often it is at mid-life that living a life based on the personality and its masculine/yang drive for outer achievements is found to be unfulfilling, and there is a yearning for a more feminine/yin, relational, and soul-centered life. In alchemy, the coming together of personality and soul signifies the first of two "sacred marriages."

The third stage, the reddening, brings about the dawning consciousness of an even higher reality, in which the soul is experienced as reflecting an even greater light: the spiritual Source, which, like the sun in the physical world, is the purveyor of all life. Masculine and feminine merge as one in the second sacred marriage: the mystical union of soul and Spirit, the achievement of the "Great Work," from which is born the enlightened self, known as the "diamond body" in Buddhism, the "resurrection body" in Christianity, and *sat-chit-ananda,* "being-consciousness-bliss," in the teachings of Yoga. A simple way to grasp this sequence is as a progression from the darkness of night to the whiteness of the moon, the redness of dawn and finally the rising of the golden sun.

RED KING AND WHITE QUEEN

One way to enter into the inner meaning of the *Prophesy of Melkin* is to view the written imagery as if it were the complex symbolic picture known as an alchemical emblem, designed for contemplation and meditation. Joseph and Mary lying in their tombs are like the Red King and White Queen in the alchemical process. The symbolism of sulfur and mercury, feminine and masculine, is clearly apparent in the two vessels that contain blood and water: the red and white fluids that represent the distillation of Christ's life essence. In esoteric Christianity, Christ is seen as the Solar Logos, or "Sun of God," who is crucified on the cross of space-time in order to mediate the divine power of his "Father," or unmanifest aspect of the divine. As mystic Geoffrey Hodson so beautifully expresses it in his book, *Kingdom of the Gods*: "He is voluntarily self-crucified, not in agony and death and downflowing sweat and blood, but in creative ecstasy and with perpetually outpoured power and life."[10]

The alchemical significance of these fluids is noted by historian Jonathan Hughes in his book, *Arthurian Myths and Alchemy:* "The red blood and white sweat of Christ were symbols for sulphur and mercury. It was considered a 'distilled medicine and a celestial quintessence which can restore the welfare of the people.'"[11]

Around the two archetypal figures are the "soothsaying spheres," perhaps containing signs of the zodiac or other symbolic images of the spiritual journey, as are found in many alchemical emblems. The promise that when Joseph's tomb is found, the area will not lack "nor water nor the dew of heaven" cannot be taken literally, since the county of Somerset has never been short on rain. It most likely refers to the alchemical *ros coeli,* or "heavenly dew," which was considered to be "divine water" sent from above to purify and fertilize the Philosopher's Stone. This process is graphically presented in an illustration from a later text, the sixteenth-century *Rosarium Philosophorum,* or the "Rose Garden of the Philosophers," which shows the sacred marriage of the Red King and White Queen. They lie joined as one in a coffin, while heavenly dew descends from spiritual clouds to purify them prior to their transformation and rebirth. As the divine grace that drops from heaven, ros coeli may be compared with the *soma* of Vedic teachings, which is experienced as a "flood of bliss" flowing down from above when the soul merges with spirit through intensive yogic practices.

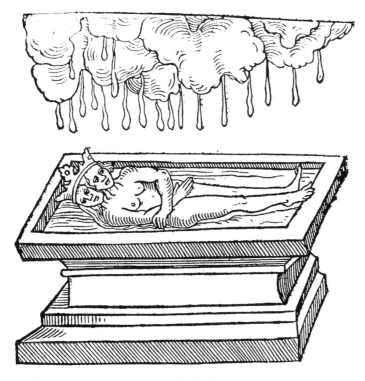

The sacred marriage of the Red King and White Queen.
Illustration no. 8 from The Rosarium Philosophorum.

In the reign of King Edward IV, a century after the *Chronicle* was published, Joseph's sacred vessels took on a new life in Glastonbury. Edward was fascinated by alchemy and surrounded himself with advisors steeped in the art. Arthurian and Grail themes also dominated the court, and Edward was proclaimed to be a "second Arthur" who would unite Britain and usher in a new Golden Age.[12] It was during these years that Glastonbury, now famous as the burial-place of King Arthur, became so popular as a place of pilgrimage. A stained glass window in Langport Church, nine miles south of the Abbey, depicts Joseph carrying the two cruets. In the sixteenth century, Richard Bere, the second-to-last Abbot of Glastonbury, devised a heraldic coat-of-arms for Saint Joseph for a window in Saint John's Church in Glastonbury High Street. It portrays the Glastonbury Thorn, shaped like a green crucifix, a medieval concept in which the cross is seen as a living Tree of Life. At its foot are the two vessels, while drops of heavenly dew pour down from above. Also in the church is a fine Victorian window stained in rich, glowing colors, showing Joseph with the two vessels in gold with a single golden chalice below.

Alchemical legend and lore continued to attach itself to Glastonbury Abbey in the centuries to come. There is an apocryphal tale concerning the famous Renaissance magician and alchemist, John Dee, and his

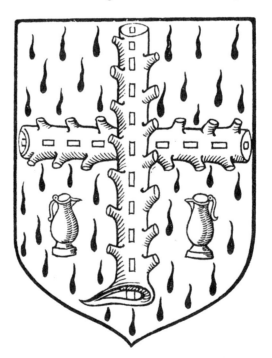

Joseph's coat of arms in St John's Church, Glastonbury

disreputable psychic assistant, Edward Kelley. The story goes that the pair was wandering through the ruins of Glastonbury Abbey when they stumbled across two phials containing a red and white powder, which Kelley believed was the Philosopher's Stone in powdered form. Kelley also claimed he found there a manuscript on alchemy purporting to have been written by the tenth-century bishop, Saint Dunstan. Had he been alive, the good bishop would no doubt have been most surprised to find himself reinvented as an alchemist.

THE RED AND WHITE SPRINGS

One of the most remarkable mysteries of Glastonbury is its red and white springs, which reflect the alchemical Grail with its red and white waters. The two springs flow in the narrow vale between Glastonbury Tor and Chalice Hill, a place of numinous power. The Tor above and the valley below form a striking contrast: above, it is all sky and sun, the masculine ascending elements of Air and Fire, while in the sheltered vale, lush with gardens and trees, the feminine, descending elements of Water and Earth prevail. The ruined tower is an upright Sword, while the valley below is a green, hollow Cup. This in itself is one mystical pairing. Another is formed by the unusual proximity of two springs, which have separate sources, yet are only a few paces apart: one red and the other white. The water of the Red Spring, also known as the Chalice Well, is rust-red, impregnated with iron. The White Spring is saturated with calcium carbonate (chalk), which coats everything it touches with a white deposit.

The White Spring, at the foot of the Tor, once flowed from a quite different source through limestone caverns, and emerged between the mossy banks of an exquisite valley, full of trees, flowers, and little waterfalls. One visitor described the waterfalls as "fairy dropping wells." Once the two springs were within sight of each other and their waters mingled into one stream that flowed down into Glastonbury town. Sadly, the White Spring's beautiful grotto was destroyed in the 1870s to build a reservoir. Its waters now flow through a windowless concrete building and are divided from its sister spring by a wall and a road. The pitiful results of this callous disregard for a place where the beauty of the feminine spirit once dwelt unfettered is an all-too-common signature of our modern age, recalling the story of the rape of the well maidens. Yet, although its natural setting has been defiled, the White Spring still retains an Otherworldly atmosphere. Its milky waters flow down through channels through the stone floor of what is, at the time of writing, a candle-lit temple to local pagan deities. It is not unlike entering an oracular cave, and it is easy to imagine that here you stand on the threshold of Annwn.

The Red Spring met with a better fate, being protected in the grounds of various religious or educational establishments through the centuries. In 1958, writer and mystic, Wellesley Tudor Pole, purchased the property and founded the Chalice Well Trust, dedicated to "preserving the well and surrounding land so that it would continue as a sacred shrine for all to visit and receive nourishment."[13] Since then, the trust has cultivated beautiful gardens around the well and stream, and the place has become a favorite destination for Glastonbury pilgrims today. In fact, the Chalice Well is one of the oldest continuously used holy wells in Britain. Archaeology has shown that the spring was used by prehistoric tribes who inhabited this land, and the site may have been in constant use for more than two thousand years. Its waters have a long-standing reputation of having medicinal properties, and miraculous cures are reported to have resulted from either drinking or bathing in the waters. The beneficial effects of the spring may stem from it being high in iron, or "chalybeate," a word that offers one explanation of the well's name. Another is that it is situated on Chilkwell Street, meaning "Chalk-well," which most likely refers to the neighboring White Spring. Yet in the minds of the many modern pilgrims who visit it today, the Chalice Well is named for the Grail, a source of healing and spiritual nourishment.

The Red Spring is also known as the Blood Spring—blood being symbolic of the essence of life. Although no female deity or saint has ever been associated with these waters in historical times, the place has an unmistakably feminine air, and those who favor a goddess-centered spirituality view the red and white streams as her blood and the milk that flows from her breast. The Christian interpretation, on the other hand, sees the figure as the crucified Christ, with the red and white springs being the blood and fluid pouring out from his sides, in a direct reference to the story of Joseph of Arimathea. Rumors of the Grail hang about the place and seem to whisper from the waters: Did Joseph bring the holy cup here and hide it for safekeeping—on the slopes of Chalice Hill, or perhaps, within the well itself?

VESICA PISCIS

The extraordinary confluence of masculine and feminine energies that cannot be ignored in this place is expressed in a symbol found throughout the Chalice Well gardens: the *vesica piscis,* literally, "fish bladder." This is a geometrical pattern in which the circumference of one circle is drawn through the center of another of the same size. Where they overlap, the inner section forms a bladder shape, hence the name.

It has been used in sacred symbolism from early times in many different contexts. The fish was a secret code for Christ among the early Christians when they were being persecuted by the Romans. In terms of the astrological Great Ages, the coming of Christ, the "Fisher of Men," also ushered in the Age of Pisces, the sign of the fish. And of course there are also symbolic resonances with the Fisher King in the Grail legend. The vesica piscis is found in many instances of medieval church architecture,

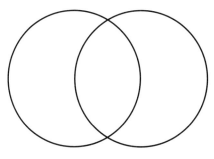

Vesica Piscis

particularly in the construction of the Gothic arch. It appears as a halo or aura surrounding the head of holy figures, and many cathedral portals display Christ or the Virgin enthroned within the vesica itself. The two circles can be seen as representing the polarities of Heaven and Earth, masculine and feminine, or spirit and matter, which converge and intersect at Avalon, the world in between. In this place, the opposites unite, not to return to a primal, undifferentiated unity, but to interact as two wholes joined in sacred relationship. Another name for the vesica is the *mandorla,* from the Italian word for "almond." The mandorla is richly symbolic, being a place of opening and becoming, a threshold of transformation where a third element, the holy child, may be born from the union of the divine couple. It has been likened to the *yoni,* or "sacred vulva," of the divine feminine who gives birth to the worlds. The Pythagoreans believed this shape represented the womb from which the first emanation of the cosmos was born.

The vesica piscis forms the design for two circular pools in the lower garden and also on the well cover at the wellhead, which is a renovation of the original one donated by the architect Frederick Bligh Bond to celebrate the end of the First World War. Bond had risen to fame as the leader of excavations at Glastonbury Abbey after it had been bought by the Anglican Church. He was also a serious student of the occult and was particularly fascinated by numerology and sacred geometry. It was his belief that the vesica piscis was deliberately incorporated into the architectural design of the Lady Chapel in Glastonbury Abbey.

Over the years, many Glastonbury pilgrims have had deep and life-changing experiences at the Chalice Well, and found the vesica to be a meaningful symbol of the meeting of the inner and outer worlds. In their book, *The Red & White Springs of Avalon,* Nicholas Mann and Philippa Glasson attribute such experiences to the alchemical powers of these waters:

> The two springs rising from their mysterious subterranean course in the axis mundi are more than a mere physical or even a symbolic representation of truths found in the inner world. They uphold the

Chalice Well Cover. Photo by David J. Watkins.

"gold" of resolved or unified matter, refine and release the individual spirit-body, and also maintain the nature, health and harmony of the land of Britain.[14]

In Glastonbury there is a unanimous hope that one day the two springs will no longer be divided, but flow as one. A great spiritual significance would attend the reuniting of the Red and White streams, whose colors symbolize the feminine and masculine elements, in the alchemical sacred marriage.

THE HALL IN THE ORCHARD

Another interweaving of the Grail mysteries and medieval alchemy is also apparent in the beautiful and mysterious verses of a traditional English ballad, *The Corpus Christi Carol*. This enigmatic song, whose imagery is strongly associated with the Wasteland theme, can be dated back to six hundred years and is probably even earlier, yet is still sung today in a number of different versions. This one is from the beginning of the fifteenth century:

> *Lully, lulley, lully, lulley!*
> *The falcon hath born my make* away.*
>
> *He bare him up, he bare him down,*
> *He bare him into an orchard brown.*
>
> *In that orchard there was an hall,*
> *That was hanged with purple and pall.*
>
> *And in that hall there was a bed:*
> *It was hanged with gold so red.*
>
> *And in that bed there lieth a knight,*
> *His wounds bleeding day and night.*
>
> *By that bed's side kneeleth a may†*
> *And she weepeth both night and day.*
>
> *And by that bed's side there standeth a stone,*
> *"Corpus Christi" written thereon.*[15]

---

*mate
†maid

The carol hauntingly evokes the tragedy of the wounded king and wasted land. A woman is lamenting that her beloved has been carried off by a falcon. The falcon is an ancient symbol with heavenly, solar qualities because of its strength, beauty, and soaring flight. In the Renaissance, a hooded falcon symbolized hope for a light to illumine the darkness.[16] The wounded knight is taken to an orchard, recalling the Isle of Apples, or Avalon. But it is "brown"—a "dead and desert" place. Here stands a hall, reminiscent of the Grail Castle, whose purple funeral drapes (pall) and bed hung with gold point to the occupant's royal status. Inside the hall, lies a knight, wounded and bleeding. He is tended by a weeping maiden, who in some versions is named as the Virgin Mary, but could equally be one of the well maidens or the bearer of the Grail.

Although "Corpus Christi" in the last line of the carol may identify the wounded knight as the crucified Christ, he could also be the Fisher King in the Wasteland. This is not mere conjecture, for in the *First Continuation* to Chrétien's *Perceval,* featuring Sir Gawain as the hero, there is a wounded king quite apart from the character of the Fisher King, who, in this narrative, is in good health. This Fisher King leads Gawain through a barren landscape to a bier on which a body lies draped in a scarlet cloth. The air resounds with the lamentations of the attendant maidens. Gawain must avenge the foul deed that will restore the bounty to the land. In one of the versions of the carol, the bed of the wounded knight is also "covered all over with scarlet so red." And in the Grail romance, *Perlesvaus,* or *The High Book of the Grail,* there is a scene also reminiscent of the one in the carol: Lancelot comes to the Grail Castle and enters a hall draped with silk cloths, in which he sees the Fisher King, "lying on a bed so rich and so finely decked that never was there seen one more splendid and there was a maiden at his head and another at his feet."[17]

Alchemy does in fact have a Christian branch where Christ is seen as undergoing the alchemical sequence of personhood, death, and resurrection of the spirit. From this perspective, the bleeding knight is Christ, who sacrifices his life in order to redeem humanity. Christ crucified and the wounded Fisher King become as one in these mysteries, while Mary contains within herself all the sorrow of the goddess of the land and her defiled well maidens.

One version of the carol in particular is filled with alchemical allusions:

> *And in that bower there standeth a bed*
> *With silken sheets and gold so red*
> *And in that bed there lieth a knight*
> *Whose wounds doth bleed by day and night*
>
> *And 'neath that bed there runneth a flood*
> *'twas half of water and half of blood*
> *And by the bed there standeth a maid*
> *She doth weep by night and day*
>
> *With silver needle and silken thread*
> *Mending the wounds where they did bleed*
> *And by that maid there standeth a stone*
> *"Corpus Christi" was writ thereon.*[18]

In this version, the wounded knight is clearly solar, being associated with "red gold" while the maiden is associated with silver, the lunar color. As he suffers during the nigredo stage of consciousness, she plies her healing skills. Indeed, the figure of Mary is frequently used to symbolize the "purified white earth" of the *albedo* stage in alchemy. She is his lunar counterpart, the alchemical queen, for among the early Gnostics, her role was very similar to that of the goddess in the pagan mysteries, who united with her son/lover in a sacred marriage of the opposites. This is the beginning of the Great Work, and the scene contains all the potential for alchemical transformation. The stream of blood and water running beneath the bed are the red and white fluids which symbolize the archetypal solar and lunar energies, or alchemical sulfur and mercury, the two primary forces of the universe. In the carol they flow together as one, as if to show that the remedy for this situation lies in their harmonious convergence.

A third version of the carol affords yet more Grail and alchemical symbolism:

> *Down in yon forest there stands a hall:*
> *The bells of Paradise I heard them ring:*
>
> *It's cover'd all over with purple and pall:*
> *And I love my Lord Jesus above any thing.*
>
> *In that hall there stands a bed:*
> *It's covered all over with scarlet so red:*
>
> *At the bed-side there lies a stone:*
> *Which the sweet Virgin Mary knelt upon.*
>
> *Under that bed there runs a flood:*
> *The one half runs water, the other runs blood:*
>
> *At the bed's foot there grows a thorn:*
> *Which ever blows blossom since he was born.*
>
> *Over that bed the moon shines bright:*
> *Denoting our Saviour was born on this night:*[19]

In this, the most clearly Christianized version of the poem, there is no dying knight. Instead, the focus is on the birth of Christ, the triumphant culmination of the last lines. The only possible reference to the crucifixion lies in the verse about the thorn, perhaps pointing to the crown of thorns. Yet that too is a symbol of hope and rebirth rather than death and suffering, for this thorn tree perpetually bears blossom to celebrate the renewing, regenerating power of Christ's birth. In fact, it may be a reference not to the crucifixion, but to the Holy Thorn of Glastonbury that blossoms at Christmastide in honor of his birth. And then there is the stone—not a gravestone, but a recumbent one— perhaps a sacred stone, or even the Philosopher's Stone, upon which the Virgin Mary kneels. Finally, a symbol that is more alchemical than Christian, is the moon, which shines over the bed to mark a time of new hope and life under the aegis of the feminine principle.

In short, the song reveals itself to be a succinct portrayal of the tragedy of the wasted land. The suffering knight represents the Western wound that is still bleeding. In alchemy, the king signifies the ego, the part of us that feels like we are the sole rulers of our individual lives and destiny. His bleeding can never be staunched, for he has chosen to split off and remain apart from the soul, which is represented by the weeping maiden who grieves at their loveless separation and tries in vain to heal him. This is what must be sacrificed before spiritual transformation and rebirth can take place.

On another level, he is King Amangons who has cruelly raped the goddess of sovereignty and, through his selfish lust, upset the ecological balance of Earth. On yet another, the wounded king is the sacrificial Christ (Spirit) who awaits resurrection and the coming of his bride, Sophia (Soul). When they unite, heaven and earth will be as one, in balance and harmony as things were meant to be. King and Maiden form a syzygy of sun and moon; if they can come together like the red and white waters flowing beneath the bed, their sacred union may give birth to a third element: the Philosopher's Child, which was another name for the Philosopher's Stone, the elixir of life.

PHILOSOPHER'S STONE

In alchemy, the Philosopher's Stone is formed in two stages. The first stage symbolizes the union of the polarized parts of our personality— masculine king and feminine queen. The fruit of this union is known as the Lesser Stone and it signifies that a state of psychological wholeness has been attained. Now the mature and individuated human being moves forward to the next phase of the evolutionary journey: to unite the individual soul with spirit, wherein the divine spark within each of us becomes one with the original Source of Light, and achieves enlightenment or unity consciousness. This is known as the Greater Stone or Philosopher's Stone. In Christian alchemy, Jesus Christ was seen as the Philosopher's Stone since he could cure diseases and bestow eternal life upon those who followed him. This is why *Corpus Christi*—"the Body of Christ"—is written on the standing stone beside the maiden or else is the one on which Mary kneels. In both cases, she represents the soul who leads the way to the sacred union with spirit.

In Wolfram von Eschenbach's *Parzival,* the Grail itself has all the qualities of the Philosopher's Stone. It provides nourishment to the company of Knights Templar who guard it; it sustains life and heals the sick. By its virtue the Phoenix is reborn out of its own ashes. Wolfram calls it by a Latin phrase, *lapsit exillis,* which does not make sense, and much ink has been spilled as to what this means. Since the stone was supposed to have fallen from heaven, one theory is that these words are a contraction of *lapis, lapsus ex coelis*—the stone fallen from the sky. Another is that the phrase was *lapis elixir,* the "elixir stone," an Arabian term for the Philosopher's Stone. Or perhaps the two words should have read *lapis exilis:* "a stone of little price," a term used in the fifteenth-century alchemical tract called *Rosarium Philosophorum* (the Rose Garden of the Philosophers):

Hic lapis exilis extat pretio quoque vilis,

Spernitur a stultis, amatur plus ab edoctis

[This stone is poor, and cheap in price/It is disdained by fools, but it is loved all the more by the wise.][20]

Alchemists often referred to the Philosopher's Stone as small and worthless, like the Old Testament verse in which "the stone that the builders rejected" becomes the capstone of the temple. This refers to the flawed and unregenerate nature of the human being before undergoing the process of alchemy when the divine spark of light within is released and he or she is revealed in the full radiance of the spiritual Self.

The Grail-Stone is said to be an emerald which fell to earth from the crown—or perhaps the brow—of Lucifer when there was war in heaven. Esoterically, this tradition is very important. There are two versions of the Lucifer story. In the more orthodox one, Lucifer leads a rebellion against God and was banished from heaven. He fell into the physical world and the underworld, where he became identified as Satan. In some esoteric traditions, however, Lucifer—whose name is Latin for "Light-Bringer"—came to earth of his own accord out of love of the human race. In this version, Lucifer was one of the seven angels around the throne of the Creator. A time came when God asked for a volunteer to descend into the material darkness of human consciousness on earth, and Lucifer took up this sacrificial task. When he entered earth, he was not welcomed by humankind, but feared and hated as the Red Fiery Dragon or the Great Serpent.

In *The Pillars of Tubal Cain,* a landmark book of occult angel lore and magic, authors Howard and Jackson declare:

> Esoteric tradition teaches us that until we find the Grail, and it should be clearly understood that it is not a physical object in this time-space continuum, Lucifer must play out his role as the sacrificial king. He is doomed to incarnate in a "cloak of flesh" as an avatar for the human race and pay the ultimate price as a scapegoat on their behalf. This is the ultimate sacrifice of being a lightbearer who brought down from Heaven the illumination of Gnostic wisdom and the primal fire of creativity. Lucifer eternally dies and is reborn to save humanity from itself. As the human race progresses spiritually so he can slowly ascend the Ladder of Lights back to the realm of the Gods beyond the Pole Star. He is the Lord of the Morning Star and the Lux Mundi (Light of the World) whose rebirth from darkness we celebrate every year at the winter solstice.[21]

Other names for Lucifer, such as Day-Star, Day-spring from on High, Morning-Star, and Son of the Morning, point to his guardianship of the planet Venus. As Venus is the morning star whose light in the eastern sky heralds the coming of the sun, Lucifer in many ways was the harbinger of the Cosmic Christ. The gemstone associated with Venus is the emerald, a color that is symbolic of life, growth, and the opening of the heart. The emerald stone, then, is a gift of great price given to us from on high for bringing healing and harmony to our planet. In *Parzival,* then, we are clearly in the realm of spiritual alchemy in which the Grail, like the Philosopher's Stone, is regarded as the power which transmutes the base metal of the egoic self into the gold of the illuminated Self.

ROSES RED AND WHITE

Perhaps the highest expression of the alchemical Grail Mysteries lies in a bed of roses. In many texts, descriptions and images of the alchemical process take place in a rose garden. This is the enclosed "Garden of the Philosophers," the Garden of Wisdom, wherein bloom red and white roses. The rose represents the blossoming and transformation of the human spirit, and in alchemy the red rose is the masculine/yang principle and the white rose the feminine/yin principle. Sometimes the mystical union of the Red King and the White Queen results in a "child" symbolized by a single golden rose, representing the regeneration of the separated essences and their resurrection on a new level, in other words, completion of the Great Work.

The alchemical emblem displayed here shows the famous female alchemist, Maria Prophetissa, pointing to a symbol of the Great Work: two Grail-like vessels pour spiritual energy from Above and Below. A vesica piscis or mandorla is formed between them like a gateway into the mysteries of life, where grows a rose-bush with blossoms, each one with five petals, symbolizing the quintessence (five-essence) of the Great Work. The bush is growing at the top of a mount, at the meeting place of Heaven and Earth.

In the fifteenth century, a rose with petals of both red and white became an important royal symbol known as the Tudor rose, for which

Maria Prophetissa from Symbola Aurea Mensae,
by Michael Maier, Frankfurt, 1617

we can again thank the alchemists. The Wars of the Roses during the fifteenth century were brought to an end when Henry VII, heir of the House of Lancaster, married Elizabeth of York, and the two roses that were the emblems of their houses were combined in the Tudor rose. The white rose of York formed the center of the flower, and the red rose of Lancaster the outside petals, to create a symbol of peaceful unity. The result of this human alchemical marriage was a flesh-and-blood "Philosopher's Child," who was named Arthur after the mythic solar king who united Britain in a Golden Age. His birth was arranged to take place at Winchester, the city believed at the time to have been Camelot. A replica Round Table was constructed with a Tudor rose at its center, to represent, in the words of historian Jonathan Hughes, "the rose of Alchemy, the philosopher's stone, the nation's soul."[22] It can still be seen today hanging in the Great Hall in Winchester Castle.

Although used as an opportune political symbol, the Tudor rose sprang from the deeper substrate of alchemical symbolism. An illustration in a famous alchemical tract of this period, *The Ripley Scroll*, shows a rose with white petals at the center, surrounded by red outer petals. The text reads:

> *Take the fayer Roses, white and red.*
> *And join them well in won bed.*
> *So betwixt these Roses mylde*
> *Thou shalt bring forth a Gloriuse chylde.*[23]

Moving beyond politics to the psycho-spiritual level, the "chylde" is the "Philosopher's Child," another name for the Philosopher's Stone, symbolizing the divine offspring born of union of the masculine and feminine forces within the psyche. The petals of the white rose represent the spiritual consciousness (Rosa Mystica) hidden deep within the red rose of the world (Rosa Mundi). This is the Western equivalent to the more well-known Eastern lotus, a flower which grows out of mud,

The Tudor Rose in Alchemy

just as higher consciousness emerges out of the ignorance of the ego. Within its heart lies "the jewel within the lotus," the *atman,* or "eternal soul."

THE ROSE CROSS

The rose re-emerged as a spiritual symbol in the seventeenth century when it appeared as the emblem of the esoteric fraternity of the Rosicrucians. The brotherhood takes its name from their legendary founder, Christian Rosencreutz, meaning "Christian Rosy Cross." The Rosicrucians studied spiritual Alchemy and healing, "Magia and Cabala," with the aim of leading Europe to a new understanding of divine wisdom under a revitalized Protestant Christianity. Although the identities of the early members were never revealed, the Rosicrucians were the inspiration behind a plethora of magical groups which arose in the following centuries, including Freemasonry, the Order of the Golden Dawn, and various groups that adopted the Rosicrucian name.

The chief symbol of the order, the Rose Cross, has multiple layers of meaning, but the underlying conjunction of the opposites is clear to see. The rose, drawn as the classic alchemical five-petal flower, represents the awakened human soul blossoming on the cross of the elements: the body, space-time, or material existence as a whole. Often the rose is shown with a golden center: the spiritual gold transmuted from the base lead of the ego. Also implied is the necessary sacrificial "crucifixion" that must occur as the ego surrenders its autonomy within the human psyche to a higher, spiritual authority.

A unique version of the Rose Cross appeared on the title-page of the book *Clavis Philosophiæ et Alchymiæ* (*The Key to Philosophy and Alchemy*) by Robert Fludd, written in 1633. It shows a huge rose blossom, whose stem is formed in the shape of a cross composed of seven circles of seven petals, above which are the words, *Dat Rosa Mel Apibus:* "the Rose gives honey to the bees." Seven implies the seven steps toward initiation, while blossom and stem together form the astrological sign for the planet Venus (♀), symbolizing the triumph of love over the pain and suffering on the cross of the world. On the right of the picture is a hive of bees, two of whom have reached the Rose. On the left is a square grape-arbor fence on which a spider has spun a web, also in seven circuits, suggesting the sticky entanglements and traps of earthly desires, which a seeker must take care to avoid on the path. The bees represent those spiritual seekers who aspire to fly beyond the hive-like business and complexity of society. Transcending the thorny challenges of life, the bees approach the nectar within the Rose of the soul. Their job does not end in mystical communion with the Rose, but rather with the return to the hive to transform the pollen into honey for the good of the whole just as, in Western esoteric tradition, the goal of the Great Work or the quest of the Grail, is service unto others.

"The Rose gives honey to the bees." The famous Rosicrucian engraving by Johann Theodore deBry (d. 1598).

THE ROSE AND THE GRAIL

Rose and Grail partake of the same symbolism. The word "chalice" comes from the Latin word *calyx,* a cup, referring to the sepals of a flower. The beauty of the rose, the number and arrangement of its petals, the intoxicating perfume and hidden golden heart deep within, is a perfect symbol for the receptive vessel of the soul, opening to receive the in-pouring of divine influence. In this, we may detect the influences of Arabian and Persian teachings from the time when Spain was an Islamic country. As Sufi teacher, Hazrat Inayat Khan, puts it:

> Just as the rose consists of many petals held together, so the person who attains to the unfoldment of the soul begins to show many different qualities. The qualities emit fragrance in the form of a spiritual personality. The rose has a beautiful structure, and the personality which proves the unfoldment of the soul has also a fine structure, in manner, in dealing with others, in speech, in action. The atmosphere of a spiritual being pervades the air like the perfume of a rose.[24]

And a twelfth-century Persian poet wrote, "Mystery glows in the rose bed; the secret is hidden in the rose."[25]

In medieval Europe the rose was pictured as growing in the heart of a fourfold sacred garden, recalling the Celtic Otherworld paradise. The earliest gardens of the desert lands of the Middle East were designed to emulate Eden, with four streams flowing out to the four directions, and a Tree of Life in the center. From Persia came gardens laid out like mandalas, surrounded by four walls, suggestive of seclusion and completion, with a fountain of crystal water in the center. The medieval rose garden was purposely laid out in this four-square design to reflect the original primal harmony of Eden, so that by the twelfth century, the rose garden had become the standard image of paradise, a word which comes from the Persian for a walled garden. Rose gardens sprang up in the cloisters of monasteries, and Cistercian scholar, Alanus de Insulis, described the earthly paradise as a place of eternal spring, flaming with roses that never faded.

ROSA MYSTICA

As well as being regarded as a form of the Grail in the Middle Ages, the Virgin Mary was also called the Mystic Rose. She shared this honor with many of the goddesses who had gone before her, including Isis, Cybele, Hecate, and Aphrodite. In the era of courtly love in twelfth-century France, the rose became the chief symbol of the newly re-emerging feminine principle, representing the beloved lady in the secular poems of the troubadours, while in the religious context, it became the flower of Mary. She herself was called the Rose of Sharon, the Rose-garland, the Wreath of Roses, and Queen of the Most Holy Rose Garden. In processions honoring the Mother of God, her devotees walked on rose petals, just as the goddesses of the pagan world were celebrated.[26] The Litany of Loreto called her "Rosa Mystica," the Mystic Rose. She was often addressed as the "Rose without a Thorn" because she was as pure as the original rose that grew in the Garden of Eden. A sixteenth-century text makes the simple yet profound analogy between the beauty and receptivity of the Rose and the divine spirit which is poured into it: "As in the morning the Rose opens, receiving the dew from heaven and the sun, so Mary's soul did open and receive Christ the heavenly dew."[27]

Mary in the Rose Garden grew to become a popular theme in European medieval art; she was frequently pictured cradling the Christ child in the peace and beauty of a medieval walled garden, a symbol of the Immaculate Conception. Around her blossom the white roses of purity and the red roses of passion, while she herself is the rose without a thorn.

THE RED AND WHITE DRAGONS

In the mysteries of Britain, the polarized red and white forces are expressed as two dragons. Dragons are symbols of the unbridled, chaotic energy of the primal life force. In alchemy, they represent the archetypal powers of the First Matter that must be brought under control of the alchemist. In the twelfth-century Mabinogi story, *Lludd and Llefelys,* a red and a white dragon cause havoc throughout Britain until they are trapped in a chest and buried deep within the mountains of Snowdonia. In a well-known story about Merlin's boyhood, the dragons are discovered fighting beneath the hill of Dinas Emrys. With his gifts of seership, Merlin understands that the red dragon represents the British in their struggle with the invading Saxons, represented by the white dragon. Medieval alchemists seized upon the political implications of this image when the first king from a Welsh line, Henry VII, brought peace to the country by ending the Wars of the Roses. As discussed earlier, Henry's emblem was the red rose of Lancaster, and the emblem of his wife, Elizabeth of York, was the white rose.

In these tales, the dragons are the equivalent of the yin and yang currents of dragon energy in Chinese "feng shui." In Western alchemy they are symbols of sulfur (a red, winged dragon) and mercury (a white, wingless dragon) or sun and moon. Their fighting is in fact an act of copulation for creating offspring, and afterward they turn into the harmonious serpents that twine around the rod, or caduceus, of Hermes.[28]

In the human body, the caduceus becomes a glyph of the subtle channel that ascends the human spine; in Yogic teachings it is called the *Shushumna,* meaning "tube" or "pipe." The two snakes symbolize the polarized serpent-like forces of *Ida* and *Pingala,* which are normally coiled like a snake at the base of the spine. Ida represents the moon and is the white, cold, feminine, current, while the Pingala is the red, hot masculine solar current. These forces can be trained to rise through the Shushumna and reach the brain, to connect the lower with the higher self and bring about a state of union with the divine. As the energy rises up the spine, it crosses back and forth through the seven subtle energy centers, or "chakras," cleansing them and opening them up, to give rise to psychic abilities and higher states of awareness. Eventually it reaches the pineal gland in the brain, so called for its pinecone shape. In Classical Greece, the caduceus was often shown with a pinecone at the tip and two wings, signifying the power of conscious flight through the higher worlds, brought about by the unfolding of the serpent fire. This technology of enlightenment was also known to the Taoist masters of China who believed that it was a means to achieving immortality.

The tip of the caduceus of Osiris shows the pinecone as the pineal gland. Courtesty of the Egyptian Museum, Turin, Italy, 1224 BCE.

It is not too difficult to discern elements of this ancient spiritual practice in the manuscripts of European alchemists, particularly in regard to the red and white polarized energies, whether symbolized as chemical substances, royal figures, dragons, or roses. The real mystery contained within Joseph's two Grail vessels of red and white fluid is nothing less than the alchemical sacred marriage: the harmonizing of the opposites within the self and the land, and ultimately, the union of soul and Spirit, which leads to the "gold" of union with the Divine.

VisionJourney VII
The Hall in the Orchard

Sit in a comfortable position, relax and quiet your mind. . . . Take some deep breaths and imagine you are breathing in a pale, misty light. Float in this light which begins to swirl around you. . . .

When the mist unfurls, you see confused shapes that resolve into the outlines of gnarled trees with bare, twisted boughs. You are walking through an orchard in a dry late autumn season; no fruit or nuts hang on the dry and brittle branches, and a few brown leaves are scattered at their roots. The air is oppressively still and the only sounds are of your soft footfall on withered grass and the occasional rustle of dead leaves. . . .

Then a rush of wings cuts through the silence of this place, and above you a falcon gives a shrill cry. You have a feeling he has been sent as a guide, and so you follow him as he glides over the trees and comes to rest on a tree before an old stone hall whose crumbling towers appear to be held together only by a mass of ivy. The walls are completely surrounded by a thorny thicket of wild briar roses, so dense you can see no way through. The falcon gives another cry, seeming to urge you onward without delay, so as best you can, you beat down the bushes to make a path through—not without incurring several painful scratches from the sharp thorns as you go. . . .

Somewhat out of breath, you disentangle strands of prickly twigs from your hair, and gaze about you. You have won through to a courtyard that breathes an air of neglect and decay. Weeds run rampant in the cracks of its once fine paving stones that are littered with rubble from fallen masonry. A dry fountain, its bowl choked with leaves, stands silent in its center.

The heavy oaken door is ajar, and creaks in protest as you push it open. At the far end of a long chamber is a huge wooden bed, draped with cloth of gold and surrounded by six white candles. By their light you can see that the walls are covered with heavy purple hangings. . . .

On it lies the figure of a crowned king, an aged man with long white straggling hair and beard and blue-veined hands clasped together on his chest. He lies motionless, as if dead, while blood from an unseen wound drips down into a Grail beneath the bed, and spills over into a channel cut into the stone floor. Behind him is a tall arched window through which can be seen the glow of the setting sun. It shines down on the still figure, bathing his face with a dull red light. . . .

In the flickering candlelight it takes you a while to realize there is another person in the hall: the glimmering white figure of a maiden with pale flaxen hair who kneels by the bed, weeping and keening a song of deep sorrow; the desolate pain of separation and endless grief for the loss of love are in her voice. Following the rise and fall of her song, you feel as if you are staring into a bottomless abyss of misery, and the memory of all the separations and losses you have endured in your own life well up within you. As she sings, the maiden's tears continually fall into a stream of water that flows down through another stone channel in the floor. You realize that you too are weeping—for your own pain, for the pain of the Earth, for all the sorrow of the world where the Two can never be made One however much love seeks to unite them. Your tears flow down and mingle with hers, and all the sorrow felt throughout time for our suffering world is poured out through these rivers of blood and tears. . . .

When it feels as if you can bear no more of this anguish, you are aware that a new light has entered the hall, for the sun has long since set. Through a small window above the door where you entered in, the moon is slowly rising and starting to show her face. Silver beams stream through the hall and illumine the scene around the bed. The maiden arises and stretches out her hands into the moonbeams. She begins to weave them like silvery threads over and about the still figure on the stone bed. Slowly, she moves as if in a solemn dance around the king, her hands continually weaving the silver threads about him. As she glides around his body, she begins once more to sing, and this time her song is low and resonant with a deep joy, such as the waves sometimes make on a long shore. . . .

You stand there mesmerized by the notes of her song and her continually moving hands, how long you cannot tell. As the maiden's face is brushed now with light, now shadow, it seems to change from young to mature, to ancient and wrinkled with untold years, and then back again. Perhaps it is a trick of the moonlight, but it seems to you as if she is joined by other figures, as faint as pale shadows that also glide around the motionless figure of the king.

And now you notice that he is beginning to change. Although he has not moved, his hair and beard seem to grow shorter and thicker, while youth and vigor fill out his face and arms. Hardly daring to breathe lest you break the spell, you watch as he visibly becomes younger and younger, while the figures about him weave their unearthly dance about him. He becomes a strong and handsome youth with curling auburn hair, bursting with health and vitality. Immediately the weaving dance stops and the shadowy dancers fade away. In the eastern window a new dawn breaks. The youth leaps off the stone bed, wreathed in smiles, and stands before the maiden. They take each others' hands and gaze long at one another in deepest love. You see the young king wears a crown of gold like the sun, and the maiden wears a crown of shimmering moonlight. They are the Red King and the White Queen: the polar forces of our world of opposites now conjoined in harmonious union.

Now become aware of the potential for a sacred marriage within your own psyche. . . . What would it feel like to be in a state of balance and harmony within yourself? To experience perfect peace and wholeness in all of your being? How would the world look and behave if all human beings attained this state of inner harmony? Take some time to clearly envision this "New Heaven, New Earth" as it might be: this is the Vision of the Harmony of Things. . . .

Now a newly risen morning sun streams into the hall and by its light you see that the red and white waters have become sparkling streams of gold and silver. The Young Queen takes up the Grail and fills it from both streams, then she and the Young King share this drink. Next she refills the Grail and hands it to you. You take a sip, aware that this is not ordinary water: it is like drinking liquid light, and you feel as if the Water of Life itself is pouring through your veins and refreshing every cell in your body.

You ask the queen what you can do in return for this precious gift. She tells you that you must go out into the orchard and water the trees with the living stream of Light. You leave the hall and fill the Grail again and again from the gold and silver river that now flows through the courtyard. You notice that the fountain has begun to send up cascades of sparkling water with a joyful sound, which is attracting butterflies and small birds. Retracing your steps through the briar thicket, you reach the orchard and pour the contents of the Grail over the roots of the dead trees, until each one puts out leaves, blossoms, and finally fruit and nuts of all kinds. The Wasteland has become a fragrant, green paradise, filled with sunlight and birdsong. When you return to the hall, you see that the briar roses have begun to give forth buds of red and white flowers.

And now the king bids you take the revivifying waters of the Grail back home to heal your own world. You ask him how it can be done and he tells you the waters of Light are rivers of healing: forces that you must allow to flow through your own heart and mind. He gives you counsel on how you can use your own unique talents in service to the earth—ways that you can protect and care for all living creatures in the mineral, vegetable, animal, and human kingdoms. . . .

As he finishes speaking a strange thing happens: king and queen merge with each other to become one Being . . . and you recognize this figure as none other than your divine Self, also known as the Holy Guardian Angel, the Perfected One who you will one day become.

Notice how it feels to be in the presence of your divine Self. Experience the power, the wisdom, and the love, and spend time in deep communion with this part of you. . . . Let your divine Self tell you what the mission of your soul is in this lifetime. . . . Let it give you guidance on how to proceed. . . .

When you return to your own place and time, make a commitment to attune to your divine Self on a regular basis, and thus create a space for this part of you to express itself through you in your daily life. Just so will the roots of your life on Earth be continually nourished and fertilized by the waters of Spirit.

8

Dion Fortune and the Church of the Graal

For centuries following its destruction, Glastonbury Abbey, once the most illustrious church in England, lay in ruins in the heart of the small town.

With the dawn of the twentieth century, the gates once more opened between the worlds, and the sleepy streets were startled awake as successive waves of notable incomers made Glastonbury their stage of artistic, musical, and spiritual endeavors. The awen flowed freely from the Cauldron of Inspiration as Alice Buckton, a pioneer of modern education, started an arts and drama center at Chalice Well in 1912, while composer Rutland Broughton inaugurated annual art and music festivals in 1914, aided by his friend, playwright George Bernard Shaw. Esotericists such as A. E. Waite and Annie Besant wandered among the abbey ruins, as did William Sharp, better known as Fiona Macleod, a poet of the Celtic Twilight.

The abbey was purchased, ironically enough, by the Anglican Church in 1907. The church hired a Bristol architect, Frederick Bligh Bond, to excavate the ruins. He achieved spectacular success by using automatic writing to communicate with the spirits of a group of medieval monks who called themselves the Company of Avalon. Unfortunately the church authorities threw up their hands in horror at his unorthodox methodology, and he was swiftly dismissed in disgrace.

The ruins of Glastonbury Abbey, with the Tor in the background.

His architectural career blighted forever, he continued working in the occult sphere for the rest of his life. He is fondly remembered at Chalice Well for his design of the iconic well-cover with its wrought-iron vesica piscis.

In 1929, a new Grail story entered Glastonbury: Katharine Maltwood's "Temple of the Stars." This young artist was engaged in creating the illustrations for a new edition of *Perlesvaus* under the title of *The High History of the Holy Graal,* when she had a vision of an entire zodiac laid out over the land in a wide circle. The outline of the constellations were marked by lanes, hedges, and streams, and other features in the landscape, both natural and manmade. This, she believed, was the real meaning of King Arthur's Round Table. The knights traveled over each sign of this landscape zodiac on their quest for the Grail. Today there are those who remain convinced of its physical reality, while others point out there is very little physical evidence to prove its existence: many of the zodiac features turn out to be formed from modern lanes and field boundaries. Maltwood also claimed the configuration was five thousand years old, a period when the area would have been entirely covered with water. Perhaps the Glastonbury Zodiac lingers just one wavelength away from the physical plane, a shimmering pattern that once was, or might have been, and whose etheric structure can still be half-glimpsed upon the land, like tracings in the sand only just washed away by the tide. Whichever reality it partakes of, physical or magical, from this time forth the Glastonbury Zodiac became firmly embedded in the geomythic landscape of Avalon.

These and many more inspired men and women became known as the "Avalonians," a term coined by one of the most famous of their number, a woman known as Dion Fortune: "We used to say that there dwelt in Glastonbury the Glastonburians and the Avalonians; the Glastonburians were those who only knew the place as a market town and a tourist centre, and the Avalonians were those who were in touch with its spiritual life."[1]

THE CHURCH OF THE GRAAL

Dion Fortune was the magical name of Violet Firth, 1890–1946, one of the foremost pioneers of modern magic, a brilliant esotericist, trance medium, seer and ritual magician, who was also a fine writer with a legacy of over twenty-five books of non-fiction and fiction to her name. After an early period of training in a series of occult orders and societies of that period, she came to Glastonbury around 1920 where she also received communications from the Company of Avalon who had contacted Frederick Bligh Bond. They told her that London was the head center of England, and Glastonbury was its heart; that the Isle of Avalon was the site of a "College of the Illuminati" and a "great center of the druidic faith" in pre-Christian times. She learned that the Isle of Avalon had always been a place of spiritual regeneration where successive generations of initiates maintained contact with inner plane powers over the centuries, and thus the door between the worlds has always been more open there than at any other place in Britain:

There has never ceased to be an open Lodge at Glastonbury. The succession has never failed; there has never been darkness there. The

Tor has never lacked its Hermit. There has always been an Upper Chamber within the bounds of the circle of the marshes, where one soul in solitude meditated upon the mysteries. Thus was maintained a focus in the flesh whereby the necessary contact could be made upon the other side. . . . Those who have functioned in this way have kept the channels open by their concentrated thought, leaving merely the thinnest film, like a psychic parchment, lest the power behind should break through into a world all unprepared, leading to martyrdom, not magic. . . . Thus at Glastonbury the contact has never been broken.[2]

Dion Fortune

In her visions, Dion Fortune could see the spiritual force that fuels this sacred landscape as a constant downpour of the Holy Spirit, flowing unceasingly from a crystal chalice high above the Tor. Inspired by these messages and by the palpably numinous power of Avalon, she acquired a plot of land that was once part of an old orchard at the foot of the Tor where she set about forming a spiritual community. In 1924 a cluster of huts were hastily erected, and Chalice Orchard, as she named it, came into being, serving both as a pilgrimage center or "hostel for Avalonians," and a sanctuary for meditation and ritual work. Here she gathered a small group, the Community of the Inner Light, which was to develop into one of the most influential magical orders

of the twentieth century, still in existence today under the name of the
Society of the Inner Light. Dion Fortune called Glastonbury "Avalon of
the Heart," and she immortalized this term in a passage from her book
of the same name: "It is to this Avalon of the Heart the pilgrims still
go. Some in bands, knowing what they seek. Some alone, with the staff
of vision in their hands, awaiting what may come to meet them on this
holy ground. None go away as they came."[3]

Dion Fortune took frequent walks up to the summit of the Tor,
which she called, "the Hill of Vision." One of her visions up there was
of a glorious parade out of Avalon's mythic past winding through the
landscape below:

> Through the valleys of Avalon moves an invisible pageant in an end-
> less procession. The darkness before the dawn is shot through by the
> magic of Merlin the Atlantean. The dark, wild men of the mere go
> past, fierce eyes gleaming under matted hair. After them come the
> white-robed Druids, with their golden sickles, bearing the holy mis-
> tletoe, and followed by the captives taken in battle, destined for the
> sacrificial niche in the Holy Well. Then comes the bowed figure of
> old St. Joseph, frail and solitary, bearing the Cup. King Arthur rides
> forth, a strong man in his strength, about his neck the crystal cross
> which was given him by the Mother of God at Beckary, Excalibur by
> his side. Guinevere rides behind him in her beauty, her golden hair
> flowing over her shoulders. . . . Behind them follows the Lady of the
> Lake, seen as if through deep water, waiting the time when Arthur
> shall return to her after the last battle, borne in the black barge,
> watched by the weeping queens, and Excalibur shall come back into
> her hands, lost to men forever.[4]

THE THREEFOLD WAY

Dion Fortune's experiences in Glastonbury led her to develop a magical system with three paths, which were symbolized by three colored

rays, each pertaining to a particular strand of tradition in the Western Mystery Teachings. They are represented in diagrammatic form as three interlocking rings.

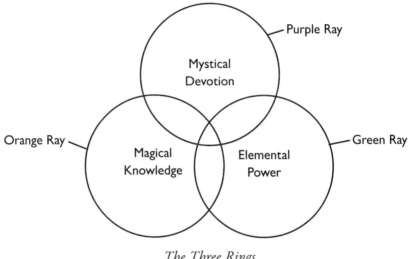

The Three Rings

The Orange Ray is the path of Magical Knowledge, the Hermetic way. It has an intellectual emphasis and focuses on working with symbolism and patterns through visualized or ceremonial forms. It was inspired by Dion Fortune's explorations of the Arthurian mythos, which seeps out of every crack and crevice of the ancient Isle of Avalon.

The Green Ray is the path of Elemental Power, which has an emotional and instinctive emphasis and is focused on Earth magic, including nature spirits, elementals, and faeries. Inspiration for the Green Ray arose out of her experience of living at the foot of the Tor, with the chthonic power of the Underworld below and the forces of wind, sun, and storm above.

The Purple Ray is the path of Mystical Devotion, focused on direct communion with the divine. The influence of Glastonbury Abbey and its pervading air of sanctity—which still lingers throughout the area like the faint fragrance of incense—provided the inspiration for this branch of the mysteries.

Although she felt herself to be more suited temperamentally to the Hermetic Ray, Dion Fortune found herself called to take a leadership role in service of the Purple Ray through a branch of her order called the Guild of the Master Jesus, which later became known as the Church of the Graal. This branch embodied an esoteric Christianity influenced in part from her early involvement with theosophical teachings, wherein Jesus was seen as a highly evolved human being (ascended master or inner plane adept) who had attained Christhood. She writes:

> The Christ is the redemptive force that harmonizes the pairs of opposites in the Cosmos, and in the individual unites the pairs of opposites—the higher and lower nature. In other words, it is the exaltation of consciousness. The illuminating power of the Christ is not a person, but a potency—the aspect of the One God aptly called the Son.[5]

The central symbol of the Guild was the Grail as the vessel of the Christ-force and receptacle for the Holy Spirit:

> . . . in the Guild of the Master Jesus you concentrate not upon the personality of the Master, but upon the Graal, because this represents a higher and more mystical symbolism than the incarnated personality. . . . The real key, then, to the Guild is in the Graal and the object of meditation should be the Graal and not the Cross; the descent of the Holy Spirit and not the historical Jesus; the present, not the past nor the future.[6]

The Risen Christ was deemed more important than the Crucified Christ, and the role of the cross assumed its rightful place in the Christian mysteries of life-death-rebirth by symbolizing the suffering and sacrifice that preceded the resurrection. Emphasis was on the eventual triumph of Spirit in the life of Jesus—and in the life of the initiate of these mysteries, who followed in his footsteps. Fortune took pains to point out that although the Grail must replace the Cross, it cannot be attained without sacrifice. The desires of the personal self must be transcended in order to follow the wiser dictates of the Higher Self.

The Church of the Graal was based on Dion Fortune's concept of the "Keltic Church" as an organization that encouraged the autonomy of each individual, man or woman, who sought God. Services were centered on a form of the Eucharist called, "the Ritual of the Cup," referring to the cup of the Last Supper, in which the Christ-force was invoked through "the calling down of power into a receptacle, that receptacle being the soul of man."[7] The service depended not only on the minister or celebrant, but on the active participation and full engagement of each member of the congregation. Through their focused visualization and intense concentration on a single theme, which included a "mighty Chalice of gold,"[8] a group-mind, or *egregore,* was formed, in order to "build up thought-forms upon the astral which shall serve as channels for the descending spiritual force."[9] The aim was that "each individual member of the group thus formed is then filled with the descending force in such measure as he is capable of receiving."[10]

The Guild of the Master Jesus also provided a training system in three courses, which marked the stages on what Fortune called the "Way of the Graal." She writes: "We seek our contacts with the tradition of Christ through the ancient Keltic Church of Britain, which, though it stands no more above ground, is eternal in the heavens. Our Holy Place is Glastonbury, 'the holiest earthe in Englande'; and in its Avalonian aspect, as the center of tradition and of the Table Round, we make contact with the Mysteries of Arthur."[11]

On the successful completion of the third course, called "the Watchers of the Graal," the initiate became a priest in his or her own right and could work with these mysteries autonomously, for "the Church of the Graal . . . is built by thought, eternal in each man's heart. Each man is his own priest, and lifts therein the Cup of the Graal, and calls down the Flame of Fire, which is the Holy Spirit."[12]

Among his or her daily devotions, the priest was instructed to build the inner Church of the Graal—"the church not made with hands, eternal in the heavens"—through the intensive formulating of an image of the following scenes, thus establishing their reality on the inner plane:

> To this end he should visualize the Isle of Avalon as it was in the days of the Coming of the Graal. He should see the Tor crowned with the circle of standing stones of the sun-worship, below it, the Well of the Wisdom of Merlin. He should see the circular Church of the Graal that enshrined the Cup, from which shines an eternal light. Around it are the cells of the twelve anchorites. Beyond, among the marshes, is the hermitage of Bride. Through and around all come and go Arthur and his knights, showing forth the ideal of chivalry. These are the Holy Places of the initiates of the Master Jesus in these islands. . . .
>
> Now the Keltic Church was built by the wise men of old; men that had knowledge, and it stands eternal in the heavens. Those who have the sight can revive it today. Let us therefore look for this Church with the eye of faith that it may live, and be built again between heaven and earth that power may come down and men may worship.
>
> In the working of the rites of the Guild we build this Church. Let us go forth by the pilgrim way up the Tor, and upon the crest rebuild the Chapel of St. Michael, and above the tower, the Star of Bethlehem. Within, the Chapel is even as our own sanctuary in black and silver, with the two pillars of positive and negative force and the Keltic cross between. But upon the altar stands the Very Graal, shining with an inner light, and above the altar descends the power of the Holy Spirit. These things we see with the inner eye, which is the eye of faith.[13]

The Grail was also at the center of the most powerful magical workings practiced by Dion Fortune and the Fellowship of the Inner Light.[14] At the worst crisis point of the Second World War, when it seemed like a Nazi invasion might happen at any moment, Dion Fortune, now working from her group's London headquarters, sent out to all her followers a weekly letter containing a lesson and the description of a symbol they were to build on the inner planes. An hour was set when, no matter where they were, everyone was to focus on this symbol as a "key-call" to the invisible guardians and protectors of the British race to enlist their aid in England's greatest time of need. Their aim was to build forms on the astral plane, which higher spiritual forces could use as channels to bring their influence to bear on the defense of the realm. Fortune likened this to becoming a radio transmitter, "through which the influence of the Masters comes through to humanity for the healing of the nations."[15]

The key powers who revealed themselves during the meditation were King Arthur, Merlin, and the Master Jesus, later joined by the figure of the Virgin Mary who bore the cup of the Grail. They appeared within Glastonbury Tor, which, on the inner planes, was seen as having four levels: the lowest was a deep cavern, with above it, a great library, called the Hall of Learning; above the library was the Chapel of the Grail, and the highest level was the Watchtower, the inner equivalent of Saint Michael's Tower in the physical world. This was guarded by a mysterious cowled figure called the Watcher who kept "perpetual vigil" on the heights.

In the meditation below we follow in the path of many who have trod this Way of Illumination before.

VisionJourney VIII
The Watcher on the Tor

Sit in a comfortable position, relax and quiet your mind. . . . Take some deep breaths and imagine you are breathing in a beautiful, silvery light like the far-distant stars. Now let yourself float in this light, which becomes like a silver mist swirling all around you. . . .

When the mist lifts, you are standing on the edge of time's spiral ready to enter into the mysteries of the Star Temple of Avalon. It is just after sunset, and you are at the foot of Glastonbury Tor in the Vale of the Red and White Springs. Their waters intertwine and mingle as they flow down through the green vale—the only sound that breaks the evening silence. . . .

Begin walking along the lane that leads to the Tor itself. The path slopes gently upward, shadowed by dark silhouettes of trees and their tracery of boughs in early springtime leaf. Cross a wooden stile and enter a broad sloping meadow open to the sky. By the sun's afterglow you can see the dark shape of the Tor as it rises before you, steeply rising from the lowlands of the Summer Country. On top is the silhouette of the ruined tower of Saint Michael like a solitary pointing finger. Above the tower shines the seven stars of the Great Bear in their slow majestic march around the Pole Star.

A narrow thread of a path now gleams whitely before you and you start to climb the Tor. Before long, you see a large reddish sandstone rock on the left of the path. This is the Living Rock. Touch it, and as you do so, you may feel it tingle slightly like electricity. . . . The landscape around you now becomes dreamlike—almost transparent—as if you have walked through a veil; and you feel transparent too, yet filled with an energy that flows through your body like a silver stream as if starlight is running in your veins. The white path glimmers like spider silk, and you see that it winds around the hill in a sun-wise direction as a luminous spiral of seven circuits.

Follow the silvery thread seven times around the Tor to the summit of the hill. . . . At each turn of the spiral, the path becomes narrower and steeper. A steady wind begins to blow in your face, forcing you to slow down. It becomes very dark, and yet whenever it seems you might lose your footing and slip off the perilously sheer slope, a faint light appears ahead of you—enough to show you where to safely place your foot. Sometimes you catch a glimpse of this Light-Bearer as a tall, cowled figure carrying a lantern: he is one of the Watchers of Avalon, the ancient Guardians of this place.

At last, you find yourself standing on top of the Tor in a high wind. Above you the black shape of the ruined tower rises in solitary splendor against the sky, which is now a deep and luminous violet blue, a fathomless sea of space wherein a million stars and planets hang like lamps. Among them you can make out the wide band of the twelve sparkling constellations that comprise the zodiac: figures of giants, gods, and animals; all dancing in a ring, rising up into the heights of the heavens, and dipping below the horizon.

One constellation in particular glows with dazzling brilliance right above the tower itself. You see by the pattern of its seven living gems of star fire that it is Ursa Major, the Great Bear, that circles around a shining orb of pure celestial light: Polaris, the Pole Star, the Gate of Heaven. As you watch, an iridescent ray of pulsating light shines out from each of the seven stars to surround the Tor with a glorious, many-hued rainbow. . . .

As the arch of the heavens opens, a gigantic figure ablaze with light appears. He reaches up to the heavens above the tower and grasps the North Star. It becomes a mighty, starry Sword of Light with a hilt and blade of dazzling shafts of laser-like beams of limitless, unbounded life force. . . .

From the tip of the sword comes forth a spiral of starlight, like a white serpent. It swirls at a dizzying speed through space toward you, and the star fire streams down like silver rain toward Earth. Within its radiance, the tower no longer appears as a ruin but a shimmering tower of starlight with all the colors of the rainbow sparkling like diamonds. It has resumed its true form on the Inner Levels as Caer Wydyr, the Crystal Tower—one of the four great Watchtowers of Logres where the Guardians of these isles keep their eternal vigil against the dark. The light is so bright that it shines like a beacon over the Tor and illumines the landscape below. And as you look down on the countryside, a glowing zodiac of starry figures slowly emerges out of the fields and meadows all around as if drawn in white fire across the land. . . a mirror of the constellations above.

The Sword of Light also gently touches your upturned brow. At first it feels like you have been brushed by an eagle feather. . . . A strong current of stellar energy spirals down through your spine . . . and you are filled with an inner radiance. . . . Breathe this luminescence into every pore of your being . . . and open yourself to the divine light of wisdom, which floods your body in wave after wave of bliss. . . .

Raise your eyes to the Great One, the Cosmic Star Father, in the heavens above. Eternities pass as you gaze into those eyes—oceans of unutterable depths radiating eternal truths. Every one of the cells of your body is filled to the brim with the heavenly light, and your entire being is suffused with the inner knowledge about many things in life and death that have previously been concealed. . . . And this engenders within you a deep and abiding sense of inner peace for now you understand that despite appearances in the worlds below. All is well. . . .

After a while, the light begins to fade, although the experience is indelibly emblazoned within your deepest Self. You are standing alone on the dark and windy hill. A soft light appears out of the night, and you catch a brief glimpse of the cowled figure who, with his lantern held high, leads you wordlessly to the head of the spiral maze that glimmers faintly below you. He stays with you until you have reached the Living Rock, then you slip through the invisible gateway and retrace your steps across the field, returning to the soft green vale where you can hear the bubbling waters of the red and white springs. When you reach level ground you find yourself back in your body, in your room, in present time with full remembrance of all that took place here. When you are ready, open your eyes and come back to present time and space.

9

The Strange Story of the Blue Bowl

Throughout the ages many have claimed the discovery of a physical Grail. Theories of the whereabouts of this elusive treasure arise equally from medieval legends, modern fads, scholarly research, and sensational hype. The *sacro catino,* "holy basin," a hexagonal green bowl in the cathedral of Genoa was one contender, until it was found to be made of glass instead of emerald, as originally supposed. Another was an agate bowl known as the Holy Chalice of Valencia, which came from Palestine or Egypt and was dated as contemporary with the Last Supper. There is also the exquisitely decorated sixth-century Antioch Chalice, recently identified as either a Eucharistic chalice or lamp bowl. Some claim the Grail has never been found: that it was the legendary treasure concealed by the Cathars in the castle of Montségur in southern France during the Inquisition, or else hidden away by the Knights Templar in Rosslyn Chapel, Edinburgh.

A GLASTONBURY GRAIL

As might be expected, a fair number of physical Grails have been linked with Glastonbury. Rumors abound that Joseph of Arimathea hid the cup of Christ somewhere on Chalice Hill or even in the Chalice Well itself. A fascinating legend clings to the Nanteos Cup, a small wooden

202

bowl discovered in the ruins of a house in the grounds of Strata Florida Abbey in mid-Wales. The legend tells how seven monks fled from Glastonbury on the eve of Henry VIII's destruction of the abbey, carrying with them Joseph's cup, their most precious treasure. It was supposedly kept at Strata Florida until its downfall, whereupon it passed into the hands of the Powell family in nearby Nanteos House. Many people in the following centuries claimed to have been cured of disease through drinking from the cup, which was considered the "true Grail."[1] Another contender is not a vessel at all but a portable altar table called the Great Sapphire. It was said to have been brought to Glastonbury Abbey by Saint David, the patron saint of Wales, in the sixth century, after he had received it as a gift while on pilgrimage in Jerusalem. Henri de Blois, abbot of Glastonbury in the twelfth century, had it set with gold and silver, and a case has been made for it being synonymous with the Grail stone in *Parzival*.[2]

In the early years of the twentieth century yet another Grail discovery took place in Glastonbury, coinciding with the newly awakened interest in the divine feminine among spiritually oriented Westerners. As we have seen, the Holy Grail is not a physical object, but an archetype imbued with so much numinous power that a genuine claim to have found it usually signifies a major psychic shift within the collective mind.

The strange story of the Glastonbury Cup, or Blue Bowl, as it was variously called, unfolded through a series of events involving a group of young spiritual seekers led by Wellesley Tudor Pole, a mystically inclined young man who later became the founder of the Chalice Well Trust. Tudor Pole lived in the nearby city of Bristol and first came to Glastonbury in 1902; he was drawn to the place after a curious and vivid dream in which he experienced himself as a monk of Glastonbury Abbey. He set forth on regular pilgrimages to Glastonbury, often timing them deliberately around the feast-day of the Celtic goddess and saint, Brighid, Bridget, or Bride, in early February. Dedicating himself to searching for the Holy Grail, he explored every inch of the area from the Tor to the Abbey, and was startled to find that he recognized all these places as if he had lived here long before. His favorite place was the Chalice Well, which was then located in the grounds of a Roman Catholic school. Here Tudor Pole first drank the waters of the Red Spring and roamed about on Chalice Hill. He experienced "a feeling of sanctity and inspiration which never left me,"[3] and had a premonition of his destiny twenty-five years later when he would become its owner and spiritual guardian. As well as feeling that Glastonbury was his true spiritual home, he also became convinced that something momentous would shortly take place here: perhaps a holy relic would be found, or else a great spiritual teacher would come forth with fresh revelations that would revitalize the Christian faith.

Wellesley Tudor Pole as a young man.
Photo courtesy of Patrick Benham.

He also felt a strong impulse to gather together three "maidens" to accompany him on his pilgrimages along a certain route that passed through all of Glastonbury's sacred shrines, believing there would be an important role for them to play in the spiritual work to come. These turned out to be Tudor Pole's sister, Katharine, known as Kitty, and two friends, sisters Janet and Christine Allen. When the Allen sisters first walked the pilgrim path in 1905, Christine knelt down to pray at Bride's Well, a holy well in the area of Glastonbury known as Beckery, a long low mound that was probably once an island. Here she saw a vision of a beautifully colored, saucer-shaped vessel being gradually raised out of the water by a woman's hand. Crystal clear water was offered to each to drink from, before it was returned to the well. Tudor Pole believed that this was a real sign that some precious relic was hidden in one of Glastonbury's wells and went searching in each of them, but to no avail. Then finally, while at work one day in his Bristol office, he had a vision of a luminous object buried within Bride's Well. Without telling them of his vision, Tudor Pole urged the Allen sisters to go to the well and see what they could find. This was no easy task in a muddy field, especially when togged out in long Edwardian skirts and coats! But miraculously, after wading through the swampy waters, the girls discovered a beautiful shallow bowl of sparkling blue glass, shot through with silver patterns. They were so in awe of its beauty and the aura of sanctity surrounding it that they washed it reverentially in the nearby Brue stream and put it back into the well.

THE DOCTOR'S DISCOVERY

A few days later, Tudor Pole received a letter from a Dr. John Goodchild, an occasional acquaintance, who was living in the nearby city of Bath. In the letter a picture was enclosed of what Goodchild called "the Cup Sign," which he had seen the day the Allen sisters found the cup. Goodchild asked for the sign to be given to the "pilgrims who had just been to Glastonbury."[4] Feeling sure this must have something to do with their adventure, Janet and Christine went to Bath and told the doctor of their find, which visibly surprised and moved him greatly. He told them he had good reason to believe that the cup was once "carried by the Master Jesus," but gave no further explanation until Tudor Pole went to see him, along with Kitty. Then he revealed the whole story.

Goodchild was a medical doctor with a thriving practice of wealthy clients in the South of France. In 1885, he was in Bordighera on the Italian Riviera when he came across the cup along with a glass platter in a tailor's shop. The tailor told him the artifacts had been found within a wall that had bordered a monastery. Goodchild took them back to England and gave them to his father, who kept them until he died. Several years later, while living in Paris, the doctor had a vision of an inner being of a high spiritual nature who appeared as a rose-colored light that sparkled with gold. The being told him that, since the Grail had once more emerged as the subject of much interest in recent years, inner agencies had decided to let it be discovered in order for certain facts about the life of Jesus to be revealed. He was also told that the cup had been carried by Jesus and "was to be a powerful influence in shaping the thought of the coming century."[5]

Goodchild was also told to take the cup to Bride's Hill, also known as "the Women's Quarter," in Glastonbury, and that a woman must be its guardian. The dream ended with the words: "Later a young girl will make a pure offering of herself at the spot where you laid down the 'Cup' and this shall be a sign to you."[6]

Goodchild spent three weeks in Glastonbury before he finally felt sure he knew where he should hide the cup. A disembodied voice awakened him from sleep and guided him to Bride's Well at Beckery. Here he placed the cup under a stone. At the time, local people were still visiting the site of the well, which had degenerated into a muddy pool. They hung ribbons and prayers written on scraps of paper from an overhanging hawthorn tree, as is the old custom when asking the spirit of a holy well for help and guidance. Pins and coins were thrown into the water as votive offerings, just as the early Celts threw precious objects into wells and lakes centuries ago. In truth, the well and tree, like so many still to be found throughout Britain and Ireland, was nothing less than the outward expression of the Well of Wisdom and Tree of Life at the heart of the Otherworld as described earlier in this book. Whether they knew it consciously or not, these latter-day pilgrims were honoring a sacred center from which deep spiritual waters flowed. And in placing his precious cup in its waters, Dr. Goodchild was performing an act of the greatest ritual significance.

Eight years passed before it was rediscovered by the Allen sisters, by which time Dr. Goodchild had given up all hope that it would be found—especially as the well had been cleared out in the meantime, and even he could no longer find it himself. During this period Goodchild became acquainted with Tudor Pole, but he swore he never mentioned the cup to him in any of their conversations. The only person to whom he told his secret was his friend, Scottish writer and visionary, William Sharp.

Sharp was the author of several highly successful books published under the name of Fiona Macleod. This was no ordinary pseudonym, for Sharp felt himself literally possessed by this female spirit, or *daimon*, who inspired him to write mystical stories and poems on Celtic or Otherworldly themes. Goodchild invited Sharp to Glastonbury on August 1, 1904. Was it just coincidence that this day marks one of the old cross-quarter day festivals known as Lughnasadh in Ireland, and Lùnasdal in Scotland, one of the four gateways between the worlds in the sacred Celtic year? The two walked to Beckery, which Sharp called the "salmon" of Saint Bride, a reference to the long shape of the mound, and also a symbolic link with the Fisher King and the Grail legend. (It is a short distance from here to Fisher's Hill and Wearyall Hill, where Joseph of Arimathea was said to have first arrived.) When they came to the old well, they found a "token" with Kitty Tudor Pole's name upon it. Strangely, Goodchild did not at the time connect this find with the sign he was told to watch out for: the young girl making a "pure offering" of herself. The token was returned with due thanks, probably via Wellesley Tudor Pole.

Unbeknownst to his friend, Goodchild set up a test for Sharp in order to sound out his psychic powers: he should either utter or write the word, "joy." Later that day, while taking a rest in the grounds of Glastonbury Abbey, Sharp fell into a reverie in which three lines of a poem came to him unbidden:

> From the silence of time, time's silence borrow.
> In the heart of today is the word of tomorrow.
> The builders of joy are the children of sorrow.[7]

This enigmatic triad carries the feeling of the sky in a hushed dawn, trembling on the verge of daylight. It must have been extraordinarily evocative to both men at the beginning of a new century, with their hopes for a renewed spiritual impulse freed from the chains of the past. Tudor Pole, perhaps influenced by this prophetic verse, later wrote of the paramount symbol for the longed-for New Age as a "cup of joy."

ICON OF A NEW DAWN

After Goodchild told his story, Kitty went down to Bride's Well and, despite it being a chill, rainy October day, she pulled off her shoes and waded through the mud until her foot touched the cup. She raised it out of its humble hiding-place for the last time and brought it to the Tudor Poles' home in Clifton, Bristol, where they created a special oratory for it, hung with white drapes. Here she and the Allen sisters held communion services at which they offered the cup filled with consecrated wine. The three young women firmly believed that they were the new guardians of the most sought-after holy vessel the West had ever known. In Janet Allen's words:

> It was with a deep feeling of reverence and awed feeling of responsibility that I realized the Vessel we had brought to light was the Holy Graal. I wondered many times why such an event should have come into my life, feeling a keen sense of unworthiness to be called as one of the custodians of this Sacred Relic.[8]

It was not long before a host of visitors, many from foreign lands, made pilgrimages to the sisters' home to meditate upon the cup or receive a healing from it. Some reported seeing a luminous beam of light, which seemed to emanate from the center of the cup and surround it like a halo. Another saw a dove hovering over it, and another, tongues of white flames. Many described a radiant beam of white light which coalesced into the form of a veiled woman who raised the cup in outstretched hands and poured forth a blessing on all those present.[9]

Many were convinced that the Holy Grail had been found, and the news even hit the headlines of a national newspaper. When the cup was first examined by an expert, there was great excitement as it was pronounced as old as the time of Christ, but when a later analysis led to the announcement that it could have been made as recently as the nineteenth century, public enthusiasm for the whole affair soon died down. Since then numerous experts have tried to determine its date and place of origin, but no definite conclusions have ever been drawn. On the other hand, all the clairvoyants who saw the cup declared it to be of ancient and sacred origins. Tudor Pole never let go of the possibility that it could very well have been the cup of Christ. It remained of central importance throughout his life, both in its physical presence and also as a symbol of an imminent New Age, which he felt was not far away. In his book, *The Silent Road,* he declares:

> I believe that the Cup or Chalice is destined to become the symbol for the new age now dawning, and it is my hope that Chalice Well may once more fulfill the inspiring mission of acting as a gateway through which revelation for coming times may flow, radiating from there across Britain and the world.[10]

Although it looks more like a shallow bowl, Tudor Pole believed it could once have had a stem like a goblet or chalice, and referred to it as "the Cup," or else "the sapphire blue bowl." He also called it "the Cup of Peace," "the Cup of Avalon," or "the Jesus Cup" and spent many years searching for evidence of its antiquity in Constantinople, where a psychic had told him that scripts proving the cup's ancient origins were hidden. He felt strongly that the cup possessed a life and individuality of its own, and that an invisible guardian was attached to it. He saw himself as a "watcher" or mediator of this guardian, who would help carry through its communications to the physical plane. However, to his disappointment, the physical evidence he sought never materialized.

On founding the Chalice Well Trust in 1959, the cup was kept at his home in the gardens surrounding the well, which is now a retreat center for Glastonbury pilgrims. Today, it is occasionally brought out for meditations into the sanctuary at the top of the house, which Tudor Pole designated "the Upper Room" after the place where Christ and his disciples gathered for the Last Supper. Since his death in 1968, the Glastonbury Cup, or Blue Bowl, as it is more often called nowadays, is in the care of the Chalice Well trustees who ensure it remains in the keeping of a woman, as instructed by Goodchild's supernatural visitor. It has become a latter-day Grail that emanates an aura of peace and healing to many who come into contact with it.

BRIDE OF BECKERY

The Glastonbury Cup is a potent symbol of the rise of feminine spirituality after thousands of years of one-sided masculine dominance. This cultural sea-change began when spiritually oriented Victorians—noticeably in England and Northern Europe, the Protestant countries—became aware of a growing need within the collective psyche for the feminine aspect of the divine. They felt more than ready for her return to a world that had been in a sorry state of imbalance for centuries in terms of religion and culture, particularly in the last two hundred years of arid scientific materialism and soulless industrial development.

Dr. John Goodchild was one of those who staunchly believed that the sacred feminine should be restored to Western religion and culture. He expressed his beliefs in a book, *The Light of the West,* published in 1898, in which he set out to show that the Celtic peoples were originally matrifocal and that ancient Ireland was the center of a religion that venerated a Great Goddess. The leader of this cult was the Mor Rigan,* or Great Queen, whom Goodchild viewed as a historical person rather than a mythological figure, as she is usually portrayed.[11] He believed all the wisdom teachings of the druids and bards stemmed from this goddess, and that her cult later became attached to the figure of Bride. Bride became the personification of the Gaelic "folk-soul," one who integrated ancient pagan ways with the new religion of Christianity.[12] Let us take a look at this ancient aspect of the divine feminine who is so intimately associated with the Glastonbury Cup.

Bride is a name for Brigit, Brighid, or Brigid, who was originally a Celtic goddess. Her name comes from the Sanskrit, meaning, "the Exalted One," from the root *brig:* "flame, force, and vigor." She was associated with the life-giving qualities of both the sun and the Earth. She ruled over everything that fostered human life and happiness: crops in the field, dairy animals, brewing and weaving, the shelter of the home, and the warmth of the hearth-fire. Her festival is in early February when the days begin to grow longer after winter and the sun brings back life to the Earth.

Brigit was said to have "two sisters" of the same name, which points to her originally being a triple goddess. The first was the patron of smithcraft: transforming ore into valuable weapons and beautiful artifacts was very important to the Celts and regarded as a magical craft. The second was the muse of poetry and prophecy, the mantic arts of the druids. Brigit's third function was healing; she was said to have made the first cloth in Ireland, into which she wove healing threads.

In the Christian era, the universal adoration given to Brigit was transferred to a holy woman of the fifth century, who today is known as Saint Bridget or Bride. This flesh and blood woman may have originally been named after the goddess, since it seems likely that her family belonged to the tribe of the Brigantes, whose tutelary deity was Brigit. Pagan elements weave through many of the stories of her life. She is described as the daughter of a druid who founded a religious community

---

*This was Goodchild's spelling for "Mórrígan."

in Kildare ("the Church of the Oak") under a sacred oak tree, which was quite likely the site of an earlier pre-Christian shrine. Here a perennial sacred flame burned in a fire sanctuary, tended only by women, recalling the Vestal Virgins of Rome.* Devotion to the goddess-saint continued undiminished throughout the centuries, and as late as the nineteenth century in Scotland and Ireland, Saint Bride was called "the Mary of the Gael," or "Foster Mother of Christ," for in many ways she was still regarded as the Great Mother of her people. Many holy wells were dedicated to her, some of which became known as "Brideswells." Pilgrims have visited these wells for centuries and many are still sought by those in search of healing and blessings. It was within one such well Dr. Goodchild hid the Glastonbury Cup.

Saint Bride was said to have come to Glastonbury in 488 CE and settled on the small low-lying island of Beckery. Some scholars consider the name to come from the Irish *bec Eriu,* meaning "Little Ireland," while others believe it comes from *beocere* and *ieg,* meaning "bee-keepers island."[13] The latter is not unlikely since Bride is linked with bees in Irish tradition, especially under the name of Saint Gobnait, which means "honey-bee." Gobnait's feast-day is on the same day as Bride's in early February (allowing for calendar changes). Like Brigit, Gobnait also has "two sisters"; she is associated with fire, was head of a women's religious community, and kept bees. At her church in Ballyvourney, County Cork, is a statue of her standing on a beehive.

Medieval chronicles describe Saint Bride's chapel as built on the site of a previous oratory dedicated to another famous holy woman: Saint Mary Magdalene. We are told that Bride founded "a monastery of holy virgins," which became known as "the women's quarter." It is tempting to speculate that this may have continued the tradition of a pre-Christian community of priestesses in Glastonbury. Excavations on the site have uncovered the remains of earlier structures, but so far, nothing older than the tenth century has come to light.

The chapel was under the protection of Glastonbury Abbey and

---

*In the 1990s, Brigit's sacred flame was relit in Kildare by two sisters of the Brigidine order. See www.solasbhride.ie/.

The Celtic Cross at Beckery.

was "sumptuously restored" in the thirteenth century. Since it was located close to one of the main causeways into Glastonbury in medieval times,* pilgrims on their way to Glastonbury spent the night in vigil at the chapel before processing onward to the abbey. If they were in need of healing, they would have crawled through a round healing hole in its southern wall. On display at the chapel were various items including a wallet, necklace or rosary, and weaving tools, said to have been left behind by Bridget when she returned to Ireland shortly before her death. The chapel fell into ruin after the Reformation, but the area still retained the name Brideshay, and the fields around there are called "Brides" on old maps. The ruins of Bride's chapel were still visible in the late eighteenth century, but since then the place has been sadly despoiled by industrial development. The holy well dedicated to Bride, once a popular destination for pilgrims in search of healing, has also disappeared; it is marked only by a stone carved with Celtic knotwork, which has been moved several yards from its original location.

Although nothing remains at Beckery but a low grassy knoll, now known as Bride's Mound, Brigit herself is not too far away. High up on the inside of the ruined tower on Glastonbury Tor is a stone carving that depicts her milking her totem cow. Another, much fainter, one

---

*This is Pomparles Bridge over the River Brue, which was the "Pont Perilous" of Arthurian legend.

can be made out on the arched doorway leading into the Lady Chapel in Glastonbury Abbey. This image has its roots in the most ancient traditions concerning Brigit as a Great Mother who provided her people with milk. In Scotland she was called "Milkmaid Bride," and was said to have suckled the Christ child from her own breast. She is often described as accompanied by a white cow that is sometimes said to have red ears, showing its origins in the Otherworld. In fact, Brigit's connection with the cow most likely has its origins in the Indo-European cow goddesses of antiquity.

THE LIGHT OF THE WEST

Since one of Bride's cult centers was Glastonbury, this confirmed Goodchild's theory that the deepest roots of Western spiritual life were in the West rather than in the East, a concept that was in part a reaction to the recent fashion for all things Eastern cherished by the Theosophists and their offshoots. In *The Light of the West,* Goodchild explains why the sacred feminine is so crucial to the world: "The Light of the West is the beauty of womanhood. It inculcates the hatred of warfare, and of empires established by the greed of nations or rulers. It preaches woman's desire for the empire of love."[14]

William Sharp was another believer in the redemptive power of the Goddess. Coming from Scotland, where Bride was still loved and revered by many of the country people (especially in the Roman Catholic communities of the Highlands and Islands), it was natural enough that he should regard her as the supreme embodiment of the divine feminine. He was well aware of Bride's ancient lineage which predates the saint of popular Scottish tradition. In his view, her legend:

> . . . goes further back than the days of the monkish chroniclers who first attempted to put the guise of verbal Christian raiment on the most widely-loved and revered beings of the ancient Celtic pantheon. Long before . . . ever the first bell of Christ was heard by startled Druids . . . the Gaels worshipped a Brighde or Bride, god-

dess of women, of fire, of poetry. . . . one whom the Druids held in honor as a torch bearer of the eternal light. . . .[15]

Writing as Fiona Macleod in his book, *The Winged Destiny,* he described this longed-for event as likely to happen on the Scottish island of Iona, with which Glastonbury is said to have strong psychic and spiritual links:*

> I believe that though the Reign of Peace may be yet a long way off, it is drawing near; and that Who shall save us anew shall come divinely as a Woman—but whether through mortal birth, or as an immortal breathing upon our souls, none can yet know. Sometimes I dream of the old prophecy that Christ shall come again upon Iona; and of that later prophecy which foretells, now as the Bride of Christ, now as the Daughter of God, now as the Divine Spirit embodied through mortal birth—the coming of a new Presence and Power; and dream that this may be upon Iona, so that the little Gaelic island may become as the little Syrian Bethlehem. But more wise is it to dream, not of hallowed ground, but of the hallowed gardens of the soul, wherein She shall appear white and radiant. Or that, upon the hills, where we are wandered, the Shepherdess shall call us home.[16]

The pun on Bride's name, which suggests she is the Bride of Christ, occurs frequently in Fiona Macleod's work. She is also called the "Shepherdess of the Flocks" the complement of Christ the Good Shepherd. In the same book Macleod also penned one of the most powerful invocations of Brighid:

> I am older than Brigit of the Mantle, I put songs and music on the wind before ever the bells of the chapels were rung in the West or heard in the East. I am Brighid-nam-Bratta, but I am also

---

*Wellesley Tudor Pole and others believed in a sacred triangle of three holy places: Glastonbury, Iona, and Devenish Island in Ireland.

Brighid-Muirghin-na-tuinne, and Brighid-sluagh, Brighid-nan-sitheach seang, Brighid-Binne-Bheule-lhuchd-nan-trusganan-uaine, and I am older than Aone, and as old as Luan. And in Tir-na-h'oige my name is Suibhal-bheann, and in Tir-fo-thuinn, it is Cú-gorm; and in Tir-na-h'oise it is Sireadh-thall. And I have been a breath in your heart, and the day has its feet to it that will see me coming into the hearts of men and women like a flame upon dry grass, like a flame of wind in a great wood.[17]

This extraordinary incantation of Brighid's names reveals how deeply Macleod was able to penetrate into the essence of this goddess and saint, tracing her origins to a time long before Christian era. *Brighid-nam-Bratta* means "Brighid of the Mantle," a traditional reference to her cloak, which is sometimes described as golden, sometimes as green. As can be seen in the folk-tales, the golden mantle refers to her identity as goddess of the sun and fire, bringing warmth and life to all; while the green mantle identifies her as the Earth Goddess who created the fertile, grassy meadows and hills. *Brighid-Muirghin-na-tuinne,* "Conception of the Waves," *Brighid-sluagh,* "Brighid of the Faery Host," and *Brighid-Binne-Bheule-lhuchd-nan-trusganan-uaine,* "Brighid the Melodious Mouthed of the Tribe of the Green Mantles" all point to her origins in the faery world, lore which Sharp claimed he got from his old Highland nurse. Writing as Macleod, he goes on to recite a further litany of evocative names from the Scottish Otherworld, known as *Tir-na-h'oige,* "Land of Youth," *Tir-fo-thuinn,* "Country of the Waves," and *Tir-na-h'oise,* "Country of Ancient Years." Here Brighid is known as *Suibhal-bheann,* "Mountain Traveler," *Cú-gorm,* "Grey hound," and *Sireadh-thall,* "Seek beyond," this last being an invitation to seek her beyond the material world. This is the ever-changing face of the Great Goddess that William Sharp, John Goodchild, and the rest of those hopeful seekers saw as setting the West on fire with her beauty, love, and wisdom.

This theme was taken up by others, who despite—or perhaps, because of—the horrific and senseless orgy of destruction that was the First World War did not give up hope that One would come who embodied these supernal qualities. Among these was the anthroposophist, Eleanor Merry, who wrote an inspirational book, *The Flaming Door,* on "the Celtic folk-soul," in which she calls Bride the "soul of the ancient Mysteries" and "the Virgin-Sophia, the Virgin of Light whom the Bards once met among the stars." [18] She goes on to say:

This Woman, who is "older than Bride" and "clothed with the Sun," is the Virgin Wisdom of the world, who gives birth to all men. She has reigned in every religion in every age. She has been called Demeter, Isis, Ceridwen, Herta, Kwan Yin, Kwannon, Sophia, Bride. . . . Dante calls her the "daughter of God." From her hand man is able to receive, even today, a healing gift for every ill that exists, if he knows how to seek with spiritual insight, in the kingdoms of the plants and the minerals—and in his own soul. [19]

Quoting Fiona Macleod's passage above, Merry concludes:

The Celtic folk-soul is no longer the soul of a *people,* but the soul of the spiritual awakening of mankind. The blue mantle of Bride is his banner shaken out over the expectant heavens. "King Arthur" will not be roused by the blast of the horn of any national egotism, though it may shake the Earth; he will awaken only at the touch of the Woman of Beauty who will "come into the hearts of men and women like a flame upon dry grass, like a flame of wind in a great wood." [20]

The Allen sisters experienced a foreshadowing of the return of the Goddess when they first made a pilgrimage to Glastonbury in 1905. After visiting Bride's Well, they walked beyond the Tor to the evocatively named Maiden Croft Lane, where Christine heard the voice of the Virgin Mother herself, saying, "I, the Mother of Life, am now with you. Here you learn the Divine Lesson of the Creation. Here is created in you, all Divine Things. Here the Mother Soul seeks to find expression."[21]

These words suggest that the divine feminine herself was actively seeking expression through the cup. Perhaps this powerful archetypal force engineered the whole sequence of events that followed, using sensitively attuned human protagonists as her vehicles. For the story of its discovery is nothing less than a modern Grail legend, with every event imbued with deep ritual significance. It was inevitable that the young women who retrieved the cup were three in number, like so many faery women in Celtic and Arthurian story. Many years later, Dion Fortune was to write in *Avalon of the Heart* an imaginative version of the Grail legend in which it was guarded by three maidens:

> . . . the dusk of the Dark Ages drew on, and men were too wicked to be entrusted with the sacred relic, so the Fisher king took it to keep in his treasury, an underground chamber in the heart of Chalice Hill. . . . There the Cup was guarded by three pure maidens, who watched it day and night. . . . Whosoever drank of it never thirsted again, for it was to him a wellspring of the Waters of Life within his soul.[22]

In the last chapter of the book, "The Vision of Avalon," the three maidens appear again in the great procession of characters from history and legend that forever moves through the valleys of Avalon. They are "robed in white, and amid them a glory that is not of any Earthly fire"—the glory of the Grail.[23] Dion Fortune's vision may have been influenced as much by the magical work of the Tudor Poles and the Allen sisters in the early years of the twentieth century as by the medieval Grail myths, for each springs from the same source of mystical power, which lies outside of time.

The girls actually took on the archetypal role of Grail Maidens in their Oratory in Clifton. One of the most startling features of the medieval Grail legends is that the bearer of the Grail is a young woman, yet the participation of women in religious ceremony was strictly forbidden by the Roman Catholic church. This prohibition was still in force when Kitty Tudor Pole and the Allen sisters presided over the cup as celebrants and priestesses. Excerpts from the service-book make it clear these were no orthodox services, but showed contemporary influences, notably from the work of Fiona Macleod and the rituals of the Hermetic Order of the Golden Dawn:

To the Bride:
O Thou Most Holy Virgin Bride, we greet thee.
Thou who comest robed in the Greater Glory of the Holy Spirit
Bride of Supreme Wisdom, Beauty and Truth.
Come on Wings of Deliverance, bearing the shield of a Dove.
Whisper to the saddened heart of My Humanity that Redemption draweth nigh.
Come O Bride, My Servant to Wait
Come O Bride, My Servant to Wait
Come O Bride, My Servant to Wait
Come in the Light of the Shining Moon,
Come in the Dawning of the Day,
Hear our cry, O Bride. Most Glorious Virgin of Supreme Loveliness
Be gracious unto thy servants.[24]

As Patrick Benham, author of *The Avalonians,* the excellent book that chronicles these events, concludes: "Plainly they felt they had inaugurated the Church of the New Age, a church in which woman was in the ascendant and Bride, the Celtic embodiment of the Universal Feminine, was restored and harmonized with a mystical understanding of the tenets of the Christian faith."[25]

THE CHALICE AND THE CROSS

More than forty years after these events took place, in the summer of 1954, Wellesley Tudor Pole was staying near Carbis Bay, St. Ives, North Cornwall, when he received an intensely vivid vision that he was to count among the most memorable experiences of his life. Over the bay appeared the figure of Saint Michael, flanked by a great semicircle of angels and backed by a radiant light. The vision unfolded even more remarkably:

> In the foreground but beyond the confines of the Bay, an immense Cross was apparent reaching toward the sky and implanted in the sea. A Chalice rested on its crossbar, the base of the Cross acting as its pedestal. A gold and jeweled Crown could be faintly seen above the Chalice.
>
> An aura of intense and dazzling light surrounded the head of the Archangel and his arms were held out horizontally with his hands joined together palm to palm and resting just above the apex of the Cross. It was possible to see a flow of what appeared to be clear liquid fire, passing through St. Michael and from his hands down into the Cross, filling to overflowing the cup or chalice that rested on its crossbeam. As this stream of illumination permeated the Cross itself, the opaque outlines of the Cross became transparent so that one could see the figure of the Archangel through it.
>
> The Chalice gradually became more vital and imposing as the Cross upon which it rested disappeared from view. When this happened, the Archangelic hosts began to sing in celestial harmony and triumph, as if in celebration of a mighty victory.[26]

Tudor Pole's vision operates on three levels, with the Cross acting as the axis mundi between the Above and Below, Fire and Water. The Chalice is positioned in the Middle World, suggestive of the unifying nature of this symbol. The Crown represents the glory and supremacy of the One Supernal Light.

The Cross is a symbol of duality, of the descent of spirit into matter, and the inevitable separation and conflicts that ensue within the world of opposites. But in this vision Earth becomes illumined, shot through with a radiant light, as the true nature of matter is revealed as spirit, and all suffering is redeemed. As the Cross disappears into the light, the Chalice emerges as the primary symbol for our times. The Cross of suffering and discord is replaced by the Chalice of joy and unity. To Tudor Pole, the progress of the Chalice to the foreground of the emerging spiritual stage prefigured nothing less than the restoration of the divine feminine to the world. He explains, "The Chalice is the symbol of the uprising from the duality of the cross to the unity on which all God's creation is based, the ultimate goal of human endeavor . . . the veritable Holy Grail and the central symbol for the coming age."[27]

For all their welcoming of the return of the feminine, the Avalonians never made the mistake of promoting a one-sided spirituality. They were well aware that the key to wisdom both within the individual and within society lies in the dynamic balance of both feminine and masculine. William Sharp, writing as Fiona Macleod, made it clear that he was fully conscious of the need to apportion equal worth to masculine and feminine, for this reflects the nature of the universe itself, including, of course, the human soul. Sharp's own struggle to integrate the masculine and feminine forces within his own psyche gives his words a certain poignancy as he declares, "There is the divine, eternal feminine counterpart to the divine eternal male, and both are needed to explain the mystery of the dual spirit within us—the mystery of the Two in One."[28]

And John Goodchild himself had an interesting psychic experience in the summer of 1906, which brings this theme into sharp focus. He saw a vision of a sword suspended in the eastern sky, and made a sketch of it with the caption: "the Sign of the East." This was followed the next day by a vision of a cup in the Western sky, with five balls of light hovering over it. He also drew this, giving it the title of "The Sign of the West." The sword appeared on Sunday (the sun's day) while the cup appeared on Monday (the moon's Day).[29] This was the sign he sent to Tudor Pole, which led the girls back to Bride's Well. Once more the alchemical Solar-Lunar mysteries of the Chalice and the Sword appeared, and this time on the threshold of the modern age, pointing the way to the sacred marriage that will bring about the healing of the world.

VisionJourney IX
Brighid's Flame

Sit in a comfortable position, relax and quiet your mind. . . . Take some deep breaths and imagine you are breathing in a beautiful, amber light. The light fills your body and swirls around you like a mist. . . .

When the mist lifts, you see a huge orange sun low down on the horizon, turning the sky a deep rose-pink. You find yourself standing in the thick grass of a low-lying green island in the lee of Wearyall Hill. This is Beckery, the Beekeepers Island, sacred to Bride, Queen Bee of the Isle of Honey— the first name ever given to this land. You see several round beehives of coiled straw where the bees are flying purposefully in and out as they gather and store the nectar from the many flowers that blossom in this place: foxgloves, clover, buttercups, wild roses, and honeysuckle. . . .

On the summit is a mound surrounded by a grove of ancient trees. They stand with a knowing, quiet presence as if they are fully aware that they are guardians of this place. As you approach the grove you see two gnarled old oaks on the edge, standing with a space in between them as if to form a gateway. As you enter the archway of the trees, the light becomes dim and dusky purple, and all around you are the shadowy shapes of other trees: hollies, alders, and hazels. In the center of the grove is a clearing, pierced by a few amber shafts of light from the evening sun. . . .

In the middle of the circle of trees is a stone carved with twisting Celtic knotwork into an equal-armed cross. On it burns an ashless flame of bright yellow tinged with violet. Standing over the flame is a woman, Bride of Beckery. She is dressed in white, and around her shoulders is a mantle of forest green. Around her head is a glowing orb of golden light. Beside her is a pure white cow with a brilliant star glittering between the wide curve of its horns. . . .

As she turns to look at you, she smiles and in that moment you see that her mantle has become vast and endless, spreading out in every direction, for it has become the wide green earth and in it you can see every animal, bird and living creature that ever walked, crept or flew, and all the trees and plants that ever grew are flourishing here. . . .

You feel a great longing to be sheltered under her mantle too, and she wraps it about you so you feel encircled with her warmth and deeply protected by her loving arms. You remain in this peace for what seems a very long time, and then you feel drops of moisture falling upon you. Looking up, you see that the face of the goddess is deeply anguished with sorrow and she is weeping, as one after another, the animals and birds, the plants and trees beneath her mantle go out like flames extinguished one by one. Bride is weeping for the folly of her human children and the dreadful damage they have done in rending the fabric of her mantle by slaughtering so many of her beloved children, even to the point of extinction.

Her tears pour down the mound and become a small pool that will ever after be known as Bride's Well. But one of her tears falls upon the ashless flame on the carven stone, which is suddenly extinguished, and in that instant Bride is no longer there. In fact, all manifest creation has vanished and you are alone in the utter darkness of empty space. For what seems like an eternity, you float in the vast sea of infinite night, utterly alone and separate. . . .

Then a point of light pierces the darkness and begins to grow. The voice of the goddess speaks:

"I am the Flame that comes forth out of the darkness."

The flame grows in size and brilliance and now you can see that it is streaming out of Bride's heart. As the universe lights up in glory all about you, she scatters her fire on every living being to call them to awaken to the glory of her creation. It is the green fire that forges springtime out of winter's sleep and rouses the human race from the sleep of fear, and the nightmare of separation, violence, and despair. See now the world on fire with Bride's power of inspiration, healing, and renewal like a flame upon dry grass, like a flame of wind in a great wood. . . .

You are swept up in the wind of the firestorm and swirled through space like a leaf, with no choice but to surrender to this inexorable power. Then suddenly you are right-side up and standing once more in the quiet grove *of Beckery with nothing but the gentle rustling of leaves and the low hum of the bees. The ashless flame burns bright upon the stone and Bride is standing before you. . . .*

The goddess looks into your eyes with a piercing gaze and you know she can see all that you are or have ever been. She motions you to step into the flame, for this is a sacrificial fire that purifies the heart and mind of dross. You are deeply afraid, yet you know you must pass through the fire of purification for your soul's sake. As you step into the flame, Bride looks at you with ancient wise and loving eyes. Although the fierce pain may take your breath away, you remain steadfast of purpose. Then above the crackle of the flames, you hear a new sound—Bride is weeping because of your pain and all that you have ever suffered in your life or many lives, for she is the Mother of the World, and there is not one whose pain she does not feel as if it were the sorrow of her own child. The fire has become a roaring furnace of flame that now engulfs you. When you feel as if you can go on no longer, two hands firmly clasp your own and Bride leads you out of the flames to the other side. She carries you down to her spring and bathes you in its healing waters and you emerge feeling refreshed and made anew. . . .

You return to the grove and Bride invites you to take some of the flame before you depart. You place your cupped hands into the flame and now there is no pain. She tells you to place the flame in your heart, which you do, breathing it in deeply, so that the flame grows and glows within you with a clear lambent light. The goddess has awakened your soul flame, your true essence, and illuminated the core of your being. . . . You know you will never forget who you are again. Bride smiles and gently smooths some honey from her bees upon your lips so that you may always speak the truth. . . .

Now into your mind come images of people or other beings, or places that are especially in need of Bride's fire of healing and regeneration. Cupping your hands, you take some of the flame in your heart and send it to the ones in need as many times as it takes. . . .

Then Bride swirls her green mantle around you and you are engulfed in its whirling folds as if borne away by a green wind. Through this vortex, you can see the tiny image of your familiar room. It becomes bigger and bigger and then you come all the way back, in light and in peace.

You may wish to end this journey with an old Irish prayer to the goddess:

> Bride, spread your mantle about me,
> and keep your protection about me
> and all living beings on Earth.

10

The Grail of the Heart

In the center of the Castle of the Grail, our own body, there is a shrine, and within it is to be found the Grail of the heart. We should indeed seek to know and understand that inhabitant. It is the fragment of the divine contained within each one of us—like the sparks of unfallen creation. . . . This light shines within each one, and the true quest of the Grail consists in bringing that light to the surface, nourishing and feeding it until its radiance suffuses the world.[1]

"Temples of the Grail,"
At the Table of the Grail

We open this chapter with these words from John Matthews, writer and authority on the Grail Mysteries, to lead us to the great truth of the Grail: that for all the mythic images, romantic notions, religious ideas, and conspiracy theories that accrue to it, the Grail is ultimately to be found within the core of each human being. The "Grail of the Heart" is the human soul. We have referred to the soul many times in these chapters, but let's look at this word again in order to get a clear understanding of what it means to each of us. The soul originates in Spirit (Divinity, the Absolute, Godhead, Creator, Great Spirit, Tao, etc.), which is the primordial Ground of All Being. It is one and indivisible, but it casts forth "sparks" from the fire of its divine nature, so that other worlds and other beings can come into existence. The human soul is one of these sparks, knowing itself to be divine, yet also separate from the One.

Although timeless itself, the soul proceeds on a great journey into time and space. It descends into many cycles of incarnation through what has been called the Arc of Involution, or as Buddhists say, "the wheel of death and rebirth." As it becomes more and more identified with physical existence, the soul forgets its divine origins altogether. When it has travelled on this arc to the furthest point of separation, there comes a turning-point when it begins its long return journey along the Arc of Evolution, growing and evolving through many more incarnations until eventually it finds its way home again to the Source.

THE QUEST FOR THE SOUL

The soul is the true Self of each of us which has existed before birth and after death. Every lifetime is designed to maximize the soul's growth, evolution, and maturity. When we are born, the soul clothes itself in a body and personality. We come into a family and an environment designed to provide the most effective experiences for the soul to learn and evolve. When the soul has evolved to the point where it no longer needs to incarnate in a human body, it will return to the divine Source from which it came, only now fully conscious and Self-knowing. The task for each of us is to allow the soul to emerge from the narrow confines of the ego, the mind-body-personality system formed from a combination of genetic and cultural factors, its focus limited to the temporal world.

The soul, like the Grail, is hidden away in the dimly-lit, tangled forest of the ego, sometimes glimpsed only as a gleam of light in the far-off window of a castle. Like Perceval's initiatory adventures, the quest for the soul entails many of life's challenges and rites of passage, yet the discovery of the Grail, or soul, is only half the story. In alchemy, the stage of knowing one's true self to be the soul rather than the personality is known as the "Lesser Work." Philosopher Titus Burkhardt writes: "Whereas the "lesser work" has as its goal the regaining of the original purity and receptivity of the *soul,* the goal of the "greater work" is the illumination of the soul by the revelation of the Spirit within."[2] For the soul is a receptacle for Spirit—a chalice that must be filled from the highest spiritual influences if it is to be of any value.

In the Christianized Grail narratives, the shining figure of Christ is often portrayed within the Grail. This is an image of the radiant force of Spirit—sometimes called the Cosmic Christ—entering the soul. The supernal force is also pictured as a light descending into the vessel. The beam of light is a masculine symbol: the highest transmutation of the Sword as a pure ray of the spiritual Sun: the first Light that emanates from out of the Void as the creative energy that gives rise to all the worlds. This is the Light that pours down from above into the chalice of the soul, known to different traditions as the Vedic Soma, the Christian Holy Spirit, or the alchemical Heavenly Dew. The masculine Sword has become a ray of pure Light streaming out from the Source of All to enter the feminine lunar Chalice. When the Light descends into the Grail, the ultimate goal of the spiritual seeker has been achieved. It is the supreme union of Soul and Spirit: the Divine Marriage, the Union of Opposites, the *Conjunctio,* or Alchemical Wedding—the apotheosis of the Grail Quest.

THE HIGHER SELF

It will take most of us countless lifetimes to attain the union of Soul and Spirit, an achievement we usually associate with a few exceptional men and women like Theresa of Avila, Meister Eckhart, Ramana Maharshi, or the Buddha—those whom we call mystics or enlightened ones who have achieved a state of direct union with the Divine. Yet we do in fact have access to a high spiritual source through a Higher Self (sometimes called the Divine Self), which resides within each of us and with whom we can make a connection. In some esoteric circles the Higher Self is called the Holy Guardian Angel, and regarded as one of the angelic kingdom who resides outside of ourselves and who walks by our side as a guide and mentor from birth to death. Yet, as Dion Fortune writes, it is not a separate entity at all: "The Higher Self is a single, unified whole, which builds up around the Divine Spark, which is the nucleus of each human manifestation."[3]

This spiritual force emanates from the highest Source, yet is "stepped down" in frequency so that the human nervous system can handle the energy. For readers familiar with the Qabalistic Tree of Life, this is the equivalent of raising one's consciousness to the level of the sphere of Tifaret where the spiritual force can flow down from Keter and be grounded at Malkut on the Middle Pillar.

Once you have been able to sense a connection with your Higher Self you will find it is always present to be of help and guidance when called upon, especially if you are in crisis. You may experience it as male, female, neither, or both. It is a wise and loving mentor and guide, ever present to help each of us grow and evolve to our highest capacity in the current lifetime. The Higher Self is not as interested in what you are doing as much as who you are becoming, how much you are willing to open to the light of Spirit and let it shine through all that you do and are while you are here on Earth. It is the personal tutor of your soul, whose role is to gently instruct, encourage, and awaken you to compassion, wisdom, harmony, and inner peace. The Higher Self is the one that heightens our consciousness at those times when the world seems shot through with an otherworldly beauty and joy; or we feel inspired and ennobled, and can see beyond all doubt the perfect unfolding of the tapestry of our lives, and perhaps even catch a glimpse of the Weaver at work on the loom of the universe. The Higher Self is also present in times of difficulty, giving comfort and strength, and acting as a patient mentor as we slowly learn the painful lessons that enable the soul to grow. The Higher Self is, in fact, always there, waiting for us to open to the pure, unconditional love and healing it has to offer us on our earthly journey.

When we quiet the ego enough so that the soul opens, allowing the Light of Spirit to shine in via the Higher Self—we fill our inner

Grail with divine energies. The processes described in this chapter will give you a way to open these channels and begin to make contact with the divine being within you. After that, your progress is entirely dependent on how willing you are to make a commitment to your spiritual growth, which requires a great deal of one-pointed intention and disciplined practice. Even more important is the willingness to surrender our little self to the higher, despite the determined resistance of the ego!

SEEING WITH THE EYES OF THE SOUL

Wellesley Tudor Pole writes: "One great truth has become my constant companion. I sum it up thus: 'Empty yourself if you would be filled.' The Waters of Life can never flow through me until I have surrendered my whole self."[4]

Each of us is already connected with the soul within—after all, the soul is who we really are! The challenge is to consciously know this at more than the intellectual level: to be living our lives as much as we can from the perspective of the soul. There are as many different ways of doing this as there are spiritual paths, East and West, and such methods usually come under the heading of meditation. There are of course many different varieties of meditation, and one of the simplest and most effective methods is a practice called Inner Silence. It is a way of learning to see with the "eyes of the soul." Practicing the Inner Silence meditation allows the mind to process and release material that has been buried in the subconscious for a long time. The psyche becomes less encumbered and cluttered with unwanted patterns of thinking, negative programming, and old psychological issues. This is what Tudor Pole means by "emptying yourself" so that you can become a clear, still channel able to receive spiritual influence from a higher plane of being. It is a subtle form of meditation—simple, but not easy—but is an essential first step toward disengaging from the constant clamor of the egoic mind in order to identify with the serene and unperturbed field of the soul, and come to know that this is truly who you are.

Meditation
The Inner Silence

Sit in a comfortable position, take some deep breaths, and relax every part of your body.

Now, begin to watch the screen of your mind and observe all the thoughts as they go by. Thoughts include ideas, memories of the past, plans or worries concerning the future, daydreams, desires, likes and dislikes, emotions and feelings—in other words, everything that goes on in your mind.

You will find yourself becoming caught up in the endless parade of thinking and feeling, because this is how your mind functions. The mind automatically wants to follow the dramas as they play out on the inner movie screen. It will want to control the thoughts that make you feel uncomfortable, and indulge in the pleasant ones. Every time this happens, gently withdraw your attention back to watching the thoughts and feelings rather than identifying with them. Above all, just let your mind continue on with its processing; don't try to control what comes up, or suppress the thoughts in any way. Keep observing from a calm, detached position. The difference is between being swept away down a turbulent river as distinct from sitting on the riverbank in warm sunlight, enjoying watching the river, feeling calm and peaceful.

This meditation can be done with eyes closed, eyes open and eventually, in your everyday life. If you practice it on a daily basis for about twenty minutes per session, you will start to get a sense of yourself as the self-aware, peaceful soul, as distinct from the personality with its never-ending stream of thoughts and emotions. Instead of being whirled about like a leaf in the wind by life's dramas, many of your problems and fears will naturally melt away in the light of the soul's higher perspective. Eventually you will come to know without a doubt, from the inside, that your true identity resides within the soul.

When practiced regularly, you will be able to drop into the Inner Silence in preparation for the following exercises in just a few moments.

Exercise
Connecting with the Higher Self

Forging a relationship with your Higher Self will enable you to develop a sense of an indwelling spiritual presence wherever you are. If you are alone, you will feel centered, light, and peaceful. You may be aware of benevolent spiritual energies about you, so there is never any sense of loneliness. The following exercise will show you how to make a connection with your Higher Self on a daily basis, preferably in the morning, in order to set the tone for the day ahead.

Light a candle and sit in an upright position facing it.

Gaze at the flame and begin a slow, deep rhythmic breathing pattern.

Close your eyes. As the breath opens your chest area, focus on your heart and see a corresponding golden glow there.

With each breath you take, the golden glow gently grows brighter and expands, opening like the cup of a flower.

Mentally invoke the presence of your Higher Self. This does not have to be elaborate: You can simply say, for example, "Higher Self, are you there?" If you prefer, you can call this presence your Holy Guardian Angel. Use the same words every time. They will be your own unique "key-code" that opens the door to admit this Being.

Sense the presence of your Higher Self as a wise and loving Being, centered a few feet above the crown of your head.

Greet your Higher Self and ask for guidance for the day ahead. You may find it helpful to write down the response, which you may either hear as words with the inner ear, or receive through a sense of "knowing." Unless you have a specific question or issue to ask about, you may simply feel yourself imbued by feelings of inner peace, lightness, warmth, or a quiet joy, which you can take with you into your day.

Thank your Higher Self, visualize the golden vessel of Light within your heart shrinking to a small glow, and open your eyes.

Reconnect with your physical body and outer environment. As you

go about your day, remain subtly aware of this golden glow within
your heart.

BECOMING A GRAIL BEARER

The aim of all spiritual work is to open the soul like a chalice to be filled with divine energies and to offer it to the world in service. This is what it means to become a Grail-bearer. Wellesley Tudor Pole intended his vision of the Chalice replacing the Cross (see chapter 9) to be applied in a practical manner for world healing. In his own words:

> Each one can become a chalice into which is to be poured the Light of the Presence of God. When entering the Silence, hold up the chalice to be filled, and in faith, humility and thankfulness, know that the Light will find its own way to use you for the fulfillment of its destined purpose. . . . In Silence, stand aside, let the Light shine, and rejoice, for it is through silence and thankfulness that the Light of the Presence can bring freedom, understanding and peace to each one of us, and to the whole world.[5]

There are many different ways of becoming a Grail Bearer. You do not have to think of yourself as a "healer" in order to have a beneficial effect on the lives of those around you at home or at work. Simply by aligning yourself with your Higher Self on a daily basis, you will enable others to feel a blessing in your presence, as the Light of the Grail will raise the frequency of any energy field it enters into. If you feel called to become a Grail Bearer in a more direct way, the following practices will enable you to go deeper into its Mysteries and prepare you to carry out the Work of the Grail for yourself, your community and the wider circle of beings on our planet. Margaret Lumley Brown, Dion Fortune's successor in the Society of the Inner Light, explains, "This is the Age of the Aquarian Grail—the highest spiritual teaching of which this age is capable. It is the Age of the coming of the Cosmic

The Grail Mysteries are pictured in A. E. Waite's Tarot Cards. On the left is the image of the Ace of Cups, in which the dove, representing the Holy Spirit, descends from on high to place a communion wafer in the chalice, from which streams of spiritual waters flow. On the right is the image for Temperance, in which the Archangel of the Sun, Michael, pours the waters of spirit from above to below, representing the union of masculine and feminine. The waters form the zodiac sign of Aquarius, the coming astrological Great Age. Courtesy of Random House Archive & Library.

Christ, not to any special group or Church but to the individual Spirit of Man when he shall have attained to worthiness of it."[6]

The first process shows you a way to devote yourself to the Grail Mysteries through a rite of dedication. This involves creating an inner Temple of the Grail, an astral form you can build using strongly focused and charged visualizations and ritual (meditation in motion). The goal is to set the Grail as a symbol within your heart, the "seat of the soul," able to receive the living Light of Spirit. This is a way to connect with the Higher Self by bringing down the radiant Light of Spirit into the Grail of the soul. Glastonbury author Chris Trwoga writes: "In the same way that Wolfram's Gral is a fragment of Paradise . . . the Grail is a spark that comes from our innermost self, lighting the way back. When we see that light, we will know that you and I are One, that the Earth and the Sky are One, that the whole sphere of existence is our Spirit and Soul."[7]

Building the symbol of the Grail within your heart is no simplistic ritual, but an act of sacred magic which has reverberations throughout the worlds, inner and outer. Gareth Knight explains, "This is a subjective test of the validity of the candidate's suitability in Mystery tradition and a sign that he is accepted by inner teachers. . . . The building of this symbol aligns one with the whole Eucharistic tradition, going back to pre-Christian days of the sacrament of bread and wine."[8]

Although the Grail resides in many different kinds of places from the plain to the grandiose, the one you will enter here is a simple chapel which stands in the heart of a vast and ancient forest. Through performing this rite, you will be allying yourself to an age-old stream of magical tradition which has its own specific inner contacts. You will meet two of them here: the Guardian of the Grail and the Grail Bearer. Once you have formulated the Grail Temple on the inner planes, you can explore further on your own, or you may wish to further your studies through the Avalon Mystery School.*

If possible, set aside a room for inner work. This will then become the outer "shell" of the inner temple. If you cannot dedicate a room entirely to this purpose, you can use any room in your house that is generally fairly quiet, uncluttered, and where you won't be disturbed, such as a bedroom. The "props" you use can be stored away and brought out only when required.

---

*For more information about the Avalon Mystery School see www.avalonmysteryschool .net.

Rite
Dedication to the Grail Mysteries

Preparation

For this magical working, you will need a chalice which can be made of any natural material: ceramic, metal, or wood.

Set up the room as follows:

In the center, an altar, preferably square, covered with a white cloth.

Place a chair in the West, facing East.

A pillar candle in the center of the altar, preferably made from beeswax.

On a side table within reach of the chair:

> A bell or chime
>
> The chalice
>
> Matches and thin taper
>
> A candle snuffer
>
> Incense (choose one which contains frankincense).
>
> A small bottle or vial of water from a pure source,
> preferably from a sacred spring, but otherwise, from
> any clean natural stream or river. Fresh rainwater will
> also do. (If you are unable to collect this yourself, then
> buy a bottle of natural spring water.)

Before you begin, light incense and carry it around the room in a sun-wise (clockwise) direction to cleanse the space. Replace on side table. Take a few deep breaths and compose yourself.

The Opening

Ring bell or chime once.

Light the taper and approach the altar.

Draw a Celtic Cross over the altar with the lit taper as follows:

Make a vertical line by raising the taper above the central candle, saying:

"In the name of the Starry Beings of the Heights."

Then lower taper, saying:

"The Shining Ones of the Deep Earth."

Draw a horizontal line from left to right to cross the vertical line, saying:

"And all the Clan of the Green World."

Draw a circle around the cross, saying:

"One Circle of Being."

Light central candle, saying:

"In Light reborn."

Extinguish the taper, and replace it on the side table. Be seated.

Gaze at the candle flame, then close your eyes.

Building the Chapel of the Grail

Using your powers of visualization, build the chapel around you with the inner eye: *It is twilight and you are walking through an ancient forest in the early part of the year. Many of the trees are bare and their branches form an interlacing tapestry against a pale sky. There is no sound of birdsong, and all the animals have not yet stirred from their winter sleep. A deep silence pervades the land. Even your footsteps on the brown damp earth of the path make no noise.*

The trees thin out and the path leads into a glade in the very heart of the forest in which stands an ancient chapel, a simple foursquare building made of blocks of old grey stone, covered in places with lichens and moss. The entrance is to the West: a rounded archway is set in a sturdy wooden door. You walk up to the door, and clasp the round iron ring which is cold to the touch. You turn it and the door slowly creaks open and you walk over the threshold, closing the door behind you. A heavy curtain of burgundy velvet covers the door on the inside and you gently push this aside and find yourself standing on the stone flags of the chapel.

The chapel walls are set with four great windows in the four cardinal directions. Before you to the East is a tall window of glowing pale-gold stained glass, depicting the giant figure of the Archangel Raphael.

On your right, to the South, is a window of scarlet stained glass depicting the giant figure of Archangel Michael.

On your left to the North is a soft green window with emerald lights, in which the giant figure of the Archangel Auriel can be seen.

You take a few steps into the chapel, turn around, and gaze up above the door through which you entered at a glowing deep blue stained-glass window that portrays the giant figure of Archangel Gabriel.

Turning around again, you see that the Chapel is simply furnished, with a bare stone altar in the center, an ancient structure that looks like it was carved from a single rock. It is bare of all ornament except for one white pillar candle in the center.

Now, still keeping the image of the Grail Chapel clearly before you, stand and walk slowly to each window in turn, strongly visualizing the window, the Archangel, and the Light.

Go to the East. Raise your arms up and out from your sides to head level, palms facing forward. Say:

"Blessed be the Light arising in the East!"

Spend a few moments visualizing the pale gold light of dawn lighting up the window.

Lower your arms.

Go to the South and raise your arms. Say:

"Blessed be the Light increasing in the South!"

Visualize a bright noonday sun streaming through the window and dappling the stone floor with splashes of fiery color.

Lower your arms.

Go to the West and raise your arms. Say:

"Blessed be the Light descending in the West!"

Visualize a dusky blue twilight tinged with the crimson afterglow of the setting sun softly illumining the circular window.

Lower your arms.

Go to the North and raise your arms. Say:

"Blessed be the Light returning in the North!"

Visualize the deep indigo of a midnight sky speckled with sparkling starlight.

Lower your arms.

Turn to face the altar. Raising your arms, say:

"Blessed be the seventh of the Seven Ways, where all goes forth and all returns!"

Lower your arms and return to your seat.

Meeting the Servants of the Grail

Now watch as a small door in the northeast corner of the chapel opens quietly and a figure stands there—a slight elderly man with a white beard and a chaplet of oak leaves about his head. It is the Hermit of the Chapel, who is the Guardian of the Grail, and even though he is half concealed in the shadows, you sense a kindly and welcoming presence.

The Hermit steps out of the shadows and greets you. You greet him in return, sensing that here is a person you can ask your deepest questions and be assured of wise and compassionate answers. In a gentle, deep voice, he asks you what brings you here. You must answer from the truth within your heart. What is his response?

From the southeast corner, another small door opens quietly and the figure of a woman stands there. She is tall and slender, beautiful, grave and of wise countenance. She is the Grail Bearer. She approaches the altar and raises her hands above the candle flame. From each of the Archangels in the four windows now streams a beam of colored light, forming an equal-armed cross that intersects just above the altar: gold from the East, scarlet from the South, violet from the West, and indigo from the North. Where the beams cross, the chalice of the Grail takes shape between the cupped hands of the Grail Bearer, like a glowing jewel of pure golden light, alive with dancing iridescent colors.

A column of pure white light now streams down from above and fills the Grail to the brim. . . . The light overflows and pours down over the stone altar, illuminating carvings of plants, animals, and other figures that you had not noticed before. . . . The light has made the altar a Living Rock . . .

The Dedication

After a while, the lights withdraw back to their points of origin, but the Grail remains. The Grail Bearer raises the holy vessel in both hands and offers it to you.

Stand up to face her.

She asks you if you are ready to be one who is a Grail Bearer in your world. You may spend some time conversing with her and asking any questions about this sacred task. What is her response?

If you decide at this point that you do not want to accept the task she offers, there is no shame. In this case, go to the Closing section of this rite.

If you accept, then take the Grail from her and hold it to your heart. It enters into your body where it appears as a smaller version of itself.

Breathe deeply and send your consciousness far above your head into the vast heights of space. Let your focus come to settle on a bright Star, at its center a radiant sphere of brilliant white scintillating light.

On the next breath you take, see this starry globe shine more and more brightly. As you exhale, let it pour rivers of radiant white light tinged with gold down through the top of your head, down your spine, and into the chalice at your heart. Raise your arms out to your sides at shoulder height, palms facing upward.

Continue breathing and visualizing until it fills the Grail within your heart and streams down through your whole body and out through your hands and feet. You are drenched in this Light. Let it cleanse and purify you from all unwanted negative energy . . .

When the negative energy has been cleansed, be aware that every cell in your body is illumined with white Fire. The Grail in your heart is sparkling with iridescent rays.

Take up your chalice and place it on the altar. Fill it with your holy water.

Raise it up in both hands and go to each direction in turn as follows:

In the East:

"I dedicate myself to the work of the Grail in the name of Raphael."

Anoint your brow with water.

In the South:

"I dedicate myself to the work of the Grail in the name of Michael."

Anoint your heart.

In the West:

"I dedicate myself to the work of the Grail in the name of Gabriel."

Anoint your abdomen.

In the North:

"I dedicate myself to the work of the Grail in the name of Auriel."

Anoint your feet.
Replace the chalice on the altar.

The Grail Prayer

Recite the following:

> **"I bear the Light: the Light of the Grail;**
> **I raise this Light above your path**
> **to show you a Way in the darkness.**
> **If you will take it, I pass you the Light**
> **for you to kindle your own Lamp.**
> **If not, I illumine your steps upon the Way;**
> **May the eternal Light of the Grail**
> **be your lodestar, guiding you home."**

Communion with the Inner Powers

Sit down again and spend some time receiving any communications about your future work as a Grail Bearer. The information may come from the Grail Guardian, the Grail Bearer, or any other inner contacts that might appear.

The Closing

When this process is complete, ring the bell or chime once.
   Say firmly:
"It is done."

Stand and go to each of the four directions, starting at the North and proceeding in a counterclockwise direction. Raise your arms as before, then turn the palms to face each other and make the gesture of a curtain being closed over each window. Lower your arms between each window. Say:
"May the Way of the North be still and silent.
May the Way of the East be still and silent.
May the Way of the South be still and silent.
May the Way of the West be still and silent."

Face the altar with arms outstretched, palms down. Say:
"Blessed be the seventh of the Seven Ways, where all goes forth and all returns."

Raise your right (or dominant) hand above the candle flame, pointing with index and middle fingers held together in the Sign of Blessings. Say:
"We give thanks to the Starry Beings of the Heights."

Lower your fingers, saying:
"The Shining Ones of the Deep Earth."

Draw a horizontal line from left to right to cross the vertical line, saying:
"And all the Clan of the Green World."

Draw a circle around the cross in a sunwise (clockwise) direction, saying:
"One Circle of Being."

Extinguish candle flame, saying:
"In Peace Unending."

Ring the bell or chime once.

Afterward, write down your experiences. Plan to visit the Grail Chapel as often as possible to receive more guidance on your life and the work you are to do in service to the Grail, or simply to converse further with the Grail guardian and Grail Bearer. You may also wish to print out the Grail prayer on a card, place it by your altar and read it out loud whenever you wish to affirm and strengthen your intention to be a Grail Bearer.

A PATH OF BALANCE

Of working with the Grail, Dion Fortune reminds us, "The Cup is the mystically exalted soul of man, held up to receive the influx of the Holy Ghost; and when receiving this influx from on high we stand with our feet set firm in the very heart of Nature, thus affirming the natural basis of all things in the Earth our Mother."[9]

Note that she stresses the importance of having a stable foundation on the earth: the Chalice of the soul must have a firm base on the physical plane so that we may successfully mediate the highest and purest spiritual energies (here referred to as the Christian "Holy

Ghost") into our world. We must be strongly grounded in physical reality. Working as a Grail Bearer is not about escaping from life's difficulties, but about bringing the Light of the Grail to our troubled world. Integrating the four "bodies" that make up each human being—the physical body, mind, soul, and spirit—is essential, so that one does not become "top-heavy" and ungrounded by focusing over much on higher energies.

THE HEXAGRAM MEDITATION

The following simple exercise uses the symbol of the hexagram, or six-pointed star, as a way to experience the four bodies in a balanced way while at the same time centering you firmly at the heart. The hexagram has been used in religious and magical contexts for centuries to denote wholeness and harmony. It is also known as Solomon's Seal and was used by the alchemists to denote the Philosopher's Stone, the completion of the great work. It is composed of two intersecting triangles, one pointing downward and the other pointing upward.

The downward-pointing triangle represents the descending, feminine element of Water. In the context of the Grail Mysteries it is the chalice of the Grail within the heart.

The upward-pointing triangle represents the ascending, masculine vertical force of Fire and can be imagined as the point of a Spear, which, like the Sword, is a symbol of higher aspiration and spiritual will. Together they represent the divine union of masculine and feminine.

Downward-pointing triangle   *Upward-pointing triangle*

When the two triangles are brought together and established within the inner body at the heart center, they interlock to create the hexagram, the Western equivalent of the Chinese yin-yang symbol.

The hexagram

When the two triangles merge into the hexagram, the alchemical symbols for Earth and Air are also formed, so all four elements are present, encoding another layer of meaning to this rich symbolism.

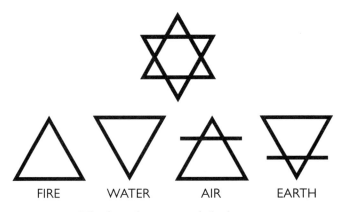

FIRE   WATER   AIR   EARTH

The four elements and the hexagram

The hexagram also contains the four elements in perfect balance, which in terms of the four bodies are as follows:

Earth: Physical Body—The experience of the self as the body living in the world of space-time, governed by the laws of physics, chemistry, biology, and so forth.

Water: Mind or Ego—The experience of the self as a personality comprised of a ceaseless flow of thoughts and feelings: ideas, desires, aversions, memories, and more, which continually change with each moment.

Air: Soul—The experience of the self as the "Knower" or "Witness" above and beyond the Ego, which is serene, unperturbed, and unchanging: the "clear sky" self.

Fire: Spirit—The awareness of the self as a divine spark of the Radiant Mystery—the "Light of Ten Thousand Suns" or "Divine Fire"—which includes the experience of the Higher Self as a stepped-down frequency of this Source.

Meditation
The Hexagram Meditation

This simple exercise shows you a way to use the hexagram to create a feeling of harmony and balance in body and mind.

Sit in a quiet place, take some deep breaths and relax. Light a candle if you wish.

At the center of your chest, without actually touching your body, draw a small, downward-pointing triangle with your finger. You can visualize it in the traditional color of deep blue if you wish, although this is not essential.

As you do this say:

"Blessed be my body and my mind."

Pause a few moments to send a heartfelt feeling of gratitude to these two aspects of yourself, which should respond to the blessing by giving you a good, warm feeling inside.

Now at the center of your chest again, draw a small, upward-pointing triangle over the first figure, which can be visualized in a fiery red if you wish.

Say:

"Blessed be my soul and my spirit."

Pause a few moments to tune into these two energies and send a feeling of deep respect and gratitude to these two aspects of yourself. Enjoy the response that is sent in return.

Focus on the hexagram in its entirety and feel the breath flow in and out of this area.

Say:

"Blessed be the wholeness of my being in all four worlds."

As you do so, see the Light of the Grail emerge as a central glowing point within the hexagram. Enjoy the feelings of balance, harmony, and integration.

You can use this exercise to center yourself anywhere you happen to be, saying the words mentally if others are present. It can be used at a moment's notice in a crisis situation. It is particularly good as a preparation for healing work or any activity that requires you to be aligned with the wholeness of yourself.

HEALING WITH THE GRAIL

If you already work in the healing arts, or else feel a call in that direction, you can use the following processes to heal yourself or others, either on their own or in conjunction with other modalities.

Rite
Drawing Down the Light in the Grail

This is the same process you used in the Rite of Dedication. It is a way of charging your body with potent spiritual energies in order to transmit them to any part of yourself that needs healing or to others. It can be practiced regularly since it has the effect of revitalizing, refreshing, and re-energizing the entire mind, body, and spirit, while raising your vibratory rate. Once a day is recommended.

Healing Yourself
Relax, establish a deep breathing pattern and enter the Inner Silence. Each time you exhale, send the breath down through your legs and out through the soles of your feet to create a good solid connection with the Earth. If it helps, you can imagine yourself strongly anchored to the iron core deep within the Earth's body.

Now let the breath open up your chest and focus your attention there. Visualize the Grail within your heart as an open vessel upturned to receive spiritual influence from above.

With the next inhalation, send your consciousness far above your head into the vast heights of space. Let your focus come to settle on a bright Star, in whose center is a radiant sphere of brilliant white scintillating Light. Charge this starry globe with energy with every breath you take so that it becomes brighter with every second.

Draw it down until it touches the crown of your head. Focus on its scintillating radiance vibrating with intense dynamic spiritual energy. The next time you exhale, let it pour rivers of radiant Light through the top of your head, down your spine, and into the bowl of the Grail within your heart.

Continue breathing and visualizing until it fills the Grail, streams through arms and legs, through your whole body, and out through your feet and into the Earth. Let the light wash away any unwanted or negative energy as it leaves so that you feel cleansed and purified on many levels.

When the purification process is over, you can visualize this luminous light streaming from the Grail into any parts of your body or mind that need healing.

When you are ready to close, see and feel the light within your body flowing away down into the Earth. See the beams of light returning to their source far above you, then let the star fade back into outer space.

Continue to sit quietly, breathing into the Grail at your heart, which shrinks in size to become a small, steady light like a candle flame that burns with a soft luminous glow.

Each time you rekindle the light of the Grail within your inner body, you can use it for healing.

Healing Others

Follow the steps below to use the "Drawing Down the Light in the Grail" ritual to heal others.

Light a candle, sit quietly, and center yourself, taking some deep breaths to relax deeply.

Practice the "Hexagram Meditation" (see page 245)

Perform "Drawing Down the Light in the Grail" (above), and when you are able to visualize the inner Grail as full to overflowing with higher energies, send this potent living energy to other people, places, or beings in need of blessings or healing, through visualization charged with strong and focused intention.

You can also use this practice as a way of generating healing energy for someone in your presence. Have this person sit or lie in front of you in a relaxed position with their eyes closed. When the Grail in your heart is full, see and feel the living light of the Grail stream down both your arms and hands; you can then direct the living light to the person to be healed. Continue to breathe deeply to allow this energy to pour through you as long as it feels comfortable. To end the session, let your breathing resume a normal pattern and close as described above.

Ritual
A Group Healing Ceremony of the Chalice

Group meditations and rituals that have a specific focus can be immensely powerful, as the attention and energy contributed by each group member grows exponentially rather than by simple addition. In this ceremony, the group itself becomes a Grail of Healing.

An ideal number for a group would be between six and ten people, but it can also be effective with only two or three if necessary.

You will need a chalice or bowl to place in the center of a table or stand around which the group will be seated, plus pens and paper to write the names of those to receive healing.

The script for the ceremony is based on one used by the twentieth-century mystic and seer, Geoffrey Hodson. Elements of the ceremony can be changed or adapted to suit any spiritual path or religious context: Pagan, Christian, Buddhist, or whatever is your group's particular preference. Chanting, music, poems, or prayers can be added as desired.

Procedure

Before you start, purify the room by burning frankincense, sandalwood, or a blend of incense that has each. You may also wish to light one or more candles.

Write the names of those in need of healing on pieces of paper.

They can be individuals, groups, organizations, or nations; creatures, places on the planet, or other beings in the web of life. Place the names in the chalice.

When you are ready to begin, the leader rings a bell or chime, and there is a short space of silence in which everyone can center themselves and settle in. The leader invites each member to visualize a sphere of protective white light around the whole group.

Leader: *Within this Sphere of Light we open to form a Chalice to be filled with the power of healing.*

We call upon the Lord of Light, Healer of the World;
We call upon the Lady of Wisdom, the Blessed Mother of the World;
We call upon the Inner Convocation of Light;
We call upon the Angels and Archangels of healing;
We ask for your aid.

(Pause to allow these Presences to enter in.)

Pour forth your healing power into those whose names we now present to you.
To every mind be peace,
To every heart be comfort,
To every body wellness.
May the rising tide of Life bring radiant health to all,
as by your healing power both soul and body are restored.
Leave with each an angel watcher, to heal, to comfort, and protect;
To ward away all ill, to hasten returning strength,
until health returns, or Life departs,
And lead to peace when life is done.
May healing be given to . . . (speak the names clearly with a short pause between them. Remain silent for a time.)

May the Infinite Light of Eternal Love enfold them forever.

Supernatural Father, strengthen us with the Power of your Presence.
Help us bring the souls of humankind to awaken to the truth of your

Love that there may be peace and justice for all.

Great Mother, Lady of Wisdom, lead us with the pure light of your love and compassion. Grant us, your willing helpers, to be channels for your healing power to the world, pure instruments in your service.

(Pause)

We will now turn our thoughts toward the animal kingdom, especially those in pain or suffering.

Lady of the Green Earth and Ocean Deeps, Lord of the Wildwood and the Mountain Heights, whose care and loving kindness are over all Creation, breathe into us your spirit of compassion and care toward all the creatures of this Earth. Teach us to look upon these, our kindred spirits, as a divine trust, that the day may be hastened when humankind shall neither hurt nor disrespect nor destroy the Earth's creatures but live with them as one community.

Let us focus our attention on . . . (examples: RSPCA, Humane Society, International Fund for Animal Welfare, Friends of the Earth, Defenders of Wildlife). *May they be strengthened and protected in their work.*

(Pause)

Let us see our circle as a Chalice of Healing, with each of us seated around its rim. Let us visualize the chalice filled with the radiant living Light of the Great Beings who are here with us today and see that Light flowing out to where it is needed.

Silence and long pause for all to visualize this. When the leader senses the completion of this process, he or she says a closing prayer or blessing. The ones I have included here are the short and longer versions of what has come to be known as the "Celtic Blessing" adapted from the writings of Fiona MacLeod:

Celtic Blessing (Short Version)

Deep Peace of the Quiet Earth to you,
Deep Peace of the Running Wave to you,

Deep Peace of the Flowing Air to you,

Deep Peace of the Shining Stars to you,

Deep Peace of the Spirit of Peace to you.

Celtic Blessing (Long Version)

Deep peace I breathe into you,

Deep peace, a soft white dove to you;

Deep peace, a quiet rain to you;

Deep peace, an ebbing wave to you!

Deep peace, red wind of the east from you;

Deep peace, grey wind of the west to you;

Deep peace, dark wind of the north from you;

Deep peace, blue wind of the south to you!

Deep peace, pure red of the flame to you;

Deep peace, pure white of the moon to you;

Deep peace, pure green of the grass to you;

Deep peace, pure brown of the earth to you;

Deep peace, pure grey of the dew to you,

Deep peace, pure blue of the sky to you!

Deep peace of the running wave to you,

Deep peace of the flowing air to you,

Deep peace of the quiet earth to you,

Deep peace of the sleeping stones to you!

Deep peace of the Yellow Shepherd to you,

Deep peace of the Wandering Shepherdess to you,

Deep peace of the Flock of Stars to you,

Deep peace from the Son of Peace to you,

Deep peace from the heart of Mary to you,

From Bridget of the Mantle

Deep peace, deep peace![10]

Leader rings chime to signal end.

Leader: ***Let us dissolve the Sphere of Light and give thanks to those Beings who have heard our call and been present with us today.***

Pronunciation Guide to Celtic Words and Names

Please Note: *This guide is meant to serve as an approximation only.*

Áes dána	*ays dahna*
Áes sídhe	*ess shee*
Afagddu	*ah-vahg-thee*
Ailbe	*ahl-byeh*
Annwfyn	*AN-oo-vuhn*
Aone	*eu-nyuh*
Baile in Scáil	*bal-uh in skaw-il*
Bealltainn	*byahl-tin*
Bec mac Buain	*bec muk boo-ain*
Belenos	*bel-ay-nos*
Bendigeidfran	*ben-dee-gaid-vrahn*
Brân	*brahn*
Bran mac Febal	*bran muck FYEV-ul*
Brânwen	*brahn-wen*
Brighid	*breej*
Brighid-Binne-Bheule-lhuchd-nan-trusganan-uaine	*breezh-bin-ya vee-uhl hlookhd-nan-troos-gan-an-weu-nyuh*

Brighid-Muirghin-na-tuinne	*breezh-MWIR-in-nah-TWIN-eh*
Brighid-nam-Bratta	*breezh nah MRAT-uh*
Brighid-nan-sitheach seang	*breezh-nahn-SIH-yahkh-shang*
Brighid-sluagh	*breezh-SLOO-ah*
Brigit	*brig-it*
Brú na Bóinne	*BROO-nuh BAW-nyuh*
Caer	*kye-er*
Caer Golud	*kye-er gol-eeth*
Caer Loyw	*kye-er loy-oo*
Caer Ochren	*kye-er okh-ren*
Caer Rigor	*kye-er ree-gor*
Caer Vandwy	*kye-er van-dwee*
Caer Vedwit	*kye-er ved-weet*
Caer Wydyr	*kye-er wee-der*
Cailleach	*kal-yakh*
Cairbre	*car-bruh*
Caledvwlch	*kal-ed-VOOLKH*
Caradog	*kar-AD-og*
Ceridwen	*ker-ED-wen*
Clíodhna	*CLEE-uh-na*
Creirwy	*KRY-roo-ee*
Cúchulainn	*koo khul-in*
Cú-gorm	*koo-gorom*
CuRoí	*coo-roy*
Cwn Annwn	*koon AN-oon*
Diurnach	*dyer-nakh*
Dyrnwch	*dern-ookh*
Efrawg	*evrowg*
Eithne	*eth-na*

Emhain Abhlach	*evan av-lakh*
Ériu	*AY-ryoo*
Fionn mac Cumhaill	*finn muk coo-wil*
Flaith Érenn	*flah- AIR-enn*
Gobnait	*gob-net*
Gwenhwyfar	*gwen-hoo-ee-var*
Gwenhwy-vach	*gwen-hoo-ee-vakh*
Gwenhwy-vawr	*gwen-hoo-ee-vowr*
Gwion Bach	*gwee-on bahkh*
Gwyn ap Nudd	*gwin-ap-neeth*
Lir	*leer*
Llyn Tegid	*hlin teg-id*
Llŷr	*hleer*
Lochlann	*LOKH-luhn*
Logres	*LOH-gress*
Luan	*LU-en*
Lugh	*loo*
Lughnasadh	*LOO-nuh-suh*
Lùnasdal	*LOO-nuhs-duhl*
MacGréine	*muk gren-ya*
Mair	*mire*
Manannán	*man-an-awn*
Manawydan	*man-a-widden*
Medb	*mayve*
Morfran	*MOR-vrahn*
Pair	*pire*
Pair pur vonhedd	*pire peer von-heth*
Pedryvan	*PED-ruh-vahn*
Peredur	*per-ed-eer*

Preiddeu Annwn	*PRY-thee AN-oon*
Prydwen	*PRID-wen*
Rhiannon	*hree-an-on*
Ruadh mac Righdonn	*rua muk ree-don*
Samhain	*sow-en*
Samhuinn	*sah-vin*
Sídhe	*shee*
Sidi	*see-dee*
Sireadh-thall	*SHEER-eh-hawl*
Sliabh na Caillighe	*shlee-uv nuh kal-ee*
Suibhal-bheann	*SIV-ul ven-yuh*
Taliesin	*Tal-YES-in*
Tír fo Thuinn	*teer fo hwin*
Tír na nÓg	*teer-na-noge*
Tir-na-h'oige	*teer-na hoy-guh*
Tir-na-h'oise	*teer-na-hoyshuh*
Tír-na-Sorcha	*teer-na-sor-kha*
Trioedd Ynys Prydein	*tree-oyth uh-nis pruh-dine*
Tuatha Dé Danann	*TOO-a-ha dyay DANan*
Ynys Witrin	*uh-nis wit-rin*

Notes

INTRODUCTION

1. See: Loomis, *The Grail*; Carey, *Ireland and the Grail*.
2. Baring and Cashford, *The Myth of The Goddess*, 50–51.
3. Evans, *In Quest of the Holy Graal*, 100.
4. Evans, *Holy Graal*, 102.
5. Carey, *Ireland and the Grail*, 88.
6. Evans, *Holy Graal*, 105.
7. Eliot, *The Waste Land and Other Poems*, 29.
8. Ibid., 44.
9. Anne Baring, "Lecture 5: Re-balancing the Masculine and the Feminine," www.annebaring.com/anbar12_lect05_mascfemine.htm (accessed July 9, 2012).

CHAPTER 1.
SEEKING THE CAULDRON

1. Loomis, *Wales and the Arthurian Legend*, 177.
2. From the suggestions of Celtic scholars Haycock, "'Preiddeu Annwn' and the Figure of Taliesin," 52–78; Koch and Carey, eds. *The Celtic Heroic Age*, 291; and Loomis, *Wales*, 155. There is no universal agreement because the language of this text is so obscure.
3. Cross and Slover, eds., *Ancient Irish Tales*, 223.
4. Eliade, *Shamanism*, 57.

5. Koch, *Celtic Culture,* 358.

6. Carey, *Ireland,* 87.

7. Ford, *The Mabinogi and Other Welsh Tales,* 184.

8. Koch and Carey, *The Celtic Heroic Age,* 290.

9. Ford, *The Mabinogi,* 19.

10. Green, *Symbol & Image in Celtic Religious Art,* 35–36.

11. Carey, *Ireland,* 88–90.

12. O'Rahilly, *Early Irish History and Mythology,* 326.

13. Gimbutas, *The Civilization of the Goddess.*

14. Eliade, *Shamanism,* 77.

15. From the Metrical Dindshenchas, quoted by McHardy, *The Quest for the Nine Maidens,* 113.

16. Clarke, ed., trans., *Life of Merlin,* 101.

17. McHardy, *Nine Maidens,* 84.

18. Loomis, *Wales,* 155.

19. McHardy, *Nine Maidens.*

20. Markale, *Women of the Celts,* 81.

21. McHardy, *Nine Maidens,* 23.

22. Rees and Rees, *Celtic Heritage,* 138.

23. Haycock, "Preiddeu Annwn," 62.

24. Campbell, *Popular Tales of the West Highlands,* 138.

25. Lincoln, *Death, War and Sacrifice,* 78.

26. Harrison, *Prolegomena to the Study of Greek Religion,* 659–60.

CHAPTER 2.
THE CUP AND THE BRANCH

1. Mac Cana, "Aspects of the Theme of King and Goddess in Irish Literature."

2. McKillop, *Dictionary of Celtic Mythology,* 270.

3. Enright, *Lady with a Mead Cup.*

4. Rees and Rees, *Celtic Heritage,* 74.

5. Stokes, ed., trans., "Echtra mac nEchach Muigmedóin," 190–207.

6. Kalweit, *Dreamtime and Inner Space,* 209.

7. Ibid., 210.

8. Gen. 9:10 (Revised Standard Version).

9. Rev. 1:2 (RSV).

10. Loomis, *Wales,* 148–49.

11. Eliade, *Shamanism,* 169.

CHAPTER 3.
SWORDS OF LIGHT AND DARKNESS

1. Martin Luther King Jr., "'Where Do We Go from Here?' Delivered at the 11th Annual SCLC Convention Atlanta, Ga., 1967," Standford.edu, http://mlk-kpp01.stanford.edu/index.php/encyclopedia/documentsentry/where_do_we_go_from_here_delivered_at_the_11th_annual_sclc_convention/ (accessed July 9, 2013).

2. Gray, ed., trans., *Cath Maige Tuired,* 25.

3. Bromwich, ed., trans., *Trioedd Ynys Prydein,* 241.

4. Malory, *Le Morte d'Arthur,* 14.

5. Ibid., 45.

6. Ibid., 46.

7. Ibid., 77.

8. Bromwich, *Trioedd,* 380.

9. Ibid., 154.

10. Cavendish, *King Arthur and the Grail,* 54.

11. Wace and Layamon, *Arthurian Chronicles,* Eugene Mason, trans., 209–11.

12. Matarasso, *The Quest of the Holy Grail,* 99.

13. Rhys, *Celtic Folklore, Welsh and Manx,* 496.

14. Loomis, *Arthurian Literature in the Middle Ages,* 68–69.

15. Robinson, *Two Glastonbury Legends,* 53.

16. Fry, *A Sleep of Prisoners,* 49.

CHAPTER 4.
WOMEN OF THE GRAIL

1. Baring and Cashford, *The Myth of the Goddess,* 652.

2. Matarasso, *Holy Grail,* 43.

3. Ibid., 52.

4. Markale, *The Grail,* i, 121.

5. Loomis, *The Grail,* 122.

6. Baring and Cashford, *The Myth of the Goddess,* 653.

7. Yeats, "The Collected Poems of W. B. Yeats," 67.

8. Loomis, *The Grail,* 149.

9. Von Eschenbach, *Parzival,* 129.

10. de Troyes, *The Story of the Grail,* Nigel Bryant, trans., 50.

11. Goetinck, "The Quest for Origins," Mahoney, ed., 136.

12. ní Dhomnaill, "Sheelagh in Her Cabin," *From Beyond the Pale,* 55.

13. See Virginia Satir, *Peoplemaking.*

CHAPTER 5.
TRIALS AND INITIATIONS

1. de Troyes, *Perceval, or The Story of the Grail,* Ruth Harwood Cline, trans., 89.

2. Goetinck, "The Quest for Origins," 137.

3. Smith, *The Burning Bush,* 333.

4. MacAlister, ed., trans., *Cath Maige Tuired,* 251.

5. Raine, *Yeats the Initiate.*

6. Wood, "The Creation of the Celtic Tarot," suggests Waite was actually drawing on the ideas of folklorist, Alfred Nutt.

7. Weston, *From Ritual to Romance,* 187.

8. Goetinck, "The Quest for Origins," 136.

9. Loomis, *The Grail,* 78.

10. Kahane, Kahane, and Pietrangeli, *The Krater and the Grail.*

11. Eliot, *The Waste Land,* 45.

12. Bryant, *The High Book of the Grail,* 46.

13. Plato, *The Symposium,* http://classics.mit.edu/Plato/symposium.html (accessed August 9, 2013).

14. Bryant, *The High Book of the Grail,* 113.

15. Koch, *Celtic Culture,* 487.

16. Bryant, *The High Book of the Grail,* 132.

17. Hill, *Masculine and Feminine.*

18. Knight, *Pythoness,* 183.

19. Holmes and Klenke, *Chrétien, Troyes, and the Grail,* 35.

CHAPTER 6.
THE GRAIL COMES TO GLASTONBURY

1. Carley, *The Chronicle of Glastonbury Abbey,* 29.

2. Powys, *A Glastonbury Romance,* 285.

3. Lindahl, McNamara, and Lindow, eds., *Medieval Folklore,* 190.

4. Crawford, "St. Joseph in Britain."

5. Fortune, *Glastonbury*, 1.

6. Armitage, *Two Glastonbury Legends*, 34.

7. Carley, *Glastonbury Abbey*, xvi.

8. Lewis, *St. Joseph of Arimathea at Glastonbury*.

9. Ashe, *Avalonian Quest*, 23.

10. Carley, *Glastonbury Abbey*, 87.

11. Carey, *Ireland and the Grail*, 146–47, 327.

12. John 6:53–56 (RSV).

13. Carley, *Glastonbury Abbey*, 182.

14. Ashe, *Avalonian Quest*, 147.

15. Caradoc of Llancarvan, *Two Lives of Gildas*, 101.

16. Carley, *Glastonbury Abbey*, 162.

17. Carley, *Glastonbury Abbey*, 89.

18. Evans, *The High History of the Holy Graal*, 133.

19. Ashe, *The Virgin*, 242.

20. Markale, *Cathedral of the Black Madonna*, 13.

21. Ruether, *Goddesses and the Divine Feminine*, 303.

22. William of Malmesbury, *Chronicle of the Kings of England*, 33.

23. Lewis, *St. Joseph of Arimathea at Glastonbury*, 59.

24. Gray, *Western Inner Workings*, 57.

25. Carley, *Glastonbury Abbey*, 109.

26. Evans, *The High History*, 21.

27. Ashe, *King Arthur's Avalon*, 272.

28. Matthews, *The Grail*, 15.

29. *The Black Madonna*, CD-ROM by Ensemble Unicorn, text taken from liner inside cover.

30. Matthews, "The Grail and the Rose," White, ed.

31. Ashe, *King Arthur's Avalon*, 268.

32. Goering, *The Virgin and the Grail*.

33. Carmichael, *Carmina Gadelica*, 230.

CHAPTER 7.
THE ALCHEMICAL GRAIL

1. Carley, *The Chronicle*, 31.

2. William of Malmesbury, *Chronicle of the Kings of England*, 20.

3. Carley, "Melkin the Bard and Esoteric Tradition at Glastonbury Abbey," 1, 11.

4. Mann, *The Isle of Avalon*, 111.

5. Carley, "Melkin," 12–13.

6. Paracelsus, *The Hermetic and Alchemical Writings of Paracelsus*, 14.

7. A. E. Waite, "The Pictorial Symbols of Alchemy," rexresearch.com, www .rexresearch.com/alchemy5/waitsymb.pdf (accessed July 9, 2013).

8. Anne Baring, "Lecture 17, The Great Work: Healing the Wasteland," annebaring.com, www.annebaring.com/anbar12_lect17_wasteland.htm (accessed July 9, 2013).

9. Warner, "The Dark Wood and the Dark Word in Dante's *Commedia*," 1.

10. Hodson, *The Kingdom of the Gods*, 72.

11. Hughes, *Arthurian Myths and Alchemy*.

12. Gosman, Macdonald, and Vanderjagt, *Princes and Princely Culture, 1450–1650*, 104.

13. Mann, *Isle of Avalon*, 156.

14. Mann and Glasson, *The Red & White Springs of Avalon*, 43.

15. Dearmer, Shaw, and Vaughan Williams, *The Oxford Book of Carols*, 134.

16. Becker, *The Continuum Encyclopedia of Symbols*, 107.

17. Bryant, trans., *The High Book of the Grail*, 103.

18. Traditional English folk-song: *Looly, looly,* performed by Archie Fisher, Topic Records, 1976.

19. Dearmer, Shaw, and Vaughan Williams, *Carols*, 134.

20. Jung and Von Franz, *The Grail Legend*, 149.

21. Howard and Jackson, *The Pillars of Tubal Cain*, 68.

22. Hughes, *Arthurian Myths*, 307.

23. Jung, *Psychology and Alchemy*, 77.

24. Hazrat Inayat Khan, "The Sufi Message of Hazrat Inayat Khan: Vol X The Path of Initiation," wahiduddin.net, http://wahiduddin.net/mv2/VIIIa/VIIIa_4_7.htm (accessed July 9, 2013).

25. Tergit, *Flowers Through the Ages*, 46.

26. Ibid., 43.

27. *Sermones XXI super Confraternitate de Rosaceo*, quoted by Wilkinson, *The Rose-Garden Game*, 113.

28. Abraham, *A Dictionary of Alchemical Symbolism*, 60.

CHAPTER 8.
DION FORTUNE AND THE CHURCH OF THE GRAAL

1. Fortune, *Glastonbury*, 111.
2. Ibid., 64.
3. Ibid., 2.
4. Ibid., 101.
5. Fortune, *Extracts from Communications Received.*
6. Ibid.
7. Fielding and Collins, *The Story of Dion Fortune*, 259.
8. Ibid., 267.
9. Ibid., *Dion Fortune*, 256.
10. Ibid.
11. Fortune, *Organisation of the Guild.*
12. Ibid.
13. Ibid.
14. Fortune, *The Magical Battle of Britain.*
15. Ibid., 140.

CHAPTER 9.
THE STRANGE STORY OF THE BLUE BOWL

1. Wood, *Eternal Chalice*, 60.
2. Barb, "Mensa Sacra," 40–67. His argument is refuted by Carley, *Glastonbury Abbey and the Arthurian Tradition*, 192.
3. Tudor Pole, *The Silent Road*, 222.
4. *MS38515/6/33/8/*, 4. From the Tudor Pole section of the "Russell Papers," a collection of papers belonging to Sir David Russell, spanning the first half of the twentieth century. University of St. Andrews Library Special Collections.
5. Ibid., *MS 38515/6/33/8/1*, 6.
6. Ibid., *MS38515/6/33/8/*, 4, 6.
7. Benham, *The Avalonians*, 39.
8. Ibid., 62.
9. Russell Papers, *MS38515/6/33/8/*, 4, 8.
10. Tudor Pole, *Silent Road*, 223.
11. Benham, *Avalonians*, 17.
12. Ibid.

13. Carley, *Glastonbury Abbey,* 110.

14. Benham, *Avalonians,* 21.

15. Blamires, *The Little Book of the Great Enchantment,* 307.

16. Macleod, *The Winged Destiny,* 213.

17. Ibid., 209.

18. Merry, *The Flaming Door,* 209.

19. Ibid., 211.

20. Ibid., 288.

21. Benham, *Avalonians,* 49.

22. Fortune, *Glastonbury,* 17.

23. Ibid., 101.

24. Benham, *Avalonians,* 52.

25. Ibid., 50.

26. "Seen over Carbis Bay, Cornwall at 7 am on 6th August 1954," quoted by Gerry Fenge, "The Blended Ray," *Gatekeeper Newsletter.*

27. Tudor Pole, *Silent Road,* 179.

28. Macleod, *Green Fire,* 279.

29. Benham, *Avalonians,* 46.

CHAPTER 10.
THE GRAIL OF THE HEART

1. Matthews, ed., "Temples of the Grail," *At the Table of the Grail,* 84.

2. Burkhardt, *Alchemy,* 183.

3. Fortune, *Practical Occultism,* 41.

4. Tudor Pole, *Private Dowding,* 31.

5. Tudor Pole, *Marching Forward,* 53.

6. Knight, *Pythoness,* 184.

7. Trwoga, *Grail Quest in the Vales of Avalon,* 169.

8. Knight, *Experience of the Inner Worlds,* 99.

9. Knight, *Merlin and the Grail,* 108.

10. Macleod, *The Dominion of Dreams,* 124.

Bibliography

Abraham, Lyndy. *A Dictionary of Alchemical Symbolism.* Cambridge: Cambridge University Press, 2001.

Armitage, Robinson J. *Two Glastonbury Legends.* Cambridge: Cambridge University Press, 1926.

Ashe, Geoffrey. *Avalonian Quest.* London: Methuen, 1982.

———. *King Arthur's Avalon.* London: Collins, 1957.

———. *The Virgin.* London: Arkana, 1976.

Barb, A. A. "Mensa Sacra: The Round Table and the Holy Grail." *Journal of the Warbourg and Courtauld Institutes* 19:1/2, 1956.

Barber, Richard. *The Holy Grail: The History of a Legend.* Cambridge, Mass.: Harvard University Press, 2004.

Baring, Anne, and Jules Cashford. *The Myth of The Goddess: Evolution of an Image.* London and New York: Penguin Books, 1993.

Becker, Udo. *The Continuum Encyclopedia of Symbols.* London and New York: Continuum, 2000.

Benham, Patrick. *The Avalonians.* 2nd ed. Glastonbury, UK: Gothic Image Publications, 2006.

Blamires, Steve. *The Little Book of the Great Enchantment.* Arcata, Calif.: RJ Stewart Books, 2008.

Bligh Bond, Frederick. *The Company of Avalon.* Oxford: B. Blackwell, 1924.

———. *The Gate of Remembrance.* Oxford: B.H. Blackwell, 1918.

Bromwich, Rachel, ed., trans. *Trioedd Ynys Prydein.* Cardiff: University of Wales Press, 1961.

Brown, Arthur C. L. *The Origin of the Grail Legend.* New York: Russell & Russell, 1966.

Bryant, Nigel, trans. *The High Book of the Grail.* Cambridge: D. S. Brewer, 1996.

Burkhardt, Titus. *Alchemy: Science of the Cosmos, Science of the Soul.* Translated by William Stoddart. Shaftesbury, UK: Element Books, 1986.

Campbell, John Gregorson. *Popular Tales of the West Highlands,* vol. 3. Paisley and London: Alexander Gardner, 1890.

Campbell, Joseph. *The Mythic Image.* Princeton, N.J.: Princeton University Press, 1964.

Caradoc of Llancarvan. *Two Lives of Gildas.* Translated by H. Williams. Somerset, UK: Llanerch Press, 1990.

Carey, John. *Ireland and the Grail.* Aberystwyth, Wales: Celtic Studies Publications, 2007.

Carley, James. *Glastonbury Abbey and the Arthurian Tradition.* Woodbridge, Suffolk, UK: D. S. Brewer, 2001.

———. *Glastonbury Abbey.* Glastonbury, UK: Gothic Image, 1988.

———. "Melkin the Bard and Esoteric Tradition at Glastonbury Abbey." *The Downside Review* 99, 1981.

———. *The Chronicle of Glastonbury Abbey.* Suffolk: Boydell and Brewer, 1985.

Carmichael, Alexander. *Carmina Gadelica.* Hudson, N.Y.: Lindisfarne Books, 1992.

Cavendish, Richard. *King Arthur and the Grail.* London: Weidenfeld and Nicolson, 1978.

Clarke, Basil, trans. *Life of Merlin (Vita Merlini).* Cardiff: University of Wales Press, 1973.

Crawford, Deborah. "St. Joseph in Britain: Reconsidering the Legends, Part I." *Folklore* 104: 1/2, 1993.

Cross, Tom Peete, and Clark Harris Slover, eds. *Ancient Irish Tales.* Dublin: Figgis, 1936.

Darragh, John. *Paganism and Arthurian Romance.* Suffolk, UK: Boydell and Brewer, 1994.

de Troyes, Chrétien. *Perceval, or The Story of the Grail.* Translated by Ruth Harwood Cline. Athens: The University of Georgia Press, 1985.

———. *The Story of the Grail.* Translated by Nigel Bryant. Suffolk, UK: D. S. Brewer, 1996.

Dearmer, Percy, Martin Shaw, and Ralph Vaughan Williams. *The Oxford Book of Carols.* London: Oxford University Press, 1964.

Eliade, Mircea. *Shamanism: Archaic Techniques of Ecstasy.* Princeton, N.J.: Princeton University Press, 1964.

Eliot, T. S. *The Waste Land and Other Poems.* New York: Harcourt, Brace & Co., 1958.

Enright, Michael. *Lady with a Mead Cup: Ritual Prophecy and Lordship in the European Warband from La Tène to the Viking Age.* Dublin: Four Courts Press, 1995.

Evans, Sebastian. *The High History of the Holy Graal,* vol. 2. London: J. M. Dent and Co., 1898.

———. *In Quest of the Holy Graal.* London: J. M. Dent and Co., 1898.

Fenge, Gerry. "The Blended Ray," *Gatekeeper Newsletter* 21, 2004, 3.

Fielding, Charles, and Carr Collins. *The Story of Dion Fortune.* Leicestershire, UK: Thoth Publications, 1998.

Ford, Patrick. *The Mabinogi and Other Welsh Tales.* Berkeley: University of California Press, 1977.

Fortune, Dion. *Extracts from Communications Received.* London: Guild of the Master Jesus.

———. *Glastonbury: Avalon of the Heart.* Wellingborough, Northamptonshire, UK: The Aquarian Press, 1986.

———. *The Magical Battle of Britain.* Oceanside, Calif.: Sun Chalice Books, 2003.

———. *Organisation of the Guild.* London: Guild of the Master Jesus.

———. *Practical Occultism.* Leicestershire, UK: Thoth Publications, 2002.

Fry, Christopher. *A Sleep of Prisoners: a Play.* New York: Oxford University Press, 1951.

Gimbutas, Marija. *The Civilization of the Goddess: The World of Old Europe.* San Francisco: HarperSanFrancisco, 1991.

Goering, Joseph. *The Virgin and the Grail—Origins of a Legend.* New Haven: Yale University Press, 2005.

Goetinck, Glenys. "The Quest for Origins." In: *The Grail: A Casebook.* Edited by Dhira Mahoney. New York: Garland, 2000.

Gosman, Martin, Alasdair Macdonald, and Arjo Vanderjagt. *Princes and Princely Culture, 1450–1650* vol. 2. Boston: Brill, 2005.

Gray, Elizabeth A., trans. *Cath Maige Tuired.* Kildare, Ireland: Irish Texts Society, 1982.

Gray, W. G. *Western Inner Workings.* Cape Neddick, Maine: Samuel Weiser, 1983.

Green, Miranda. *Celtic Goddesses.* New York: George Braziller, 1995.

———. *Symbol & Image in Celtic Religious Art.* London: Routledge, 1992.

Harrison, Jane Ellen. *Prolegomena to the Study of Greek Religion.* Princeton, N.J.: Princeton University Press, 1991.

Haycock, Marged. "'Preiddeu Annwn' and the Figure of Taliesin." *Studia Celtica* 18/19 (1983–84): 52–78.

Hill, Gareth. *Masculine and Feminine: The Natural Flow of Opposites in the Psyche.* Boston and London: Shambala, 2001.

Hodson, Geoffrey. *The Kingdom of the Gods.* Adyar, India: The Theosophical Publishing House, 1952.

Holmes, Jr., Urban T., and Sister M. Amelia Klenke. *Chrétien, Troyes, and the Grail.* Chapel Hill: University of North Carolina Press, 1959.

Howard, M., and N. Jackson. *The Pillars of Tubal Cain.* Somerset, UK: Capall Bann, 2000.

Hughes, Jonathan. *Arthurian Myths and Alchemy.* Stroud, UK: Sutton Publishing, 2002.

Jung, C. G. *Psychology and Alchemy.* London: Routledge and Kegan Paul Ltd., 1953.

Jung, Emma, and Marie-Louise Von Franz. *The Grail Legend.* London: Hodder and Stoughton, 1971.

Kahane, Henry, Renee Kahane, and Angelina Pietrangeli. *The Krater and the Grail: Hermetic Sources of the Parzival.* Champaign: University of Illinois Press, 1965.

Kalweit, Holgar. *Dreamtime and Inner Space: The World of the Shaman.* Boston and London: Shambhala, 1988.

Knight, Gareth. *Dion Fortune and the Inner Light.* Leicestershire, UK: Thoth Publications, 2000.

———. *Dion Fortune and the Threefold Way.* London: SIL Trading Ltd., 2004.

———. *Experience of the Inner Worlds.* Cape Neddick, Maine: Samuel Weiser Inc., 1993.

———. *Merlin and the Grail.* Oceanside, Calif.: Sun Chalice Books, 1999.

———. *Pythoness: The Life and Work of Margaret Lumley Brown.* Oceanside, Calif.: Sun Chalice Books, 2000.

Koch, John T. *Celtic Culture: A Historical Encyclopedia.* Santa Barbara, Calif., and Oxford: ABC-CLIO, 2006.

Koch, John T., and John Carey, eds. *The Celtic Heroic Age: Literary Sources for*

Ancient Celtic Europe and Early Ireland and Wales. Malden, Mass.: Celtic Studies Publications, 1994.

Lewis, Lionel Smithett. *St. Joseph of Arimathea at Glastonbury.* London: James Clarke and Co. Ltd., 1955.

Lincoln, Bruce. *Death, War and Sacrifice.* Chicago: University of Chicago Press, 1991.

Lindahl, Carl, John McNamara, and John Lindow, eds. *Medieval Folklore: An Encyclopedia of Myths, Legends, Tales, Beliefs, and Customs.* Oxford: Oxford University Press, 2002.

Loomis, R. S. *Arthurian Literature in the Middle Ages.* Oxford: Clarendon Press, 1959.

———. *The Grail.* Cardiff: University of Wales Press, 1963.

———. *Wales and the Arthurian Legend.* Cardiff: University of Wales Press, 1956.

Mac Cana, Proinsias. "Aspects of the Theme of King and Goddess in Irish Literature." *Études Celtiques* 1955–56, 1958–59.

MacAlister, R. A. S., ed., trans. *Cath Maige Tuired.* Kildare, Ireland: Irish Texts Society, 1987.

Macleod, Fiona. *The Dominion of Dreams.* London: Archibald Constable and Co., 1899.

———. *Green Fire.* New York: Harper and Brothers, 1896.

———. *The Winged Destiny: Studies in the Spiritual History of the Gael.* London: William Heineman, 1913.

Mahoney, Dhira, ed. *The Grail: A Casebook.* New York: Garland, 2000.

Malory, Sir Thomas. *Le Morte d'Arthur.* New York: Random House Inc., 1994.

Mann, Nicholas. *The Isle of Avalon.* St. Paul, Minn.: Llewellyn Publications, 1996.

Mann, Nicholas, and Philippa Glasson. *The Red & White Springs of Avalon.* Sutton Mallet, England: Green Magic, 2005.

Markale, Jean. *Cathedral of the Black Madonna: The Druids and the Mysteries of Chartres.* Rochester, Vt.: Inner Traditions, 2005.

———. *The Grail: The Celtic Origins of the Sacred Icon.* Rochester, Vermont: Inner Traditions, 1999.

———. *Women of the Celts.* Rochester, Vt.: Inner Traditions/Bear and Co., 1986.

Matarasso, P. M. *The Quest of the Holy Grail.* Baltimore: Penguin Books, 1969.

Matthews, John. *The Grail: Quest for the Eternal*. New York: Crossroad, 1981.

———. "The Grail and the Rose," *The Rosicrucian Enlightenment Revisited*. Edited by Ralph White. Hudson, N.Y.: Lindisfarne Books, 1999.

Matthews, John, ed. *At the Table of the Grail*. London: Routledge and Kegan Paul, 1984.

McHardy, Stuart. *The Quest for the Nine Maidens*. Edinburgh: Luath Press, 2003.

McKillop, James. *Dictionary of Celtic Mythology*. Oxford: Oxford University Press, 1998.

Merry, Eleanor. *The Flaming Door*. Edinburgh: Floris Books, 1936/1962.

ní Dhomnaill, Nuala. "Sheelagh in Her Cabin." In From *Beyond the Pale: Art and Artists at the Edge of Consensus*. Dublin: Irish Museum of Modern Art, 1994.

O'Rahilly, T. F. *Early Irish History and Mythology*. Dublin: Dublin Institute for Advanced Studies, 1976.

Paracelsus. *The Hermetic and Alchemical Writings of Paracelsus*. Translated by A. E. Waite. Sioux Falls, S.Dak.: NuVision Publications, 2007.

Powys, John Cooper. *A Glastonbury Romance*. London: MacDonald and Co., 1955.

Raine, Kathleen. *Yeats the Initiate*. Portlaoise, Ireland: Dolmen Press, 1986.

Rees, Alwyn, and Brinley Rees. *Celtic Heritage*. London: Thames & Hudson, 1961.

Rhys, John. *Celtic Folklore, Welsh and Manx*. New York: Arno Press, 1980.

Robinson, J. A. *Two Glastonbury Legends*. Cambridge: Cambridge University Press, 1926.

Ruether, Rosemary. *Goddesses and the Divine Feminine*. Berkeley: University of California Press, 2005.

Satir, Virginia. *Peoplemaking*. New York: Souvenir Press, 1994.

Smith, Edward Reaugh. *The Burning Bush: Rudolf Steiner, Anthroposophy, and the Holy Scriptures*. Hudson, N.Y.: Anthroposophic Press, 1997.

Stokes, Whitley, trans. "Echtra mac nEchach Muigmedóin: The Adventures of the Sons of Eochaid Mugmedón." *Révue Celtique* 24 (1903): 190–207.

Tergit, Gabrielle. *Flowers Through the Ages*. London: Charles Skilton Ltd., 1972.

Trwoga, Chris. *Grail Quest in the Vales of Avalon*. Glastonbury, UK: Speaking Tree Publications, 2001.

Tudor Pole, Wellesley. *Marching Forward*. Chalice Well Trust Archives.

———. *Private Dowding.* London: J. M. Watkins, 1917.

———. *The Silent Road.* London: Neville Spearman Ltd., 1960.

Von Eschenbach, Wolfram. *Parzival.* New York: Random House, 1961.

Wace and Layamon, *Arthurian Chronicles.* Translated by Eugene Mason. London: Dent, 1962.

Warner, Lawrence. "The Dark Wood and the Dark Word in Dante's *Commedia,*" *Comparative Literature Studies* 32, no. 4 (1995): 1.

Weston, Jesse L. *The Quest of the Holy Grail.* New York: Haskell House, 1965.

———. *From Ritual to Romance.* Princeton, N.J.: Princeton University Press, 1941.

White Ralph, ed. *The Rosicrucian Enlightenment Revisited.* Hudson, N.Y.: Lindisfarne Books, 1999.

Wilkinson, Eithne. *The Rose-Garden Game.* London: Victor Gollancz, Ltd., 1969.

William of Malmesbury. *Chronicle of the Kings of England.* Edited by J. A. Giles, translated by Rev. John Sharpe. London: George Bell and Sons, 1904.

Wood, Juliette. "The Creation of the Celtic Tarot." *Folklore* 109, 1998.

———. *Eternal Chalice.* London: I. B. Tauris and Co. Ltd., 2008.

Yeats, W. B. *The Collected Poems of W.B. Yeats.* London: MacMillan, 1963.

Index

271